WILD KNIGHTS IN NC

Major S
was bor
est of fc
Matthews. Jim Matthews was a Territorial Officer and in WW2 served in the Pacific with the Fijian Infantry. Daphne Matthews was an officer in the St John's Ambulance for many years.

When the Territorial units were reintroduced in New Zealand in 1949 Bruce immediately volunteered and was one of the first to be commissioned in the 1st Auckland Regiment in 1952. On commissioning, he put in an application to be seconded to the 3rd Battalion, Royal Australian Regiment, which was already in action in Korea. Accepted by the Australians, he subsequently replaced a New Zealand Duntroon graduate, who was killed patrolling in no-man's land. After Korea, Bruce spent a further 15 years in the Territorials.

Bruce and his wife Annette now live in Cambridge, within walking distance of their daughter Elizabeth and her husband Dean and four children.

CMG

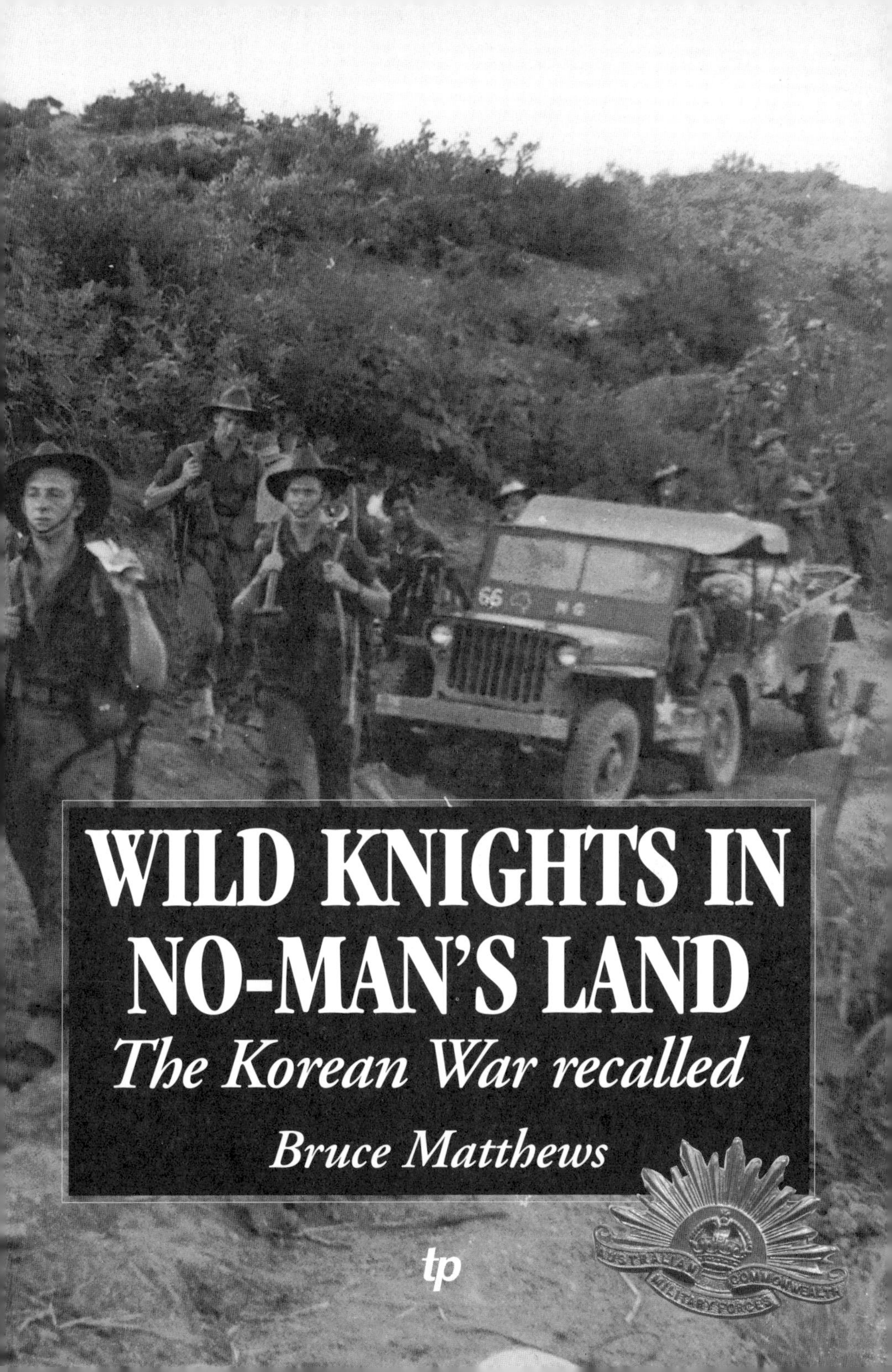
WILD KNIGHTS IN
NO-MAN'S LAND
The Korean War recalled
Bruce Matthews
tp
AUSTRALIAN
COMMONWEALTH
MILITARY FORCES
66

Dedicated to the memory of

Sergeant Bernard Cocks 2/400126 (Bernie)
3rd Battalion Royal Australian Regiment.
Killed in action 17 May 1953 aged 32, Hill 355.
He was the personification of the courageous
Australian professional soldier.

They shall grow not old as we who are left grow old,
Age shall not weary them, nor the years condemn,
At the going down of the sun and in the morning
We will remember them.

First published in 2003 by

transpress New Zealand
P.O. Box 10-215
Wellington
New Zealand

transpress@paradise.net.nz
www.transpressnz.com

Edited by Colin Bassett
Art direction by Geoffrey Churchman
Illustrations from the author's collection
Printed in Hong Kong

ISBN 0-908876-27-0 (New Zealand edition)
ISBN 0-9751532-0-X (Australian edition)

Front Cover scene: A Bren-gunner and an Owen-gunner moving into no-man's land on a night patrol. The other 14 men are probably in front and behind. (Army photo)

Title Page: Lt. Bruce Matthews leading his platoon off Pt 146 on The Hook position, 72 hours after the truce took effect. (Army photo)

Contents

Preface

When war broke out on the Korean Peninsula on 25 June 1950, I was a corporal in the New Zealand territorial force. Having volunteered for secondment to the regular force to train the first intake of CMT recruits, I was stationed in Papakura Military Camp as an instructor and a hut commander in Lt. John Brooke's platoon. As John did not have a platoon sergeant, I also carried out those duties with the added title of Admin NCO.

When we heard the radio announcement of the outbreak of the Korean War, one of the 18-year-old trainees turned to me and asked, "Will you be going, Corporal?"

"Probably," I replied. But the New Zealand Government opted to raise a regiment of field artillery for service in Korea. The volunteers marched into camp at the end of August 1950. As an infantry man, I wanted to fight as one. The answer was to volunteer for service with the Australian battalion.

But I was under pressure to complete my apprenticeship in the family business, with the intention of eventually continuing the business. This obstacle had been put in my way when I wanted to apply for entrance to the Royal Military College Duntroon, in Australia. But I was given every encouragement, including time off, to be a successful territorial soldier. By the time I finished my apprenticeship, I was half way through an OCTU (Officer Cadets training Unit) course. Then during a weekend camp soon after commissioning, Major 'Dinty' Moore M.B.E., an original battery commander in 16th Field Regiment, treated the TF officers of 1 Brigade to a lecture on the part that New Zealand was playing in the war in Korea. When he described the Kiwi gunners providing supporting fire for the 3rd Battalion Royal Australian Regiment (3 RAR), clearing the enemy off the hills with spirited attacks, I knew that I should join them. I immediately applied for secondment to 3RAR.

Two months later, Major Alf Voss M.C., D.C.M., the adjutant of the 1st Battalion Auckland Regiment (Countess of Ranfurly's Own), called me on the phone. His first words were, "Pack your bags Bruce. You're on your way."

Introduction

The Korean War is referred to as the forgotten war. Yet it was the most significant war of the latter half of the twentieth century, in that it was the first reversal for communism, which was spreading across the world like a cancer.

On 25 June 1950, war broke out in the recently divided country, not long freed from Japanese occupation.

In the last days of WW2, with the Japanese having withdrawn their occupation troops to defend Japan itself, the Russians marched into the northern end of the Korean peninsula and the Americans landed troops on the southern end. The Russians were bent on establishing a communist state, and the Americans a democratic one. They met about the middle.

Neither of the big powers would back off, so a compromise was reluctantly agreed to and Korea was divided into two separate countries at the 38th Parallel. The Russians helped the north to establish a heavily armed state by supplying them with weapons and making top-line instructors available, while the Americans encouraged the South to establish a so-called democratic state, armed with minimal strength and a lightly equipped army. They also provided instructors and left two American infantry divisions in the country.

Five years later, on 25 June 1950, North Korean troops, by now well trained and indoctrinated in communism, invaded the South. The South Korean army, even with the help of American forces stationed there for just such an emergency, could not hold them. Eventually, the South Korean and American units were driven back into a last stand position in the south-east corner of South Korea. Named the Pusan perimeter, its front line was approximately 100 miles (160 km) long. There the communists were held until other members of the United Nations Organization could send enough troops, and the Americans could reinforce theirs sufficiently for a break out.

Sixteen members of UNO responded to the request to contribute troops to restore peace, and five others sent medical units. At this stage, it was not called a war. The United Nations Organization called it a police action.

The USA mobilised WW2 reservists and quickly built up its army, airforce and naval strength in the battle zone.

Britain despatched naval squadrons immediately and moved two infantry battalions from their Hong Kong station to Korea.

Without hesitation, Australia with a population in those days of only about five million, responded with naval units and set about preparing significant contributions from all three services. The 3rd Bn. Royal Australian Regiment, being the last Australian infantry battalion serving in the occupation force in Japan, was nominated for Korea. Already a mix of battle-experienced and post World War 2 regulars, it was reinforced by volunteers from civvy street, who included a proportion of New Australian citizens from the UK and more New Guinea campaign veterans.

New Zealand, with a population of one and a half million, despatched two frigates immediately, and called for volunteers for an army unit. There was an overwhelming response and the volunteers were trained into a first-class field artillery regiment and a motor transport company to keep it resupplied. The New Zealand 16th Field Artillery Regiment and 10 Company RNZASC, having to be raised and retrained, did not arrive in Korea until 31 December 1950. Armed with 25-pounder gun/howitzers, they provided the bulk of the close artillery support for the two Australian battalions, for the rest of the war.

The famous American general, Douglas MacArthur, who was in command of the occupational force in Japan following WW2, was appointed Supreme Commander of the UNO forces in Korea and directed operations from Japan. When he was confident that he had sufficient troops in the Pusan perimeter for a counter-attack, he ordered a break out.

3 RAR arrived in Pusan just before the break out and went straight into action. Participating in the push to the Yalu, the battalion fought some sharp little battles to clear ambushes that tended to bog down the highly motorised American Army in its thrusts northwards, and some larger ones as rearguard against the Chinese army that had moved quietly into North Korea to assist the communist forces. In doing so, the Australian battalion developed into a superb fighting unit, again with a very high morale.

Early in 1952, 1 RAR arrived in Korea, having been brought up to strength for this first United Nations crisis that turned into a full-scale war. With 60% of its personnel being New Australians, some wag described it as a 'first class Pommy battalion, mucked up by a few Australians.' It is worth noting that a significant number of New Zealanders who were working in Australia also enlisted in the Australian battalions. These two comparatively small infantry contributions of 1000 men each, in a war that eventually involved millions of soldiers, quickly developed a moral ascendancy over the enemy. Over their allies too, for that matter, except for their close associates, the New Zealanders. It is my opinion that the élan of the Australian fighting man was as strong as it has ever been. Many countries attempt to train special units into that most valuable fighting spirit, but the Australian serviceman has always had it naturally.

After the two sides had pushed each other up and down the divided country for nine months, 3 RAR played a vital role in establishing the Commonwealth Division in the western sector of the Jamestown Line. After minor adjustments were made with local attacks, the situation settled into trench warfare, right across the country. We were not encouraged to take more real estate, the American terminology of the day, except to secure a tactical feature.

For two more years, the war was stalemated with neither side attacking for a decision, but trying to keep the initiative in the peace talks and their troops on their toes, by patrolling aggressively. The Chinese high command, who had taken over the strategic direction of the communist effort, sometimes attempted to gain ground by attacking South Korean divisional sectors, using North Korean troops, and using Chinese troops against American and British battalion positions including Australian. But after the battles of Kapyong and Maryang, neither the Chinese nor the North Koreans ever again attacked the Australians seriously. Other Commonwealth battalions blocking their way to Seoul were subject to severe attacks.

The constant probing by fighting patrols that characterised most of the action during the static period was rather one sided. Sixteen Australians pitted against 40 Chinese was a definite imbalance, but the aggressive attitude of the Australian patrols, backed by two Bren light machine-guns and superior hand grenades, went some way toward equalling the odds. So much so that the Chinese rarely pressed home clashes with the Australian patrols. Of course there were exceptions.

What follows is one New Zealander's firsthand account of service with the 3rd Battalion Royal Australian Regiment, in the latter part of the war.

The recounting is as accurate as my memory will allow after 50 years. But most of it is burnt into it, anyway.

The Digger

The Digger, who is he? He is the Australian soldier. Not just one, but all, of every corps of the army and indeed, by association, all Australian servicemen.

When referring to an Australian serviceman, it is 'the digger'. When identifying a unit or group of Aussie soldiers, the correct term is the 'diggers'. A private soldier is a digger, as are the non-commissioned and commissioned officers. But they are not so likely to be individually described as such. It is usually a collective reference.

The term originated in the gumfields and the goldfields of Australia and New Zealand in the early pioneering days, passing on to the subsequent coal and opal mining. It resurfaced when it was re-applied to the Anzacs in the Gallipoli campaign and on the Western Front in WW1.

"Gad sir, these colonials are great diggers."

Once the order to dig trenches for protection from machine-gun and shell-fire was given, the men experienced in digging for a living showed the others how to dig fast and efficiently. The Australian and New Zealand soldiers who weren't miners took the lesson to heart and never forgot it.

The men used the nickname when referring to their mates in their letters home. On their return from the Great War, they found that it had gained acceptance through popular usage. It was widely used by members of the public in both countries between the world wars. During WW2 New Zealanders continued to use the term when referring to their Australian mates. But not themselves. They had become Kiwis.

The Australian soldiers have re-earned the title digging-in and fighting all over the world. Friend and foe alike unreservedly respect the term Digger. But no one more than this Kiwi.

Abbreviations

2IC	Second in command
Adjt	Adjutant
Armed	Armoured
Arty	Artillery
Aust	Australian
Bde	Brigade
BEM	British Empire Medal
BHQ	Battalion Headquarters
Bn	Battalion
Bty	Battery
CO	Commanding Officer
COMDIV	Commonwealth Division
Coy	Company
CCP	Casualty Clearing Post
CP	Command Post
CSM	Company Sergeant Major
DCM	Distinguished Conduct Medal
DF	Defensive Fire
Div	Division
DMZ	Demilitarized Zone
DSO	Distinguished Service Order
ED	Efficiency Decoration
Fld Regt	Field (artillery) Regiment
FDLs	Forward Defensive Lines
FOO	Forward Observation Officer
FUP	Forming up Place
GI	Government Issue (nickname for an American soldier)
GR	Grid Reference
HE	High Explosive
HF	Harassing Fire
HQ	Headquarters
KOSB	King's Own Scottish Borderers
KSC	Korean Service Corp
MASH	Mobile Army Surgical Hospital
MBE	Member of the Order of the British Empire

MC	Military Cross
MiD	Mentioned in Despatches
MM	Military Medal
MMG	Medium machine-gun
MP	Military Police
NAAFI	Navy, Army and Air Force Institute
NCO	Non Commissioned Officer
NZ	New Zealand
OC	Officer Commanding
OP	Observation Post
OPO	Observation Post Officer
Pl	Platoon
PPCLI	Princess Patricia's Canadian Light Infantry regiment
QARANC	Queen Alexander's Royal Army Nursing Corps
RAAR	Royal Australian Air Force
RAF	Royal Air Force
RAN	Royal Australian Navy
RAOC	Royal Army Ordnance Corps
RAP	Regimental aid post
RAR	Royal Australian Regiment
RASC	Royal Army Service Corps
Regt	Regiment
RF	Regular Force
RF	Royal Fusiliers
RHQ	Regimental Headquarters
RHU	Reinforcement Holding Unit
RMO	Regimental Medical Officer
RN	Royal Navy
RNZA	Royal new Zealand Artillery
ROK	Republic of Korea
RSM	Regimental Sergeant-Major
RV	Rendezvous
TF	Territorial Force
TP	Troop
Tpt Coy	Transport Company
UK	United Kingdom
UNO	United Nations Organization

USAF	United States Airforce
USMC	United States Marine Corps
USN	United States Navy
USS	United States Ship
VC	Victoria Cross
VT	Variable Time (Fuse)
WO	Warrant Officer

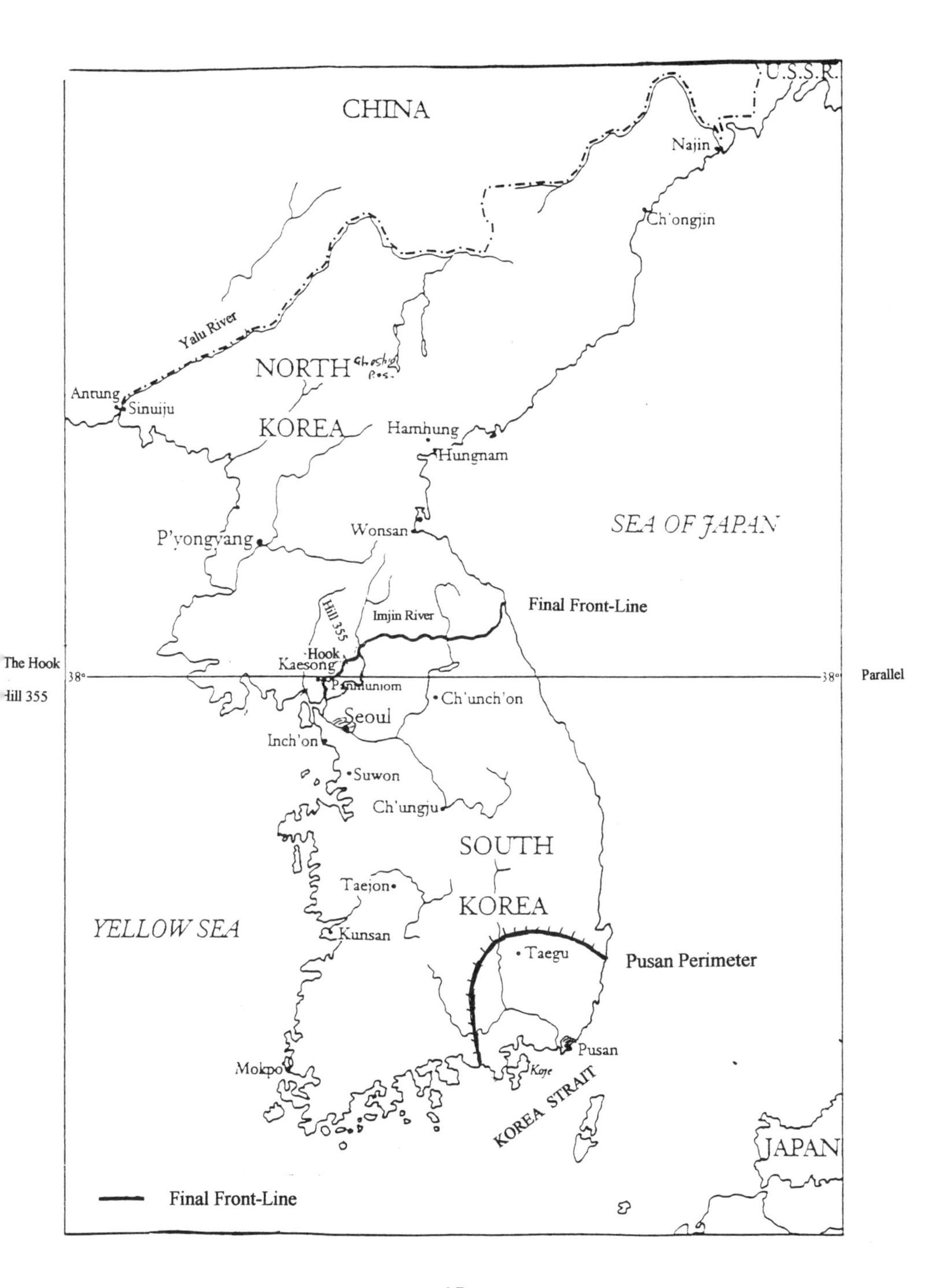
CHINA
U.S.S.R.
Najin
Ch'ongjin
Yalu River
NORTH
KOREA
Antung
Sinuiju
Hamhung
Hungnam
SEA OF JAPAN
Wonsan
P'yongyang
Final Front-Line
Hill 355
Imjin River
The Hook
Hill 355
Hook
Kaesong
38°
38°
Parallel
Panmuniom
Ch'unch'on
Seoul
Inch'on
Suwon
Ch'ungju
SOUTH
KOREA
Taejon
YELLOW SEA
Kunsan
Taegu
Pusan Perimeter
Pusan
Mokpo
Koje
KOREA STRAIT
JAPAN
Final Front-Line

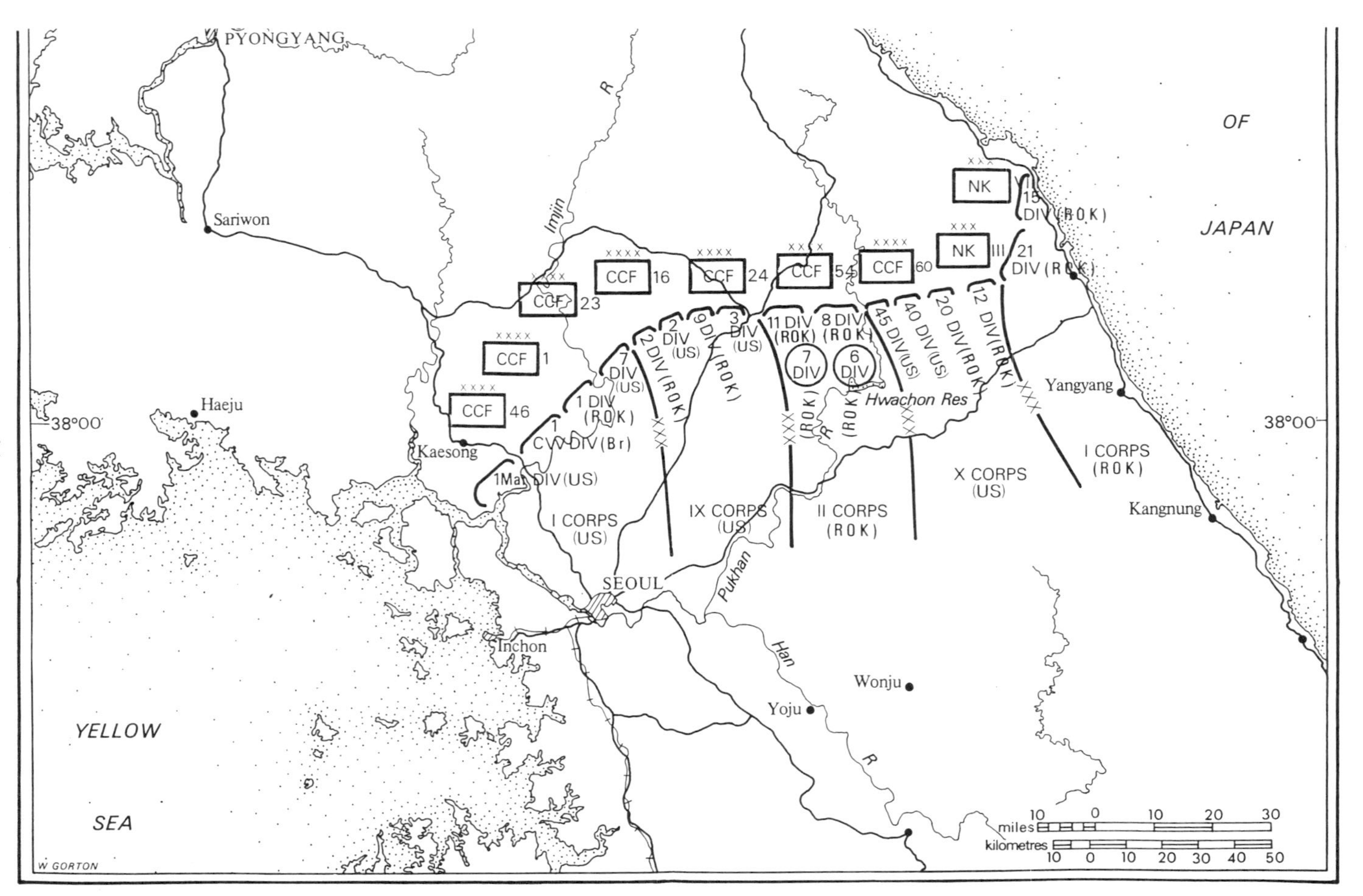

The Cease-fire Line, 27 July 1953

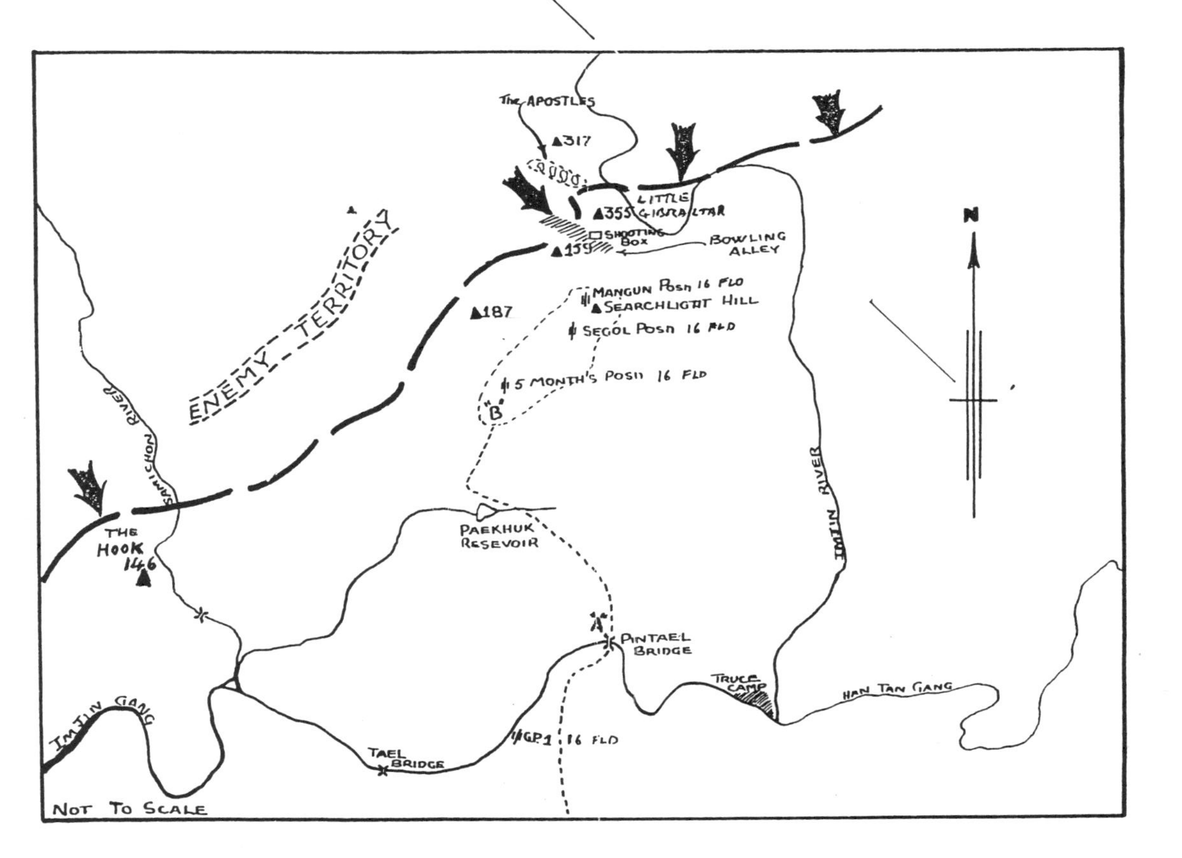
TO P YONGYANG
The APOSTLES
317
LITTLE GIBRALTAR
355
SHOOTING BOX
BOWLING ALLEY
159
ENEMY TERRITORY
MANGUN Posn 16 FLD
SEARCHLIGHT HILL
SEGOL Posn 16 FLD
187
5 MONTH'S Posn 16 FLD
"B"
N
SAMICHON RIVER
IMJIN RIVER
THE HOOK
146
PAEKHUK RESEVOIR
"A"
PINTAEL BRIDGE
TRUCE CAMP
HAN TAN GANG
IMJIN GANG
GP 1 16 FLD
TAEL BRIDGE
NOT TO SCALE
TO SEOUL AND 38° PARALLEL

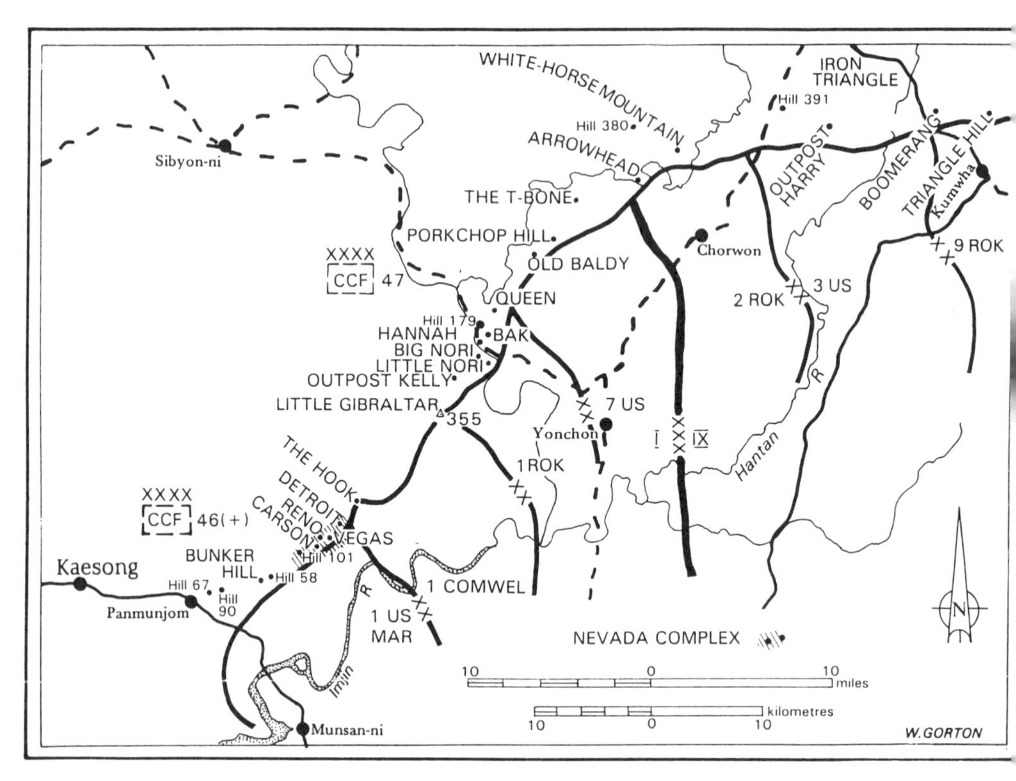

The Eighth Army Front, Western Sector, Showing Major Outposts, 1953

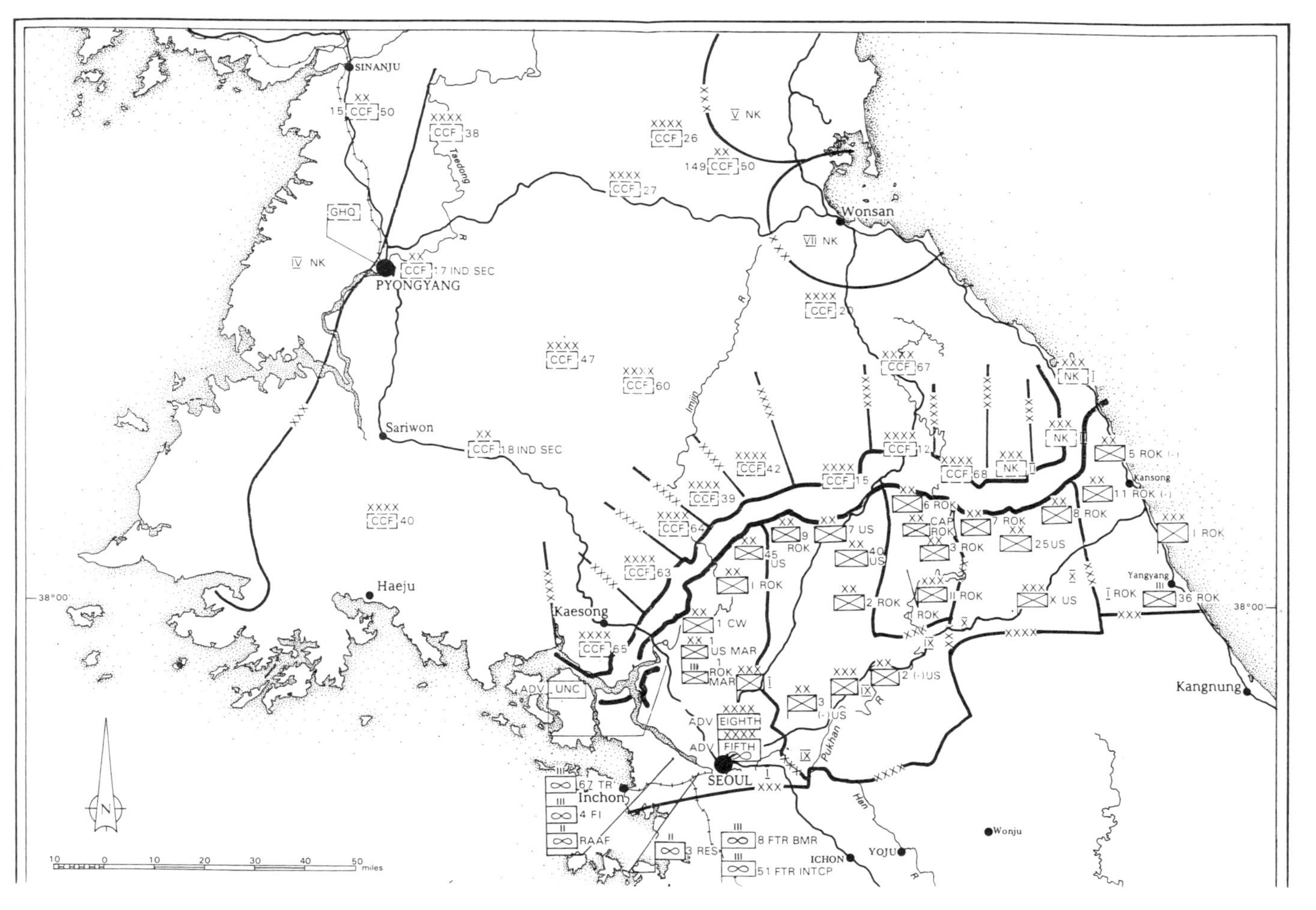
SINANJU
PYONGYANG
Sariwon
Haeju
Wonsan
Kaesong
Inchon
SEOUL
ICHON
YOJU
Wonju
Yangyang
Kansong
Kangnung
Taedong
Imjin
Pukhan
Han
38°00'
miles

– *One* –
Going to War

After my secondment to the New Zealand Regular Force, training the first intake of Compulsory Military Training (CMT), I returned to my civilian apprenticeship and completed that, in anticipation of volunteering for the Korean war. Soon after, I was put up for a commission. In the Territorial Army in those days, the officer training took a long time. After a week-long selection course in Waiouru Military Camp, it was mostly done part-time, in the weekends; plus a two-week annual camp like the rest of the Territorial training. But I thought that I should go through with it. With a commission, I reasoned, I might have more influence over my own future in action. I was not wrong.

Meanwhile, the 3rd Bn. Royal Australian Regiment, one of the first British Commonwealth units to be deployed in Korea, 'soldiered on' as part of the 27th Commonwealth Brigade. The fact that both officers and men were rotated after 12 months, combined with the casualty rate, presented the opportunity for some New Zealand Regular Force Infantry personnel to be seconded to 3 RAR. My friend, Lt. John Brooke, was the first of a total of nine sent during the whole three year war. He was posted to the battalion in July 1951, returning to New Zealand nearly 12 months later after being seriously wounded in a night raid that he led across the Bowling Alley from Hill 159, onto the Chinese position called Luke.

Nearly two years had elapsed since the American and South Korean troops had broken out of the Pusan perimeter, where they had fought hard to hold their tenuous footing in Korea with sheer guts and determination. For there was no high ground in or around Pusan and furthermore they were heavily outnumbered, until the rest of the free world sent reinforcements to save South Korea and stop North Korea from taking over the country.

General MacArthur's amphibious landing at Inchon had catapulted the US forces well up the peninsula. Leading units, encountering little opposition, advanced further north in spearheaded thrusts rather than on a broad front. Some got within sight of the Yalu River, but not for long. The Chinese were not going to tolerate foreign forces so close to their border. Anticipating the likelihood of such a threat, they had covertly marched 100,000 troops into North Korea.

Flushed with success and hyped up by the speed of their advance north, plus the apparent weakening of the North Korean opposition, the Americans grew careless. Few reconnaissance units were deployed ahead of their main forces, and those that were displayed an off-hand approach to their vital task, clearing the roads but not the hills. The result was that, when the Chinese blew the whistle (or more correctly, their trumpets for, lacking sufficient radios, they signalled with trumpet calls) they fell upon the US forward units in overwhelming numbers and the high morale of the American army evaporated. "Bug-out" became the catchword. Not all, but a considerable number, panicked. Men panicked. Officers panicked. Whole units panicked. Formations panicked. The great bug-out was underway.

The cross-country mobility of the Chinese was largely responsible for this turn of events. They were not road-bound on inadequate roads, like the American army was. They did not, at this stage of their involvement, require large convoys of trucks to bring forward their rations and ammunition. They relied, with good reason, on their coolies, maybe another 100,000 men. These travelled cross-country during the hours of darkness, carrying on A frames and stretchers all the stores and ammunition that their army needed. Further, dressed in quilted clothing like their soldiers, they were better able to withstand the rigours of the Korean winter than their opponents' trucks were. The winter of 1950 was recorded as the most severe since the Japanese had control of the country, 45 years before.

Some way behind the United State forces that had been rushing north, the 27th British Commonwealth Brigade, with old and unreliable WW2 transport carrying its stores, plodded steadily forward keeping its collective head. That was the blessing that saved the United Nations' army. The Commonwealth units were nicely placed to protect the lines of retreat from the enveloping Chinese army. Large numbers of enemy infantry had already infiltrated south behind the leading elements of the UNO forces. The snow and the sub-zero temperatures added to the misery of the American troops, who had been led to expect 'to be home for Christmas', based on a remark carelessly made by General Douglas MacArthur after the success of the Inchon landing.

Keeping the bridges intact during the retreat from the Yalu became one of the main tasks of the units of the 27th Commonwealth Brigade. 3 RAR played a major part in defending the bridges and breaking up ambushes. In his book *The Last Call of the Bugle*, Australian veteran colonel Jack Gallaway, gives a first hand, authoritative account of the battalion's role in the battles of the Apple Orchard, Broken Bridge, Chongju, Taenyong River, Pakchon, Chasan and many others. Describing these small but vital battles in detail, he brings infantry fighting to life in a way that few war histories can.

Meanwhile, the American X Corps, having been switched to the eastern side of the peninsula following the Inchon landing, had made a second landing at Wonson. Capturing Hungnam and Hamhung, the 1st and 7th US Marine Divisions pushed north to the Chosin Reservoir, a very strategic target. With the intervention of the Chinese, the marines were forced to withdraw. But they did not bug-out. In their fighting withdrawal, they suffered badly from the early onset of winter and the resulting frostbite. The British sent in the 219 strong, 41 (Independent) Commando of the Royal Marines, to keep the US Marines' line of retreat open by patrolling the hilltops. The Marines, harassed by seven different Chinese divisions along the way, made it back in a fighting retreat via Hagaru and Koto-ri to Hamhung. The British Commandos suffered a total of 98 casualties: 32 killed, 39 wounded and 27 missing.

The Chinese kept the pressure on, driving the UNO forces back down the peninsula and over the 38th parallel again. Eventually, the frontline was stabilised about 20 km south of Suwon. The retreating and the wild charges north were over. American General Matthew Ridgway had been appointed by President Harry Truman to replace the ageing Supreme Commander, General Douglas MacArthur. This did not mean that the fighting had stopped. General Ridgway lost no time in pushing the Chinese back into North Korea and establishing a defended line on defendable ground, north of the 38th parallel. The war then became static but both sides continued at each other's throats, fighting for small gains of 'real estate'. It became more a war of attrition, with each side trying to wear the other down with assaults of divisional strength or less. Meanwhile, the flag waving diplomats at Panmunjom argued the political future of the Korean nation.

On commissioning in 1952, I wasted no time in applying through my territorial CO, Lt. Col. Harry McElroy D.S.O. and bar, for a posting to 3 RAR.

I had been fired up by a lecture given by Major Dinty Moore MC, who had commanded 162 Battery of the New Zealand 16th Field Regiment in Korea. He told of "supporting the unstoppable Australian infantry sweeping the Chinese army off the hills." Great Boys' Own Annual stuff, but not far from the truth. The Australians did not hesitate to accept me. Quite surprising, I thought at the time. But on arrival I found that the attrition rate in platoon commander appointments was rather high, and that we were always short of junior officers. Within two months of tendering my application, Alf Voss rang me, and said, "Pack your bags, Bruce. You're on your way."

I marched into Papakura Military camp for kitting out and inoculations. There I met up with Captain Dick Stanley-Harris, a Duntroon graduate Regular Force infantry officer, who had also been posted to 3 RAR. We flew out of New Zealand with a K Force reinforcement in December 1952. Our landfall in Japan was the mighty Australian-run airbase at Iwakuni, from which a large part of the United Nations' air war was being conducted. An hour and a half journey by launch up the Inland Sea took us to the major Japanese naval and shipbuilding city of Kure, where what was to be the biggest tanker in the world at that time was under construction. During WW2, Kure had been a closed city where the Japanese built warships in secret. Some were still lying at the bottom of the harbour.

From Kure, the reinforcement marched the nine miles to NZ base camp at Hiro and was made most welcome by the 'old hands'. The next day Dick and I moved to the 1 Aust. Reinforcement Holding Unit (RHU), also in Hiro. The commandant was Major Jack Gerke M.C., an earlier commander of 3 RAR's C Company. It was he and his men who during 'Operation Commando' surprised and attacked two Chinese companies digging in on Hill 317, wiping them out. The capture of this relatively high and prominent position enabled the 27th Commonwealth Brigade to attack the 355 metre high hill, Little Gibraltar, from the north, as it had proven too steep to assault from the south. Hill 317 was abandoned soon after, because it did not fit into the planned new defensive line. But its capture had played its part for without 317 the Australians could not have taken 355.

Dick and I set to work to study all the available intelligence data. I found it difficult to visualise Hill 355 that the battalion was now holding. Men spoke in awe of that menacing giant, which was constantly being shelled and mortared. However, I found out soon enough that this was no Hill 60 of WW1 infamy, but a benevolent bastion for its owners, a secure and defended position dominating the enemy held features within range. It was a good hill to call home.

Meanwhile we were kitted out again. All the gear issued in New Zealand was replaced with standard British issue for the theatre of conflict, plus a slouch hat. It took two trips to carry the stuff to our quarters. We were resplendent in our new winter combat uniforms, sporting New Zealand Regiment flashes on our epaulets and the Royal Australian Regiment brassards on our right arms. We were, however, still wearing our NZ berets. Dick never did change his head-dress. But I did, as soon as I had sorted out to my satisfaction the regimental bash in my slouch hat. A felt slouch hat left for dead the beret that the New Zealanders wore in those days. It was the Australian equivalent of the New Zealand lemon squeezer, but more practical. It protected one from both the hot sun and the heavy rain. The 'bash' in the slouch hat is a crease put in the crown with the edge of the hand. Then, squeezing the sides of the crown with the fingers and heel of the hand, produces a dent each side which in turn causes the brim to curve down, front and back, protecting both the face and the neck from the sun.

The next day, impatient to join the battalion, we checked the Intelligence Office again, both to keep up to date, and spin out the afternoon. Then we headed for the mess. Turning a corner, we spotted about 70 diggers blocking the road outside the Q Store, at the far end of the row of buildings. Obviously, they were reinforcements being kitted-out for the theatre.

"Let's duck back along the other way," said Dick. "I don't want to salute my way through that lot."

"These are Australian soldiers," I laughed, "and they're not going to salute anyone other than their own officers."

"A bottle of beer on it?" suggested Dick, chuckling.

"Right," I agreed.

As we approached the group, they stood aside quietly and politely. They were reinforcements, but I was not prepared to speak to them until I had learnt more about the Australian soldier. We were close to emerging without incident, when a short thickset young fella gathered himself to his full height and saluted. With a smile on his face, Dick raised his right arm to the salute, while his left elbow jabbed me in the ribs. I paid the bet, but got the last laugh (see next chapter).

Then Dick left for the battalion to take up the appointment of 2IC D Coy, while I moved on to the Battle School at Hara Mura, about 40 km from Hiro. This was a large piece of real estate, where it was possible to carry out company size exercises with artillery and armour support without endangering the local population. It was organized into A, B and C companies, which coincided nicely with Australian, British and Canadian cadres, who each trained their own men. One of the Australian Company's instructors was Sergeant Gordon Curly, a New Zealander who had fought in 3 RAR. Gordon had bought himself out of the NZ Regular Force and joined the Australian Army to get to Korea. Some time after the Korean war he reversed the process, coming home and rejoining ours. Eventually retiring after a lifetime of soldiering, he was still training a school cadet unit voluntarily in 1993 when he died suddenly. I had the honour of saying "The Ode" at his graveside.

The officers' mess at Hara Mura was populated by a mixture of the three nationalities and all the instructors were veterans of earlier fighting in the theatre, and most had also served in WW2. Prominent among the characters in the mess was the ex-2IC of the Argyll and Sutherland Highlanders. On one occasion, so I was told, he was driving a jeep loaded with officers home from a party in Kure, when a provost stopped him. A little fazed to find a major behind the wheel, the MP nevertheless pointed out that there was a man sitting on the canvas roof of the jeep.

"Of course there is," answered the Argyll man in his cultured voice, "I always have somebody up there, he's the aircraft sentry." Only too glad to get a civil answer, if not a sensible one, the Red Cap waved him on.

I was not included in the training at the battle school, but I was expected to observe it and absorb the way things were done in this Asian war. I didn't learn much that way, but I spent a lot of time on the grenade range throwing live grenades, until I was nearly as good as

Hadlee or Lillee. One afternoon, I took an Owen gun, several magazines and a sealed tin box containing 900 rounds of 9 mm ammunition to the submachine-gun range. I practiced shooting in all positions, particularly from the hip which, although less accurate, in a patrol clash is the most likely first encounter position to fire from. I kept at it until I could flick over the safety sleeve and fire the owen as quickly and accurately as John Wayne could fire a six-gun from the hip, in the cowboy movies. After also practicing from the prone and shoulder positions, I left the range with complete confidence in myself and the Australian-designed and manufactured submachine-gun, a weapon that was much superior to the unreliable British Sten gun, on which I had been trained, and with which the poor British soldiers were still equipped.

Back at 1 Aust RHU, it was not long before I was summoned to join the battalion. Flying out of Iwakuni again, we landed at Kimpo airfield, which was overpoweringly large for those days. With my ears nearly dropping off with the freezing Siberian wind whistling around them, I hurriedly lugged my gear about a thousand metres over the frozen ground to the little shack on the edge of the field, where movement of personnel in transit was monitored. Like we have all seen in the movies, an American top sergeant requested my written orders. I had none, but told him that I was expecting transport from my unit. The name of the battalion worked wonders and an Aussie driver quickly appeared.

I was impressed with the careful way that he drove into Seoul, then north through Uijongbu and over the Pintail Bridge straddling the Imjin River, to my new and exciting home. It was not until later that I learnt that the battalion had laid down its own speed limit of 20 mph (32 km/h), to prolong the life of our clapped-out WW2 jeeps and trucks on the extremely rough roads. The theatre speed limit, imposed of course by the Americans in an endeavour to reduce wear and tear on the roads, was 30 mph (50 km/h) on the open roads and 20 mph through towns and cities. This limit was never enforced except in Seoul, from which the American Military Police rarely strayed, preferring to stay close to their Korean girlfriends. On the way north we called in at 3 Battalion's A Echelon. There I was issued with a .38 calibre Smith and Wesson pistol, a compass and a rugged Omega watch. The next stop was home, where I was cordially received into the best infantry battalion on our side, the 3rd Battalion, Royal Australian Regiment.

On 12 January 1953, a 21-year-old New Zealand Duntroon graduate, Lieutenant Bob Unsworth, was killed in action and I was summoned to replace him. It is over 50 years ago now so, hopefully, telling how Bob died will do no further damage. Colonel Hughes was very careful with the cocky young New Zealander, and arranged for a reliable and mature man, Private Laddie Lord, to keep an eye on him. After accompanying two experienced patrol leaders on fighting patrols as we all did on joining the battalion, although we didn't all have minders, Bob was judged to be ready to take out his own fighting patrol. His patrol moved into no-man's land, apparently without hassle, and proceeded to the first ambush position.

After deploying 14 of his 15 men in a circle, which was the accepted formation in the deep snow that hid more suitable cover, Bob left the patrol, presumably to carry out an unscheduled recce. Laddie went with him as ordered by the battalion commander. Unfortunately, Unsworth did not, as he should have done, pass the word around that they were leaving the ambush position. It was the responsibility of the patrol leader to ensure that this was done, regardless of who was leaving the patrol. Time passed, then he and Laddie returned without any warning, such as whistling or making some sort of sound to identify themselves, and the new fall of snow was still soft and quiet to walk on. They approached the patrol from a different direction, so it is likely that Unsworth had lost his bearings and blundered into his own ambush. No one in the rest of the patrol was aware that anyone had left it, so it was not surprising, in fact it was expected of him, that the man they suddenly loomed up in front of opened fire. Of the 20 rounds in his Owen gun's magazine, four hit Lord and 15 Unsworth. Both died instantly. The third casualty was the man who fired. He went mental and had to be evacuated to Australia.

I was blissfully unaware of the tragedy until when I arrived in the unit. Then I found that the whole of the battalion was in mourning for Laddie Lord, aged 27 with five children. He had volunteered for Korea because he believed that the communist had to be stopped. There was some thoughtful reshuffling, so that another Kiwi did not take over the same platoon. That would have been too tough on everybody.

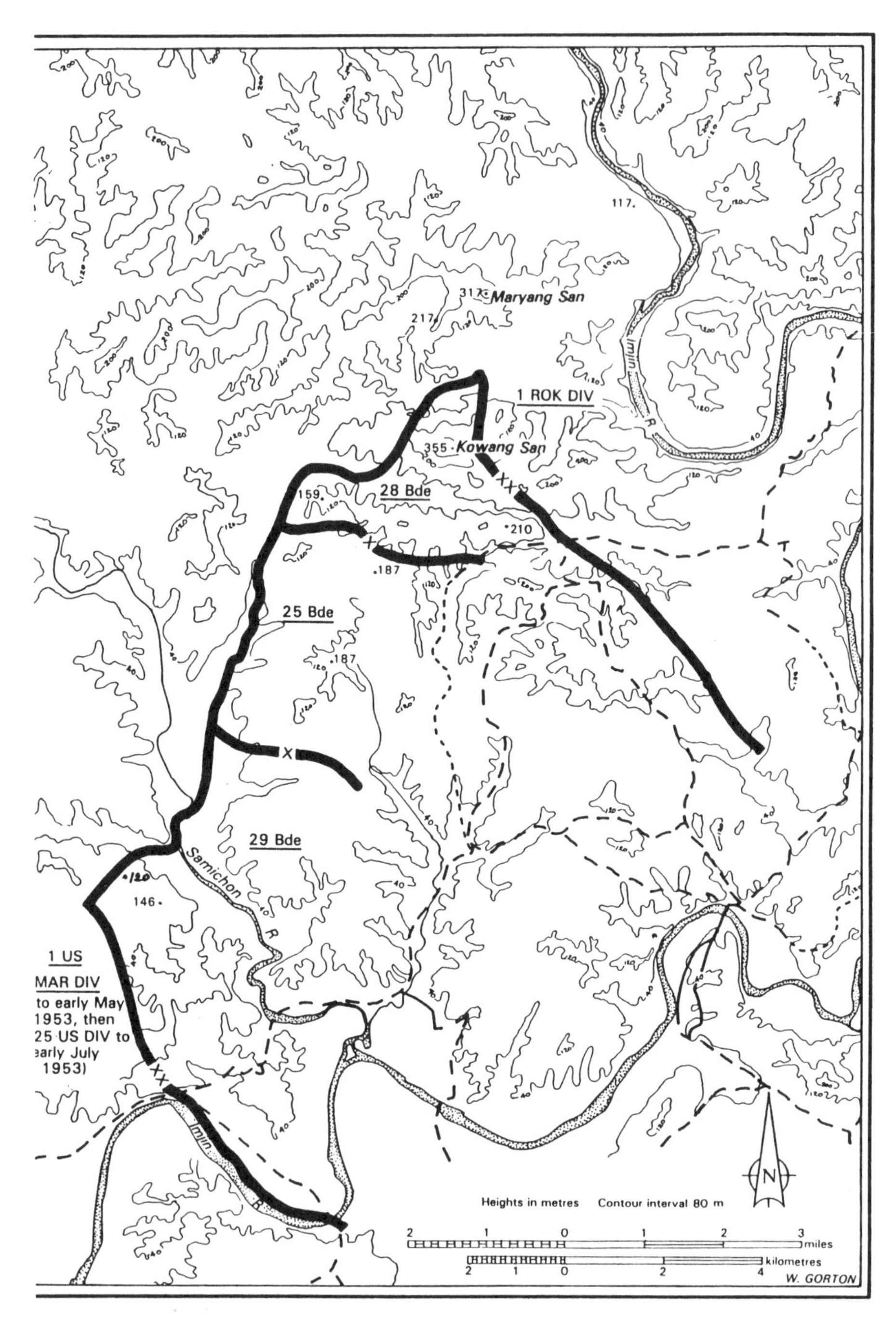

Brigade Dispositions, 1st Commonwealth Division, 8 April–9 July 1953

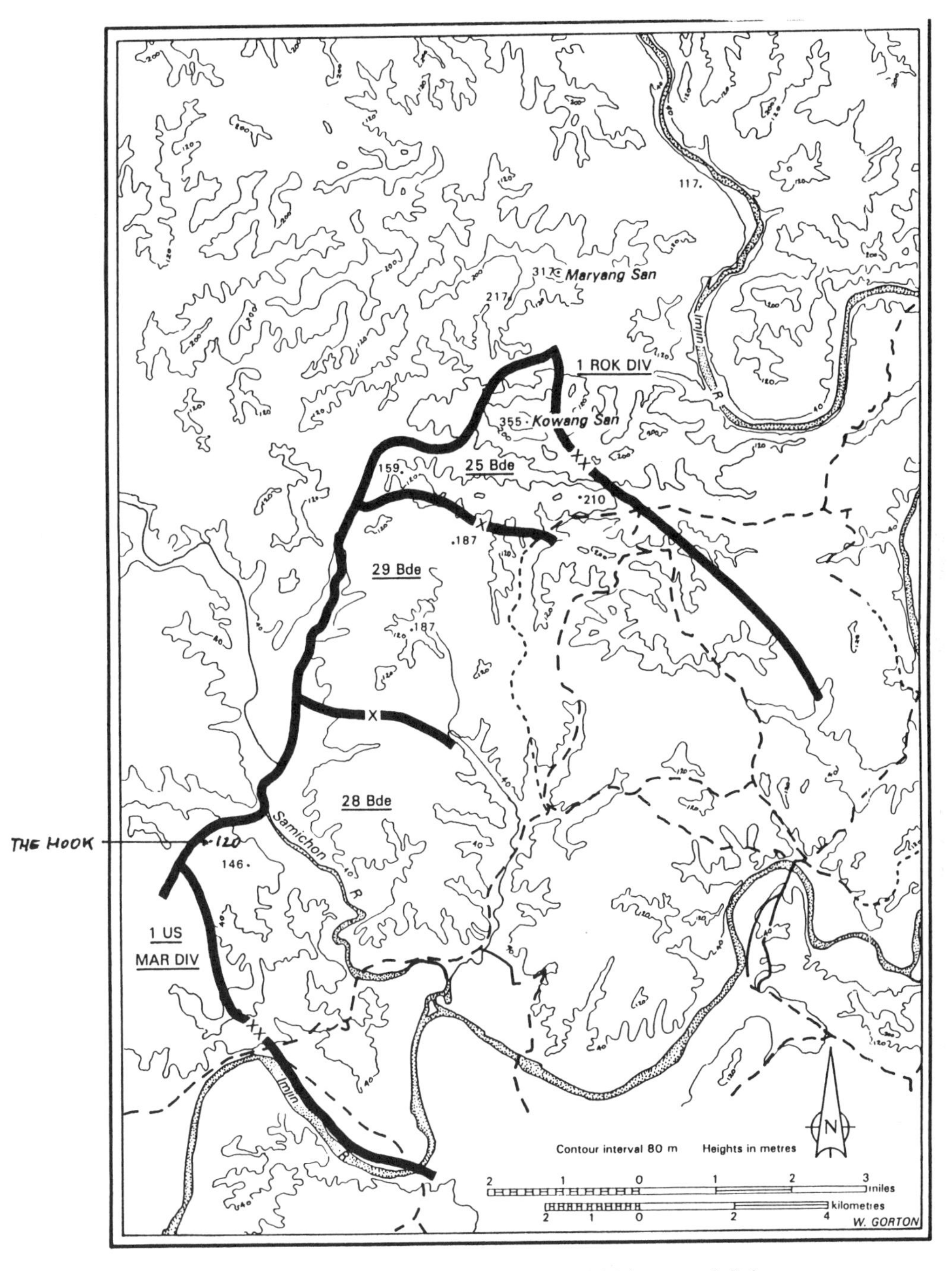

Brigade Dispositions, 1st Commonwealth Division, 10–28 July 1953

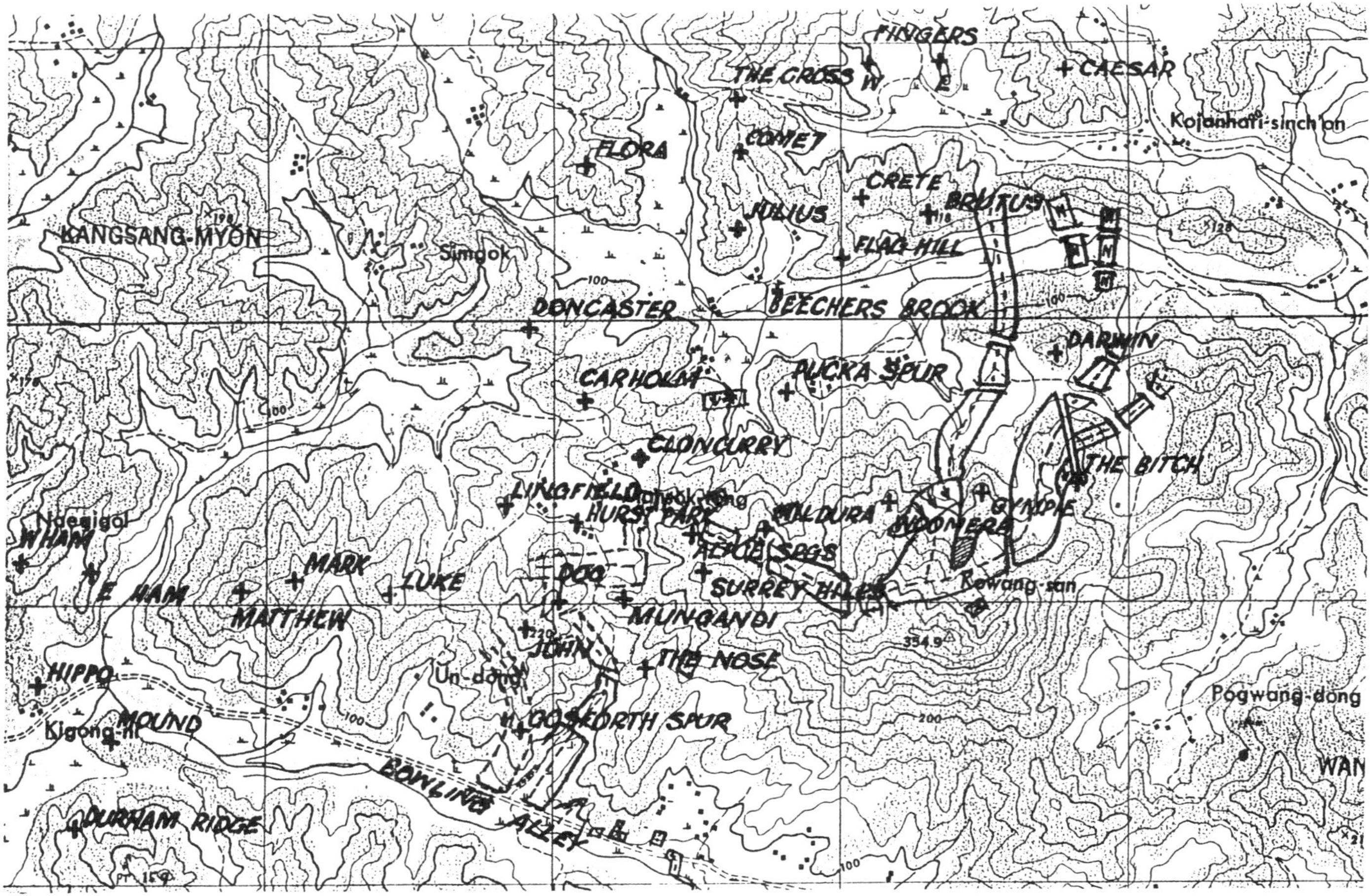

3 RAR Minefields and Topographical Code-names, Hill 355, May 1953 (battle-map of Commanding Officer, Lt. Col. A. L. MacDonald)

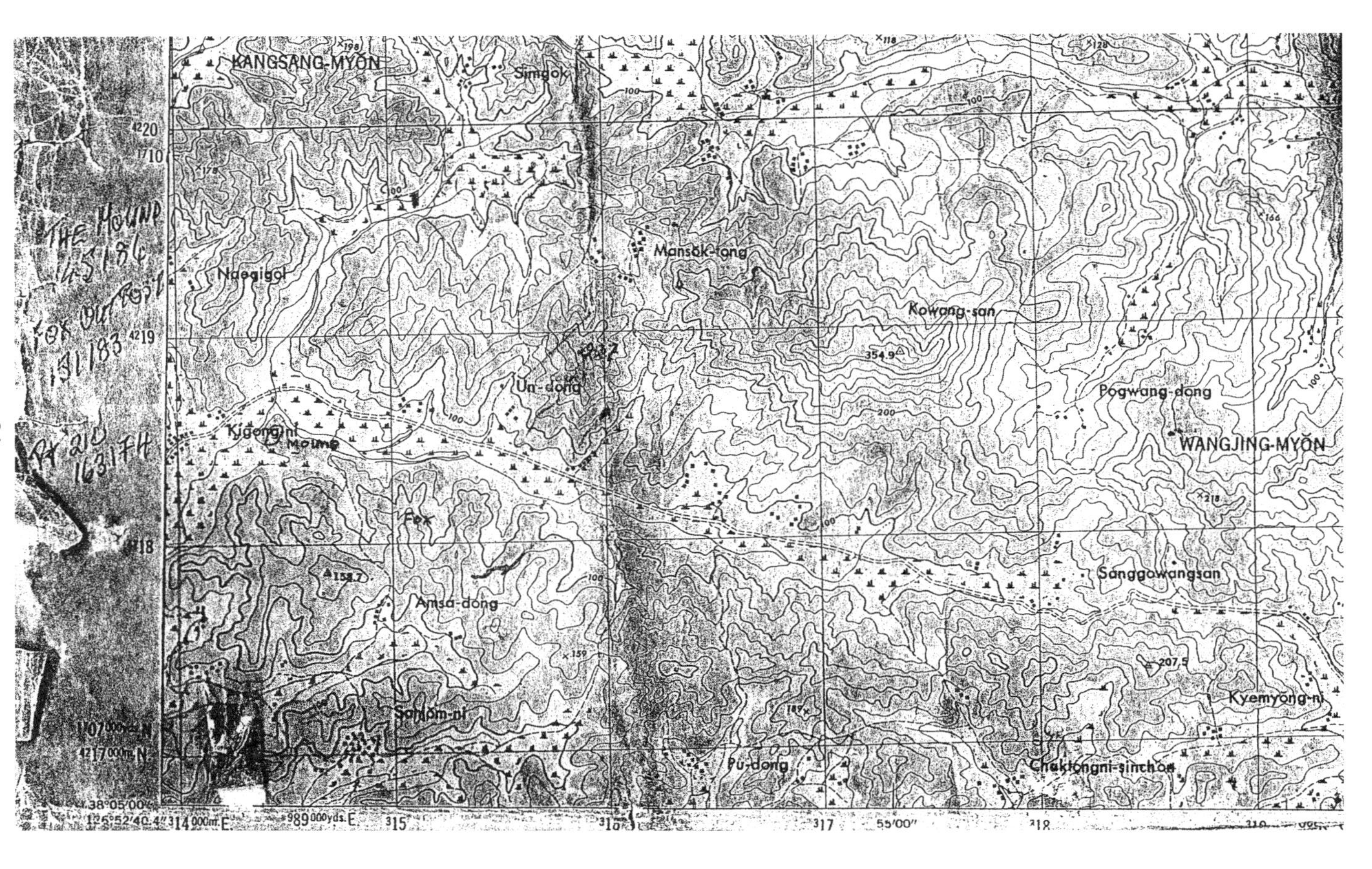
KANGSANG-MYŎN
Simgok
Naegigol
Mansŏk-tong
Kowang-san
354.9
Un-dong
Kigong-ni
Pogwang-dong
WANGJING-MYŎN
Fox
Amsa-dong
Sanggowangsan
207.5
Kyemyŏng-ni
Pu-dong
Chaktongni-sinch'on
4220
4219
4217000m.N.
315
317
318
55'00"

– *Two* –

Hill 355

Hill 355 was the right flank battalion position of the Commonwealth Division's sector, 12 km north of the 38th Parallel and about 30 km from the west coast. The front line, which had become static, was a few kilometres south of the parallel on the western coast but approximately 50 north of it where it met the eastern coast.

The esprit de corps of a well run unit is so great that it forms a bond that stays with its members for the rest of their lives. It is, I believe, stronger than in any other organisation. Colonel Hughes welcomed me at BHQ and impressed me from the start by not being patronising, particularly in view of the fact that unlike the New Zealander I was replacing, I was not a Duntroon graduate; indeed I was not even a regular. One can only speculate that my New Zealand CO, the highly decorated Lt.Col. Harry McElroy D.S.O. and bar and his also decorated and efficient adjutant, Captain Alf Voss M.C., D.C.M. must have given me a good report. Even so, the colonel had every right and indeed reason to at least remind me that the war was no push-over and caution me to take it easy until I had learnt the ropes. But he didn't. He did, however, give me as my sergeant, Mick O'Donnell, who, he emphasised, "Is the most experienced platoon sergeant in the battalion. Do what Mick says should be done, until you have found your feet."

There was nothing wrong with that; I appreciated his confidence and took his advice to heart. Of course, he would have known that I was two years older than Bob Unsworth.

I was well aware that there was a lot to learn about fighting in the Korean war. The basics were the same as the textbook but the local conditions were so different from anything previously experienced that one had to look to the example set and listen to the advice of the men who had been there long enough to know the score. Which, not having been in action before, I would have done anyway. The Battle School played an important role in preparing the reinforcements but, as we all know, there is nothing like the real thing.

I was posted to A Company, commanded by the tough and aggressive WW2 warrior, Major Jim Norrie. He believed, with good reason, that A Company was the best in the battalion. It was dark when I reported to his command post on the reserve company position, on a smaller hill to the rear of Hill 355. Jim Norrie was his usual affable self, but was busy, as the company was preparing to do a counter-attack rehearsal. He turned down my request to accompany him, explaining that, not having seen the ground, I could break my neck. He was of course right so I turned in early, bedding down in an annex adjoining the Coy HQ. The next day I took over No. 1 Platoon. For me, the war started in earnest.

Naturally, the most important thing to do on taking command is to get to know your men. In this I was lucky to have the advantage of being in the reserve company. That gave me more time to sort people out and be sorted out myself. I was most conscious of the fact that they were my men and I was their leader and therefore totally responsible for both their survival and performance. It was obvious that we were undermanned. With the fighting that had been going on, that was not surprising. However, reinforcements would bring us up to strength before we were committed again.

A day or two after I took over, Mick O'Donnell lined up half a dozen newly arrived reinforcements for me to meet. I went along the line and shook hands with each man, welcoming him into the platoon. When I came to a short but tough looking soldier named Roy Stewart, I did a double take. I recognised him, but did not have a clue why or where. "I have seen you somewhere before," I said. Then it hit me. "Yes, you're the man who saluted outside the Q Store in Hiro."

"That's right sir," he said with a huge grin. "I said to my mate George here, watch me embarrass these Kiwi officers."

"Well, Stewart, you didn't embarrass us but you cost me a bottle of beer." We all had a good laugh when I explained the full story, and he became one of the best men in a platoon of best men. 'Honest Roy' Stewart and his mate 'Square Deal George' Chandler were inseparable and made a great combination as forward scouts, without doubt the most nerve-wracking and dangerous job in night patrolling. I made sure right from the beginning that they were put in the same section. There will be more of Roy Stewart later. But I must say that I was very upset when, in hospital myself, I learnt that he had lost an eye in action. I could not visit him, as he had been sent straight home to Australia.

There were gaps in my organization that had to be attended to. The platoon was in fact, run down. Section leaders, Section 2IC and signallers were the obvious ones. Rather than rush in and get it wrong, I talked to the men individually and in groups to assess their personalities. So as not to make obvious what I was doing, I also stood back a lot, watching attitudes and performances as the sergeant sent them about their daily chores. Talking to some of the older men, I found that they had a certain respect for one of the younger ones. Likewise, some younger men expressed respect for an older man. We were all under 25, with the exception of the sergeant Mick O'Donnell and another digger, Bernie Cocks. They were WW2 veterans, but still under 30. I knew that I had to work fast, as A Company could replace a forward company at any time. In the final analysis, it came down to my own gut feeling about an individual.

Corporal Whitney retained No. 1 section, with Private Fred Wilson his section 2IC. Private Bernie Cocks, a quiet West Australian from Perth, impressed me as a real professional soldier. At 29, he was a veteran of the New Guinea campaign of the second world war, besides being on his second tour of duty in the Korean. An 'original', he had got within sight of the Yalu with the battalion. Steady and sound of judgement, Bernie was a team man with a flair for acting decisively when the situation called for it. A quiet but born leader would be the best description of this tough and resilient professional fighting man, who started as a volunteer soldier in WW2. Not only had Cocks seen a lot of action, but also somewhere along the line he had, like some of the other diggers, worked as an opal miner at Lightning Ridge. His ability to get the best performance out of the men was instinctive. I persuaded him to take over No. 2 Section, initially with the rank of Acting Lance-Corporal.

Major Norrie backed me when I pushed for substantive rank for my promoted men. Like me, he believed that if they could do the job, they should receive the appropriate pay for the extra responsibility. Temporary or acting rank attracted no pay increase. Private Kevin (Ned) Kelly became Bernie's Section 2IC. No. 3 Section was already in the capable charge of Lance-Corporal Jacky Coyle, another straight and open West

Australian, who at 22 was a little older than the average. His 2IC was Tony Johnstone. Colin Turner and Terry Chinn were made platoon signallers, and very reliable they both were. They picked up the radio techniques quickly and were each sent on a signaller's course when the chances came. As it turned out, I doubt whether my original choice could have been improved on. But, having said that, it was remarkable just how capable and how conscientious the majority of the men were. We never wanted for reliable replacements in any appointment.

Five days after I took command of No. 1 platoon, the order came for A Company to do a night relief of B Company, on the left forward company position at the western end of the mighty Hill 355. It was popularly believed that the major, wishing to keep A Company in the action, had pleaded with the colonel for the most forward position. It was a four-platoon position, in that it included Anti-tank Ridge, a low spur running south-west off Hill 355's left flank. It protected the rear of the hill from penetration along the dry paddy plain, known as the Bowling Alley, that ran south-east across the front, between the UNO position on Pt. 159 and the enemy held hills Matthew, Mark, Luke and John, which were linked into one feature and were collectively nicknamed the Apostles. The Bowling Alley carried on behind Hill 355, while the front-line turned north between it and John and then east again around the front of 355.

Lt. Jack Kelly, a first rate Duntroon graduate commanding the 60-strong anti-tank platoon that manned this vital position, attended all A Company's O Groups, receiving his routine orders there and his operational orders from BHQ. We considered Jack and his men part of A Company. The ridge they held hid A Company's jeep-head from prying eyes.

The most direct route into no-man's land from my platoon position was down Mildura Spur, running due north from my right flank, which was also the company's right boundary. It was well defined and very steep. My centre overlooked the long spur of Surrey Hills. Pointing north-westerly toward the Chinese positions like an accusing finger, it descended deep into no-man's land, which was fairly wide immediately to our front because of the nature of the terrain and the dominance of Hill 355. Surrey Hills had some tactical ground at our end, then dropped quickly, levelled out and dipped again. Two hundred metres further on, a knoll known as Alice Springs stood alone. Quite a good name really, as it was so far out. On the left of the track over Alice Springs was the outspread shape of a Chinese soldier. It could be seen from our trenches, because the lime that had been applied to the body showed up like a white shadow. The Alice Springs outpost, comprising three fighting pits connected by a crawl trench, was on the forward slope out of sight of the main position and was manned at night.

A Company's most vulnerable ground was Anti-tank Ridge and Surrey Hills overlooked by a Chinese OP known as Dog Outpost, 300 metres to the west on the slope of Pt. 227, which was nicknamed John. As the easternmost hill of the Apostle complex, it was the closest Chinese position to Hill 355. The top end of the Surrey Hills spur was in the capable hands of Lt. John Hooper's platoon. They would never get past No. 2 platoon while John commanded it. An assault up the long spur could be heavily punished with artillery fire. The artillery OP on the western end of 355 had an excellent view of it but the infantry would still have to pick off the proportion of enemy that would survive a barrage. The left forward company position had been close to being lost when the 3rd Battalion Royal Canadian Regiment was attacked in October '52. Streaming out from behind John, the Chinese advanced up the main communication trench. But a Canadian .30 calibre Browning medium machine-gun, firing down the trench from the centre company, took such a heavy toll that the attacking infantry climbed out of the trench and endeavoured to continue up the open ground on the sides of the long spur. The artillery put paid to that. Had the Chinese succeeded, it is certain that they would have poured in more men and pressed on, to invest the whole feature.

Between No. 2 Platoon's position down Surrey Hills and No. 1 Platoon on the eastern end of A Company's position, was No. 3 Platoon. Due to heavy losses among junior officers, it was under the capable command of Sergeant Jack Morrison. Jack later became CSM of A Company, with a DCM. Later still in Vietnam, he earned a bar to that. A flamboyant born leader, full of bullshit, but as game as they come, he harboured resentment against junior officers. Our company command post was to the rear of my platoon position on the reverse slope. It was therefore in dead ground from direct shellfire. However, the enemy tended more and more to favour box barrages, that is, concentrating all their artillery firepower on to a chosen area at any one time. So the CP got its share of shelling.

The platoon was well settled into the new position by mid-morning the next day, when one of the diggers tipped me off that the mortar OP was manned by a Kiwi. Arriving at the empty OP, I soon found the entrance to a nearby dugout, known in the theatre as a hutchie. Sticking my head in the entrance, I called out, "Anybody home?"

"Come in!" yelled back a cheerful New Zealand voice. I became more and more shocked as I crawled in. The bunker had taken a direct hit from at least one sizeable shell, its roof had collapsed and it had been burnt out. Within a metre of the floor the roof had stabilised and was shored up with new timbers, like pit props in a coalmine. Rubbish lay everywhere from an earlier occupation, as no one had found time to remove it. In the furthest and safest looking corner, half lying and half sitting, as there was no headroom even to sit let alone standing room, was none other than Sergeant Jack Spiers, the mortar platoon's mortar fire controller (MFC). During the previous two years, Jack had stood out among the various acquaintances that I had made among the instructors at Army Schools, Waiouru Military Camp. He and I were kindred spirits and remained so until his recent death, having been cobbers since Korea. Lack of heating in the battered hutchie was a problem, as it was no longer practical to put in a stove, which was so necessary at that time of the year. More like the home of the feathered kiwi, it was all that was available for one of the most valuable men on the hill. Luckily for us he was a tough Dunedin-ite, so did not let the cold get him down. A reunion is a reunion, and over a brew of tea we compared notes. Not having seen each other since my mortar course at the School of Infantry, neither of us was aware that the other had volunteered to go to Korea with the Aussies. There really was no time for socialising on Little Gibraltar, but while prowling around my position on the nights that I was not out in the valley, I would look in on Jack's OP for a bit of a chat. He was always on his toes, scanning the dark front, interpreting the gun flashes or sounds of small arms fire. In the event of a little excitement, I would scuttle off to either my own CP to ensure that everyone was on the ball, or straight to Company HQ, which was also within my platoon perimeter, for a more comprehensive picture and maybe orders. If all was quiet, I might share an hour of Jack's lonely vigil and sometimes the counter bombardment that his OP attracted.

The first thing that the experienced diggers taught me about surviving in the forward position was to recognise the plop of a mortar being fired at us, to judge time of flight, and when to crouch below the parapet of the trench with the studied casualness that is the hallmark of a veteran. Jack Coyle and Larry Francisco were my tutors one morning in the platoon's observation post. The enemy provided the accompaniment. Once you know what to listen for, the drill of sheltering from mortar bombs heading in your direction becomes a subconscious act. If, several seconds after hearing the plop, a fluttering whistling sound is heard, it is time to duck below the parapet and hope that the bomb does not join you. I subsequently realised that Jack Coyle was the most conscientious OP man I had. He possessed remarkable powers of observation, plus the tactical judgement to assess the importance of what he saw. He reported day-to-day changes, like fresh diggings in the Chinese lines and new dumps of defence stores, such as a load of timber. These of course made good targets for our artillery. We passed back a lot of valuable information gathered by this very able soldier.

At my first Company O Group, I was informed that No. 1 Platoon was to send out a patrol that night, leaving our FDLs at 1800 hrs. Mick O'Donnell would command it and I would accompany him as a supernumerary for my first familiarisation patrol, to start learning the ropes. It was to be a fighting patrol of one and 15; that is, one officer or sergeant and fifteen men. That was standard within the battalion and in winter time we set several ambushes of 30 minutes duration, as one could not sit still any longer without risking frostbite. As we proceeded, Mick gave me such tips as he thought necessary and the patrol passed off uneventfully, as most of them did. The next night was my finishing class, Lt. John Hooper having been detailed to take me along with his No. 2 Platoon patrol. I went happily with the man who had the reputation of being a master of the art. We went down Mildura Spur and returned through the more gradual Surrey Hills. The Mildura track had been crunched for so long by heavy boots, it had become hard and slippery ice. We had not gone far down the razorback spur leading into no-man's land when, instead of the ball of my foot, I carelessly put the heel down first. My backside was second and I slid helplessly out of control into the minefield on the right. In my surprise I dropped my Owen gun which slid into the minefield on the left. The patrol stopped. I crawled out, cursing under my breath and continued on hands and knees across the track and into the other minefield to retrieve my Owen. I knew that I had made a fool of myself, but the diggers never mentioned it. I realised later that the fields had almost certainly been laid by British units, so would have had the 5-metre free fringe inside the marker wire.

John Hooper was the finest type of officer that any army could wish for. Very capable, conscientious and affable without being cocky, both his men and his contemporaries held him in high regard. During the course of this patrol, he kept me near him and explained what he was doing and why. After the tuition patrol, which covered a lot of ground, I was considered capable of leading my own fighting patrols. I also felt confident that I could.

One morning after we had been on Hill 355 for about four days, our commanding officer, Lt. Colonel R.L. Hughes DSO, arrived at my command post and asked me to accompany him on an inspection of my platoon position. He did not concern himself with inspecting the hutchies where the troops slept. He would be well aware that the resourceful diggers had made them as comfortable as they could under the circumstances. But he did have a look at the fighting pits and bunkers. Now, it could have been that he knew that an air strike on to Pt. 227 was planned and that my position, being the best to observe from, was to be inundated with VIPs. Or was it to test my courage that, when we reached the best vantage point and he spotted an empty food can 20 or so metres up the slope behind the communication trench, he remarked that it looked untidy and was not what one would expect of a top rate platoon? He had conveniently overlooked the fact that the tin was rusty and weather-worn and that I had just occupied the position. Careful not to fall into the trap of saying, "I will have it shifted tonight," I climbed out of the 2-metre deep trench. No easy task in itself. Retrieving the offending can, I was sliding down the steep slope on my backside as fast as I could, knowing full well how visible I was to the enemy. Just before I regained the protection of the trench, a sniper's bullet zapped past my left ear and slammed into the slope, a metre behind me. Had we been on The Hook, the sniper would have been armed with a 76 mm high velocity self-propelled gun, and it would have been all over. However, the CO was satisfied and continued the inspection cheerfully. He was a bloody good bloke.

Another morning it was reported to me that a camouflage net had slipped from in front of some digging that the Chinese had been engaged in on the slopes of Pt. 227. Taking a look through my binoculars, I had no doubt that the picket had spotted something worthwhile. But rather than call artillery onto an empty hole, I decided to lay a Bren gun on fixed lines and have a go ourselves that night, when the Chinese would be working on their project. When it was fully dark and patrols were in position, there was the usual quiet period. This was the time for three of us who had set it up in the morning to act. The Bren, set on automatic, fired one round and we heard the bullet strike metal. It sounded like a shovel. But that one round was all. The Bren gun stopped. The gunner checked the change lever. It was of course on automatic. He cocked it again, fired, and the same thing happened. I lost interest in the target. I wanted to know why the gun played up. It was important to find out. We retired to a hutchie and stripped the Bren. Nothing broken, but something had to be wrong. I reasoned that as the weapon had been sitting out in the freezing conditions all day, the metal had contracted. Then the hot gas blowing back the working parts had expanded the piston, jamming it in the cylinder. We tried heating the cylinder in different ways, but with no success. I was very concerned that in the event of an attack on our position, the cold could stop our main weapons from functioning. Finally, we took another Bren out of the dugout and fired a few bursts. No trouble, and the culprit, having been kept under cover this time, fired when we tested it again the next afternoon. From then on during the cold spell, I had the Brens kept under cover until needed.

Years later, I was discussing the incident with a 24th Battalion 2nd NZEF man who had served in Italy. He told me that they had experienced the same problem in the snow conditions. They eventually solved it by taking the springs out of 36 grenades and inserting them behind the recoil springs in the butts of the Brens. The only side effect, he reported, was that it increased their rate of fire.

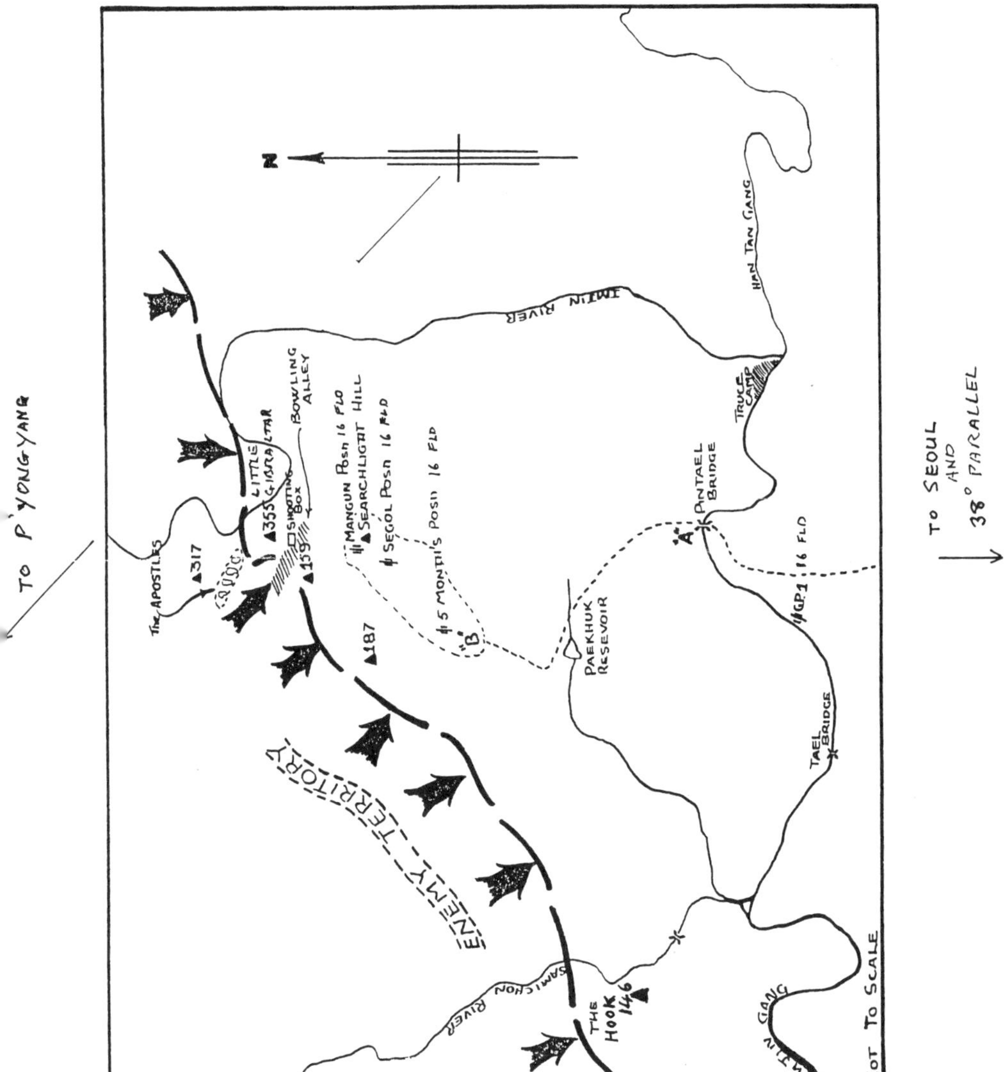

TO P'YONGYANG

The APOSTLES
▲317
LITTLE GIBRALTAR
▲355
SHOOTING BOX
BOWLING ALLEY
▲159
▲187
MANGUN Posn 16 FLD
▲SEARCHLIGHT HILL
SEGOL Posn 16 FLD
5 MONTH'S Posn 16 FLD
"B"
ENEMY TERRITORY
N
IMJIN RIVER
SAMICHON RIVER
THE HOOK
146▲
PAEKHUK RESEVOIR
"A"
PINTAEL BRIDGE
TRUCE CAMP
HAN TAN GANG
IMJIN GANG
TAEL BRIDGE
GP 1 16 FLD
NOT TO SCALE

TO SEOUL AND 38° PARALLEL

– *Three* –

Settling In

One night, before I had learned very much, I was informed by phone through Company from Battalion, that one of our patrols had chased a lone Chinese soldier into a minefield in front of my position between the Surrey Hills spur and Mildura. The patrol had spread out across the bottom of the open square.

This sounded great: we might have a chance of capturing a prisoner. I sent a runner to alert the pickets while I organised extra men. We manned the communication trench as well as the fighting pit and bunkers in that area. I was confident that, with minefields on the flanks and the patrol at the bottom of the hill, the Chinese soldier's only option was to climb to the top. My reasoning was that, from his point of view, to go back or sideways would be suicidal, whereas by climbing to the top he had a chance of evading our pickets or surrendering. After some time without results, I got restive. Taking one man with me, I checked out the reserve position that we had started digging on the higher ground behind us. From there we went even higher to our platoon OP trench. No dice. Returning to the communication trench, I figured he could be just about in front of us, boxed in by the two mined spurs, the patrol in the paddy field and our trench.

At A echelon, where I drew my weaponry on my way forward to join the battalion, I had been issued with an illuminating grenade. This seemed like a suitable occasion to use it. I warned the men, pulled the pin and heaved it. As the ground was steep, throwing it lit up a fair bit of 'real estate.' There was nothing to be seen but barbed wire and minefields. Not a thing moved, except the army system. I stood down the off-duty men and returned to my command post. A message was already waiting: "Ring BHQ at once."

Identifying myself, I was connected to an unfriendly voice.

"A flare has been observed on your frontage and you have not reported it. What is going on?"

My explanation only made things worse. It was tersely explained to me that such conduct was unacceptable, as firing illumination indicates a jumpy unit. Which is quite true. I should have sent a patrol down the track.

Another morning, we platoon commanders were sitting in the company command post on whatever we could find, in some cases the earth floor. Major Norrie was holding his daily O Group. Also present were the company 2IC, Captain Colin Brown; the company sergeant major, Jack Spiers; and a sergeant from the British field engineers. As usual the Boss was delivering his orders like a machine-gun.

"Kiwi," he said turning to me, "You will be wiring tonight. I have noticed a gap in the wire at the top of Surrey Hills between your position and Morrison's. We might as well tidy it up. I want you to field as many men as possible and put up a 'high wire fence.' Do you know what that is?"

"Yes sir. It is a dannet fence held down with extra stays, etc."

"Good. But I don't want a description now. But you do know that dannet is concertina?"

"Yes, sir. But that's what the Poms call it."

"Damn it, Matthews, don't refer to our allies like that."

"Sorry, sir."

Pointing to the Royal Engineer sergeant he said, "Well, talk to the sergeant when the O Group is over, and don't forget that he is English. Ha! ha! ha!"

Turning to Sergeant Morrison, temporarily in command of 3 Platoon, Jim Norrie continued, "Jack, I want you to provide a covering patrol to make sure that Kiwi's lot doesn't get jumped. A Chinese patrol may well hear the activity. A full one and 15, Jack. Don't go yourself. Put a corporal in charge. How does that sound to you, Kiwi?"

"Fine thank you, sir. But where do we get the stores? Wire, pickets and stuff?"

"Good point, Kiwi. That's what the sergeant is here for." Another chuckle. "Over to you, Sarg."

"Thank you, surr," replied the very English engineer. Turning to me, he said, "Surr, we will have all the gear for you at the junction of the Jeep head and the Surrey Hills trench, at 1830 hrs. Is that OK, surr?"

It sure was, because the junction was at the top of the hill, not the bottom. I thought he must have had access to Korean labour for such a Herculean task.

"First class, Sergeant," I replied, trying to sound like a pukka English officer. But I only succeeded in sounding more like a Pig islander than usual.

1830 hrs came, and the efficient Brit sergeant had delivered the goods: heavy coils of 1.4-metre diameter concertina barbed wire, two types of pickets, waratahs and screw pickets as I had requested. The latter were rolled 16 mm round steel shaped into giant corkscrews, with loops twisted into the stem to hook the barbed wire in. I took the lot with us, because no one knew which type of picket would work best in the frozen ground. I doubt that any wiring had been done in the battalion since the winter weather set in. To drive the fluted waratah pickets into the ground, a monkey was provided. Called in civy street a thumper, this is a pipe sleeve with a heavy steel disk welded on top and two light pipe handles welded on top and bottom, running parallel with the sleeve. The sleeve is slipped over the straight steel picket and, with a man on each handle, the whole contraption is slid up and then slammed down. In soft ground the picket will be driven in quickly and efficiently and without the frustration of missing that can happen with a sledgehammer. The noise could only be muffled somewhat by stuffing empty sand bags into the sleeve. However, we gave it a go, because it might have penetrated the frozen ground more easily than the screw type. The noise had to be accepted. I had briefed the men that, in the event of flares being fired in our direction, they were to freeze. It has been proven many times, in many wars, that movement is the main give-away. As it turned out, there were flares quite near us, but we were not spotted. We soon found that the ground was far too hard for the waratahs to be driven into. It was permafrost, the same as we had on the company position. The soil would have been frozen as hard as concrete to a depth of 600 mm.

Luckily, I had also had the foresight to bring along picks, so we tried digging holes with them to give the screw pickets a start. This technique worked. But it must be said that we were not able to screw them in very far. However, they were firmly enough embedded to enable us to place the rolls of concertina wire between them without them falling over. We then anchored the whole lot down with wire stays, windlassed to steel pegs that had been determinedly driven into the frozen ground with sledgehammers. Once the thaw came, the coils of concertina would bed themselves in. The finished job was two rows of concertina wire pegged down with wire stays with another roll on top, also pegged down with stays. This local pattern barbed wire obstacle was a combination of what the training pamphlets called a cat wire fence and a triple concertina fence. After six hours of hard labour on the forward slope we were all glad to finish without interruption from the enemy. I'm sure that No. 3 Platoon men were also glad when I gave them the nod by radio to pack up. They would have been freezing while we were sweating.

In the platoon command post there were only two beds, each constructed with seven waratah pickets. Two uprights were driven into the clay floor at each end and two lashed horizontally lengthwise, onto the uprights, about 2 feet (610 mm) above the floor. The seventh was cut in half and lashed crosswise at each end, to complete and brace the rectangular structure. The lashing was done with a strong type of signal wire called assault cable. The frame thus formed was then laced lengthwise and crosswise with more assault cable, making an excellent platform on which to sleep. It would almost be exaggerating to call them beds, as we slept fully dressed, boots and all, on top of our sleeping bags with our Owen guns hanging by their slings on the outside picket, by our heads. Mick owned one bunk and I the other. The verticals were high enough to hang a blanket from, stopping the light from the signaller's Tilly lantern from shining on the sleeper's face. In the CP, we kept the lamps going around the clock. The Tilly kerosene lamps were good for bright light and safety. They burned with a sound not unlike the hum of the present day computers. The radio's squelch and crackle also joined in, and combining with the quiet male tones of the signaller's voice, produced a mini-opera effect. I soon learnt to ignore the background sounds and slept my few hours soundly. In the rest of the platoon's bunkers there were top bunks as well, as the ceilings of the bunkers were 1.8 to 2 metres above the floor and at least 1.2 metres below the surface. Some hutchies were deep enough to have three tiers of bunks.

In the winter, the divisional field park at Rear Div provided each front-line battalion with an allocation of diesel/water drip stoves to heat the hutchies. Nicknamed choofers, they made life in the subzero temperatures bearable. Unfortunately, six or seven per platoon was insufficient for the strength of an Australian platoon. Our platoons were about six men larger than the British ones and, although there was no shortage of bunkers, they were not all equipped with choofers. The shortfall was made good by the resourceful diggers making wood burning choofers out of 2 inch (51 mm) mortar pressed steel ammunition boxes. The flues were fashioned from the tubes that the ammunition for the Centurion tanks' main armourment came in. Wood was by no means plentiful as the trees had all been blown to pieces, but once again they managed. If anyone came across some wood from ammo boxes, tree stumps, etc, they appropriated it for their mates.

It had been the policy in the platoon, which I did not change, to keep night and day throughout the bitter winter months, a jerrycan of water on the command post choofer. It provided the hot water for the whole platoon for shaving or making coffee. Our CP routine was as follows. As activity quietened down in the wee hours of the morning, Mick or I checked the pickets, while Battalion debriefed the one who had been patrolling, usually over the phone. We then turned in, leaving the Sig on duty to keep a listening watch and wake us if necessary. We would be up and shaved before morning 'stand to'. Then half an hour before dawn we would rouse the men, to man their posts for an hour.

My way of washing in the line had been taught me by a WW2 desert veteran. Fill one's mug with our precious water, clean teeth first, wash face second, and then shave. Wash armpits and crotch, then one boot off at a time, to wash feet and change socks. With my feet powdered with zinc powder to keep tinea at bay, they were set up for the next 24 hours. Hands were a problem to keep clean, because of the oil picked up when handling guns. I inspected every man's rifle, Owen gun or Bren gun, every day, not counting cleaning my own Owen gun and pistol. But a wipe of the hands with a sweat rag, which was part of our issue kit, helped. We were back in Camp Casey before I had a shower, nine weeks after going into the line. But to be realistic, this was not the desert. Temperatures were –25 degrees Celsius or 42 degrees below freezing point Fahrenheit. Which could be handled quite comfortably if you opened your clothing enough to allow your body to breathe when doing anything requiring exertion, like digging or walking about in no-man's land. You reduced the sweating, which was aggravated by the wind-proof nylon winter clothing, yet retained some heat by zipping up upon stopping. We were well served by our winter clothing. During the first year of the war, when winter temperatures were the lowest in Korea for 50 years, the men of the 27th British Commonwealth Brigade, which included 3 RAR, wore only the WW2 type battledress. To make their plight worse, the war was very fluid at that time so they had fewer chances of getting below ground, where there is more protection from the elements.

One morning, a little over a week after moving on to Hill 355, disaster struck No. 1 Platoon's HQ hutchie. The Sig woke us and departed to his own hutchie to clean himself up before breakfast. He was then free to sleep until lunchtime, as his relief took over after breakfast. I had, as usual, turned in fully dressed except for my nylon combat jacket, but Mick had removed his woollen shirt before putting his head down. As he walked past the stove, he brushed the lid of the jerrycan full of water, which was kept hot throughout the night, so that there was hot water for the whole platoon to shave with in the morning. Jerrycans have a lid on the pouring spout that is locked in position by curved pawls that slide into slots on the side of the spout, clamping the lid down tightly so that they can be carried without spilling. During the night the lid, which was always left open when the can was on the stove, had somehow dropped onto the spout, and the pawls had hooked lightly into their slots, holding the lid shut and causing a head of steam to build up. When Mick's touch dislodged them all hell broke loose. It was as if we had a Rotorua geyser inside the 3 x 3 x 2.8 metre hole in the ground. The dugout quickly filled with opaque boiling steam. Our issue singlets were 10-mm mesh string ones; designed to keep airspace between the skin and the shirt, to improve insulation. With my tightly woven woollen shirt over mine, I had much better protection from the steam. Reacting instinctively, we both made a dash for the trench that led to the surface. We couldn't see and collided in the bottom doorway. Mick collapsed. No wonder, with the terrible steam burns that he had suffered. I dragged him up the short tunnel to the crawl trench that circled the position and called for stretcher-bearers. My burns were superficial, but Mick had to be evacuated and did not come back. When I met up with him again in Japan, five months later, he seemed OK. But I have since been told by a chap who served with Mick later in Vietnam that his back was badly scarred.

It was bad luck for Mick, but what about the platoon? I knew that I had a problem, but it never even occurred to me to ask for a replacement sergeant.

Corporal Bernie Cocks, as he now was, was the oldest and most experienced man in the platoon, including me. He had taken a firm grip of his section and they had responded splendidly. I never saw his pay book so I didn't know whether he had held rank before or not. He was six years older than me and very steady. I approached him. He was prepared to work with me as my sergeant. I then spoke to Jim Norrie and he was in agreement with the appointment. After getting further assurance from the major of substantive rank for my new NCOs I told Bernie that he was now my off-sider. From memory, I think that Peter Gulson took over No. 2 Section, when Bernie moved into the command post.

It was an excellent arrangement from the start. I never had a cross word with Bernie. He took his soldiering seriously and was totally unflappable. He possessed a dry sense of humour, and had seen it all, although he never mentioned his past unless asked. When he joined me in running the sub-unit, it was business-like from the start, and of course there was no break in operations. Patrolling, digging and looking after the men had to be carried on regardless of the state of order or disorder.

The only hiccup that we ever had happened immediately after Bernie moved into the CP. I was informed at the Company O Group that I was to do my solo patrol that night. After the Company O group, I had to walk off the hill and back along the Bowling Alley to be briefed at battalion headquarters. In the event, the patrol took several hours. There were several sound reasons for sending patrols into no-man's land each night. The two basic types of patrols were fighting and recce. Fighting patrols were essential to a unit's security. The aim was to dominate the ground between the opposing sides so that the enemy could not probe our positions or mount a night attack without us getting prior warning. Sometimes a fighting patrol just moved around no-man's land, but we frequently set ambushes. In the winter, the temperatures dropping to –20 degrees Centigrade, necessitated setting four or five ambushes instead of just one or two. With each ambush being of 25 minutes duration, at least five minutes walking time was required to thaw out again, before setting another. In addition it took 30 minutes to move out into the valley and the same to come in again.

It went off without a hitch or, rather disappointingly at the time, a contact. But I came back in the early hours of the morning utterly exhausted. After a thorough debriefing by the adjutant over the phone, I crashed. We had, as was the drill, test fired our automatic weapons in the rear of the position before going out on patrol. I was so tired when I returned and had been debriefed, that I forgot to clean my Owen gun before turning in. Bernie happened to pick it up from where it was hanging, when we got up for morning 'stand to'. Noting from its dirty condition that it had been fired, he asked whose gun it was. He nearly had a fit when I confessed that it was mine. Rightly so, too; I never forgot again. But I knew that I had a bloody good sergeant. Life settled down nicely in No. 1 Platoon. Bernie had a very good management style with the diggers and the platoon was a happy one. We were also lucky in only suffering a couple of relatively minor casualties from 81 mm mortar fire during that period. The more so, as harassing fire from artillery and mortars was a fact of daily life.

One humorous incident occurred after a night when the enemy must have had a bad liver or blamed us for something that upset him. We got pounded with a particularly heavy artillery bombardment from 0200 hrs until 0400 hrs. There were no casualties at the time. The OC's batman was a good keen bloke, burdened with the nickname of 'Mary' bestowed on him by the other diggers by virtue of his appointment, though there was nothing like that about him. He was a red-blooded soldier doing his job and contributing, with his sense of humour, a considerable amount to the smooth running of the company command post. As usual, Mary was up before stand-to, to prepare himself for the new day. He went to the Coy HQ latrine in the pitch dark with an outside temperature of 20 plus degrees below freezing point. The latrine was a sandbagged structure, 30 metres down the reverse slope, sheltering half of a 44 gallon drum with a hole cut in the end; and dug in over the long drop. A round wooden disk set inside the rim of the drum, with a corresponding hole and a hinged wooden lid, completed the fly proofing and at the same time provided maximum comfort.

I certainly did not carry out an enquiry. Neither did anyone else. But I was personally familiar with the comfort of this loo. I reckon that because it was winter with no flies around on account of the terribly cold temperatures the users had become slack in their haste to return to the warm company command post and the practice of not putting down the lid had crept in. Mary therefore assumed that the seat's lid had been left up. It was freezing cold in the snow and the biting wind, especially at 0430 hrs. He must have been so glad to gain the shelter of the dunny that he did not notice that a shell had blown the wooden seat away. In the light of day, it was obvious that the whole edifice had been dealt a cruel blow. But not as cruel as what happened to Mary. He sat straight down onto the freezing cold steel drum. Gamely he stayed on the hill, but had to lie on his stomach for a few days to re-grow the missing skin.

Now that I was on the Big Hill, I sought out the 16th NZ Field Regiment OP. We were supported by 163 Battery commanded by Major Roy Spence, M.B.E., M.C. His senior observation post officer was Major Jock McLanachan who later commanded the battery himself. A very pleasant, quiet and unassuming New Zealander, Jock was most friendly toward the young Kiwi and jokingly had me on for opting to go to war with the infantry. I learnt later, that he himself had been in the infantry in WW2. They had heard that I was coming and Major Spence had instructed his troop commanders to enquire if there was anything that I needed. It was an offer which I subsequently took up. When my Australian issue boots lost their shape in the wet paddy fields, I mentioned it to Jock. A pair of New Zealand army boots arrived the following day. Jack Spiers received the same helping hand and backup from these great men. They were very supportive.

– *Four* –
The Environment

Typical Korean terrain is river flats and paddy fields, tucked in between masses of hills. Not necessarily precipitous, but too steep to be able to walk up comfortably. Their heights vary. The average for a dominant feature on the western or Yellow Sea side is about 200 metres, increasing steadily across the country to over 1000 metres high near the east coast, which is washed by the Sea of Japan, called the Eastern Sea by the Koreans. The country is very mountainous where the coast bulges further east and north, meeting both the Chinese and the U.S.S.R. borders just 150 km short of Vladivostok. Some hills are clustered together forming a major feature. Others, linked by saddles, form high and defensible ranges. But there are also a surprising number of individual hills rising out of the flat land, with paddy all around them.

The Koreans don't grow their crops high up re-entrants, like other rice-growing people. I believe the reason lies in their history. Various invaders have, over the centuries, ruthlessly carried out deforestation. Most recent were the Japanese, who occupied the country for 45 years before the end of the second world war, and used, as they did elsewhere, the whole of the Korean Peninsula as a source of raw material for homeland Japan. The harsh climate has denuded the unprotected hills of their topsoil and loosened boulders, which have been used by the Koreans to build paddy bunds designed to trap water and soil that is washed off the hills by the torrential monsoon rains. The result is paddy fields which are the gardens in which the Koreans grow their vegetables, including the staple, rice. The bunds are in valleys and across re-entrants. Conforming to the contours of the land, they control the flow of water from one paddy to another until it reaches a river at the lowest part of the valley.

The dearth of topsoil on the hills also meant that the combatants had only hard clay or solid rock to dig into. We blew the rock, while the Chinese used compressed air drills to good effect. They also tended to dig deeper and developed tunnel systems more than we did. But they had more men, both to do the digging and to provide cover for. However, the New Zealand Field Engineers Company dug tunnels into The Hook features.

During the spring thaw and the summer monsoon rains, the rivers carry terrific run-offs flowing from the high ground in the east, gushing and winding through the deep and narrow gorges to the western plains. There, they slow down somewhat in the meandering river beds that the rivers have carved for themselves through the flatter and wider valleys, occasionally forming a shingle and sand ford on their way to the Yellow Sea. On the eastern coastal fringe, mostly in North Korea, rivers plunge straight off the high mountain range into the Sea of Japan. In South Korea there are three large rivers, which emerge on the south coast. The biggest and most prominent during the war was the Naktong, on which the western boundary of the Pusan perimeter was held.

The largest river in the whole land is the Amnokkang, also known as the Yalu. This natural obstacle, which separates North Korea from the Manchuria region of China, was the scene of many air battles. Air bombardment of its bridges, to hinder access into North Korea from China, and high altitude interdiction of the Russian-built MIG fighter planes to stop them penetrating south, were top priority tasks for the UNO's air forces.

Of the three strategic rivers, the Naktong, the Imjin and the Yalu, the Imjin was the most fought over. It was also the only one of the three that was crossed by both sides. Running south from headwaters on the slopes of the Taebaek-Sanmaek Range near Wonsan on the east coast, it veers south-west some 64 km north of Seoul, crosses the 38th parallel and runs 12 to 16 km behind the western end of the wartime frontline, towards the Yellow Sea. It eventually joins the Han River on the west coast, 8 km short of the sea and about 18 km northwest of Seoul.

The Imjin presented us with different problems in different seasons. The winter, with its subzero temperatures, froze it solid at a fairly low level, providing a continuous bridge across which even 50-tonne Centurion tanks could trundle. So it was no barrier to enemy infantry or line crossers.

When in spring the warmer sun brought out the buds on the trees, the thaw left the paddies full and ready for planting, as water was trapped in the cleverly designed bunds. The Imjin also rose dramatically, as much as 12 metres, washing right over the top of low concrete bridges like Teal, which were especially designed to withstand it. High steel trestle bridges such as the Pintail, which held their decks above the torrent, were not too much affected in the thaw and were usually able to carry light vehicle traffic. In the late spring, the river dropped to what we considered normal, in that it was between its banks and behaving itself. At this lower level it was fordable in places, such as where the Chinese Army crossed in front of the Gloucester's position at Choksong, at the start of the Battle of the Imjin in April 1951.

Early summer monsoon rains gave the country a real saturating, providing the multitude of shrubs that had sprung up on the hills with a real boost. The river system flooded again, depositing fresh layers of silt and nutriment over the flats. The bridges could not be used at all and were lucky to stay put. Their wooden predecessors had been swept away the year before. The Brits placed Bofor light anti-aircraft guns upstream of the Pintail bridge to break up debris accumulation and explode mines floated down the river by the enemy to destroy the bridges.

The last straw in reducing a modern army's mobility was the roads. On the outbreak of war, the arterial roads shown on Japanese surveyed maps dated 1911 were the only real roads in the country. That did not appear to worry the North Korean army unduly, but it was of real concern to the motorised forces of South Korea's allies. As the rest of the non-communist world rallied to the South's aid, it became necessary to improve the existing roads and build extra feeder ones, to deploy the large number of occidental troops in their vehicles. In 1951 the Americans put their 64th Engineering Base Topographic Battalion to work compiling emergency topographical maps. Based on aerial photography dated October 1950, they were checked and edited against the Japanese ones. Those are the maps that we fought the war with. In my view they were quite adequate. They still showed more tracks than roads, but that was not the fault of the mapmakers of course; few roads existed. Of those that did, maintenance could not keep up and to make matters worse in the winter, moisture would freeze just below the road surface, forming what were known as ice bubbles. The heavy traffic chopped these up and the road surface disintegrated. When there were ice bubbles around, the roads were declared Red and only traffic deemed to be absolutely essential was allowed to move.

Despite the lack of good topsoil, the hills were not, most of the year, bare of foliage. Dead-looking trees came to life again and low scrub sprang up in the spring and early summer. They were by no means all the same species. The ubiquitous azalea beautified whole hillsides with its colourful flowers. The rest of the shrubs were a multitude of green leaves of various shades, shapes and sizes. One particular bush caught me a few times. When one's skin brushed a leaf, a large blister about 30 to 40 mm long and half as wide appeared immediately. The initial pain was like a burn from a hot stove. The blister never broke, but the severe burning sensation persisted. After two days of discomfort, both the pain and the blister just disappeared, leaving the skin undamaged. Similar plants must have made life miserable in the Burma and New Guinea campaigns of WW2 and for those who served in Malaysia and Vietnam in the fifties and sixties. The scrub flourished during the rainy season and, by the end of the dry that followed, it had grown quite large and started dying off. The fires started by shellfire vied with the snow to turn the scrub black. Before the thaw had finished, it had rotted down and the cycle started again.

Before winter was completely spent, one of the other companies had a patrol stray into a minefield. No names, no pack drill. The marker wire and pickets had been blown away by artillery fire. It was the sixth man in the file who walked into the trip wire, which was hidden by deep snow. The mine jumped to chest height before exploding. Ball bearings shot out in a 360 degree spread, causing six casualties, but there were no fatalities as far as I can remember.

With the arrival of spring, when the battalion went back into the line after our Camp Casey sojourn, the snow on the sunny southern slopes began to thaw. In a copy of the weekly intelligence report, circulated down to platoon level, our attention was drawn to a new menace. Some bodies, not recovered after clashes in no-man's land the autumn before, had reappeared and proved to be booby-trapped. A large charge had been fixed to a pin driven into the ground, with its triggering device attached to the body, which had then been placed over the explosive to conceal it. When the body was moved, the diabolical booby trap exploded. To avoid further casualties from such a practice, patrol commanders were advised to carry 20 metres of assault cable, to pull any bodies found sufficiently to trigger such a device. Soon after the warning had been promulgated, a patrol led by Charlie Yacopetti came across the body of a Canadian officer which had been hidden under the snow since the previous November. The intense cold had preserved it. Mindful of the intelligence report and as efficient as usual, Charlie produced the signal wire from around his waist and ordered his men back. He fastened the wire to a boot. Charlie was never short of guts. Carefully paying it out, he joined his men in a fold in the ground and began to pull. Unfortunately only the leg moved, detaching from the body. The story went around the battalion like a bush fire.

High and dominant as the Big Hill was, it followed that any incautious movement during daylight hours was visible from three directions and quickly punished. Naturally, the Chinese mortars and 76 mm self-propelled guns had every feature registered, large and small, gaps in the trench-lines at the top of tracks particularly. One night, I had a party thickening up the barbed wire at the top of Mildura Spur. A recent reinforcement decided to slip back to the gap in the communication trench and have a smoke. He must have been careless lighting up because, before his absence from the working party was noticed, we were picking him up. He suffered a non-serious light wound from a mortar bomb and a more serious blow to his pride. Just happening to arrive after the bomb, to check how the work was progressing, I gave him a severe dressing down for deserting his mates, followed by a lecture on the stupidity of lingering, let alone lighting up, by such an obvious reference point for the enemy artillery and mortars. Then I sent him off to the platoon medic to have his wound dressed.

In contrast to its front, the rear of Hill 355 was almost totally concealed from enemy observation. It was so steep and rugged on its southern side that the engineers had built a flying fox to the top. It supplied the centre company with its heavy stores such as ammunition and engineering equipment. A substantial piece of machinery, it was also used to evacuate stretcher cases down to the Bowling Alley. The Chinese apparently had no knowledge of it.

East of 355, the frontline turned north to the next divisional sector manned by the 1st Division South Korean Army. At this end, the big hill had a long spur similar to Surrey Hills, pointing to the north-east and another lower and wider spur that thrust due east but was less steep than the spur at the western end of 355. Because of the bend in the line, this spur was in dead ground, providing an excellent jeephead where they could be unloaded out of sight of the enemy. Naturally, the army engineers had built a road to it, over the Korean foot track that had been there for centuries. This simplified the casualty evacuation (casevac in military jargon) and food and ammunition re-supply for the company on the right flank. It also provided cover for the tanks.

The 'Tankies', as the crews were nicknamed, were able to trundle their Centurion tanks into what is known as a hull down position. With only the barrel of their 120 mm gun and the top half of the turret exposed to the enemy, they would fire off a few of their hard hitting rounds, and then pull back out of sight of the enemy.

– Five –

Routine in the Line

Some sort of activity was always going on in the front line throughout the 24 hours, with night and day duties interrelated, so it was essential to work to a platoon routine. This was fairly standard throughout the battalion. Most men managed 3–5 hours sleep in the early hours before morning 'stand to'. Those not on duty could usually pick up a couple more hours during the afternoon. They never really got enough sleep, but their natural fighting spirit sustained them.

The command post phones and radios were manned night and day, the two platoon signallers working their roster out between them. I checked it personally, to ensure that it was in place and equitable, particularly as they were still needed for night patrols. Because of the demands of O Groups, reconnaissance patrols and administration, the sergeants and I got less sleep than anyone else. I say the 'sergeants' advisedly, as during my tour of duty I had, over the 12 month period, three platoon sergeants. Each was an outstanding soldier and gallant leader of men.

Half an hour before first light, everybody on the position 'stood to'. Battle stations were manned for an hour, in case of a dawn attack. Minefield checking parties were sent out to repair or replace the perimeter marker wires and the red metal triangles that were hung from them, to warn both the enemy and our own troops of the presence of the vicious fields. The checking parties did their job and returned without delay, and standing patrols were withdrawn before it got too light to move on a forward slope. Equally important was the laying out of the air recognition panels by first light. As we had total air supremacy, camouflage from the air was not deemed to be necessary, but identification by friendly planes was very necessary, especially by those piloted by our American allies. If the situation was potentially dangerous or visibility was poor, restricted by fog or heavy rain, the standing patrols would be left out and the 'stand to' extended, usually on a 50 percent basis. That meant that one man would be withdrawn from each of the two-man fighting pits and the machine-gun bunkers, to clean up and have breakfast. They then relieved their mates. If nothing happened, and it mostly didn't, then all were stood down when it was possible to see into the 'valley'. However, the decision to 'stand down' was always a battalion one.

During daylight hours, two men manned the platoon OP and watched for any unusual activity in the immediate foreground and middle distance. I considered this a specialised task and chose the men accordingly. The change-over of observers was self-operating. When the first hour was up, one of the lookouts would leave the OP and wake his relief, returning to the OP until he arrived. An hour later, the other original lookout would go and wake his relief. This system of overlap ensured continuity in the surveillance plus having the obvious advantage that two people tend to keep each other awake when engaged in monotonous work.

After morning 'stand down' the position was cleaned up. This could in fact mean anything, depending on the night's activities, but under normal conditions it was sweeping the trenches. Sounds crazy? Not so. The constant scuffing by army boots on the clay type subsoil produced an amazing amount of dust, 150–200 mm deep in 24 hours. When walked through, it generated clouds, which attracted hostile fire. Add rain and you had mud. In the wet season, the mud itself required the main effort. Major clean up tasks, such as a blown in trench or collapsed hutchie, would be assessed and tackled immediately or, if under observation, after dark.

Because we were living cheek by jowl with rats, bad company because of their disease carrying capacity, sanitation was extremely important. Ours was primitive but effective. Each company appointed a sanitation man, whose responsibility was keeping the long drop toilets clean and limed. He was invariably a good bloke, who could work without supervision. Recesses were incorporated at intervals in the communication trenches, and soak holes were dug. Into these were set tubes that the tank shells were delivered in. They certainly had many uses. The top ends were screened with fine mesh wire netting, to keep out the flies. These makeshift urinals, known as gonophones in WW2, we called pissaphones. They too, were sprinkled with lime every day by the sanitation man. The chores finished, we all washed and shaved; and I mean all. The men preferred to be clean-shaven except for their moustaches, which were very popular. One felt better, as the bristles trapped a lot of grime which did not always get washed off at night but came away easily on a razor the next morning. As close to 0800 hrs as possible, breakfast would arrive courtesy of the sturdy Korean porters and the company cooks.

The Commonwealth Division's battalions enjoyed the backup provided by the South Korean Government in the form of porters from the KSC (Korean Service Corps). These comprised men who were too young or too old to serve in their fighting units, that is, they were under 15 years of age or over 50. About 30 KSC were attached to each company of the battalion and were usually controlled and led by a digger who had less than two months left to serve of his 12 months tour of duty as frontline infantry. In our company, the diggers themselves chose him for this task, as a bloke who had always pulled his weight and deserved a break. There was a lessening of risk for him, in that he was not required to go on patrol or do any other front line duties. The Australians are naturally democratic in the true sense of the word, and the diggers were always right in their choice. Rain, hail, snow or shells, we were never let down. With another national characteristic, their penchant for nicknames, the Aussies called him "The Noggie Basher."

That was of course a deliberate misnomer, although he might have had to kick a backside occasionally. *Noggie* is the Japanese word for man and was a carry-over from the Allies occupation of Japan after WW2. The basher always made sure that his charges were fed, and not exposed to unnecessary danger. I don't recall any casualties among the porters but he kept them moving with phrases like *Hubba hubba*, or, *Hubba hubba ano-nei?* Which translated meant 'Hurry up' and 'Hurry up won't you?' Or words to that effect. These people worked hard, tramping half to a full kilometre each way, up and down the steep tracks of the front line hills, sometimes under fire. On his A-frame each man carried the maximum load of food, water or ammunition of which he was physically capable.

An A-frame consisted of two wooden staves lashed together at the top end and spread two thirds of the way down by a cross piece, thereby forming a bipod. At the level of the cross piece, two arms were lashed at right angles to the main staves, parallel to one another. With the A-shaped bipod held against the man's back by rope slings, these arms protruded rearwards. Upon them was stacked the load. On the march he leant on a stout birch sapling with a fork at the top, over which he kept a secure grip with his thumb. This staff assisted balance and gave leverage, both going up and coming down the steep and narrow paths. To take off the A-frame, he crouched until the legs of the frame touched the ground. He then placed the fork of his staff under the apex, turning the bipod into a tripod and was then able to slip safely out of the slings. The A-frame is a time-honoured tool of the Korean people and was as universally used in Korea as the yoke in most other East Asian countries.

Our cooks always seemed to be able to produce excellent meals despite the conditions that they had to work under. In the summertime, breakfast consisted of cereals, bacon and scrambled eggs made from egg powder reconstituted with milk which itself was powder reconstituted with water. A dry ration for lunch was sent up with the breakfast. Food suitable for the cold conditions was provided in the winter, such as porridge with bacon and eggs for breakfast and hotboxes of soup and bread for lunch, and plenty of meat and vegies for the evening meal, regardless of the season. The menu had variety by the day, but not by the week. The food had, of necessity, to be prepared in a manner that ensured it could be distributed equitably. I never heard anyone complain. We ate well. Apparently, someone was impressed with the physique and vigour of the Australian troops, as we had a ration scale of eight rations per man, for seven days, five Australian and three American. This generosity usually meant we had turkey drumsticks three times a week. These were not only most acceptable but were easy to dish out. Interestingly, Trevor Lynch who served in 16th New Zealand Field Artillery Regiment, has since told me that when on occasions the gunners received turkey, it was only the meat off the body. I used to wonder about the fate of the other parts of the birds. We ate an awful lot of drumsticks. Our ration also included powdered potato reconstituted with water, a mess well known to those who served in the Pacific theatre during WW2. Every evening meal included Korean cabbage. This looked like anaemic broccoli, but was closer in flavour to kim chee which, anyone who has tasted that traditional Korean delicacy will testify, must be the most bitter dish in the world.

Throughout the day, several more trips by the Korean porters resupplied us with machine-gun and rifle ammunition, hand grenades and fresh phone and radio batteries. They also lugged up jerrycans of diesel for the choofers in the winter, plus the hundred and one items that are needed to keep a modern army running. But most important of all was drinking water, in 5 gallon steel jerrycans. Fancy having to carry them up those hills? That was not lost on us. We wasted not a drop.

Every day after breakfast, while the weapons were being cleaned, I visited each hutchie with the respective section leaders. It was the most convenient time to issue and supervise the swallowing of the anti-malaria paludrine tablets and inspect the men's feet for frostbite, trench feet and tinea. A revolting task as you might imagine but very necessary, as both malaria and tinea are preventable and frostbite and trench foot can be treated if recognised in time. Battalion policy was that the platoon commander was responsible for enforcing the precautions, and he would be court-martialled if malaria or frostbite occurred in his platoon. We were therefore careful to keep special notebooks, recording the dates of our personally administering the paludrine tablets and inspecting each man's feet. Red tape it was not, but a hell of a job, looking between over-worked and sometimes dirty toes! Especially as some diggers, not wanting to be evacuated, would try and hide a problem by making only a token gesture of parting their toes. To inspect the likely area of infection, you had to separate the toes yourself. But it kept our fitness level high and very few cases had to be evacuated. Those sent out were usually suffering from trench foot caused by prolonged periods standing in wet boots, either in paddy fields or flooded trenches. Tinea was also a common complaint and difficult to avoid but, if detected or reported in time, it could be dealt with in the line by the application of the ointment that the medical services supplied. Zinc powder was issued constantly, being one of the best preventatives that you could put on such hard-worked feet. Once a week we dusted our clothes with anti-mite powder. This hardly needed supervision, as everyone was made well aware of the consequences of not doing so. The mites, on the fleas on the rats, were carriers of the dreaded disease haemorrhagic fever which was prevalent on the peninsula and, if contracted, invariably fatal.

For the rest of the morning, with the exceptions mentioned, the men slept. Meanwhile, the platoon commanders attended Company O Groups. In A Company these were pleasant occasions. Not only did the Officer Commanding have good signallers in the CP who could be relied on to be cheerful, it was a chance to compare notes with fellow platoon commanders. Often as not one would be a sergeant, as we so frequently had gaps in our junior officer ranks due to casualties. But the sergeants were good blokes in their own right.

Major Jim Norrie was bluff and outgoing. Mind you, he stood no nonsense, but inspired confidence, which is an important characteristic in a commander. He should have been good. After service in World War 2, he was appointed to the Royal Australian Military College, Duntroon as an instructor. He also became their rugby coach. Most of my colleagues called him 'Poodle' behind his back, his nickname from the college. I never did so, not so much because of my undoubted respect for him, but because I didn't want to be misunderstood by my graduate fellow officers.

Early in the morning, Major Norrie would have attended an O group at BHQ or, if things were fairly quiet, have received instructions over the field telephone. When I first joined A Company, fighting and recce patrols were planned and co-ordinated by the battalion and passed on by the adjutant. When we came out of the line for a spell at Camp Casey the CO, Colonel Hughes, had to return home on compassionate grounds and Lt. Colonel MacDonald was sent from Australia to take command of the battalion. Captain Dick Stanley-Harris replaced the Scottish adjutant, and the policy changed. The commanding officer still decided the patrolling program, but a company commander could submit a patrol plan to battalion and, if approved, it would be incorporated in the patrolling schedule. 3 RAR never used a patrol master in the battalion while I was with it.

We platoon commanders received our orders at the Company O Group, collecting a new 'password' and 'countersign' for the battalion that night, plus the air panel code for the next day. This was followed by orders regarding the command and manning of fighting patrols, recce patrols, standing patrols and the flying squad. The briefing of the fighting patrol leaders would be done individually later. Sometimes, the battalion would consider that a particular patrol warranted a briefing by the IO, and the patrol leader would report to BHQ for his detailed briefing. Any company-initiated patrol plan also had to be sanctioned by Battalion headquarters.

Patrol orders for each platoon would include:

1) The task, time and duration of the patrol.
2) Routes out and in. They were usually different, to avoid being ambushed.
3) Grid references or place names at which our own ambushes were to be set, with code names allotted to them for radio security.
4) Sit reps (situation reports) information on patrol activity in our sector the previous day.
5) Int. reps (intelligence reports) were distributed once a week. They made great reading and gave us something to tell the men about other units' 'highs and lows'. Sometimes there would be new information which came to light as a result of a patrol action or enemy pressure on a nearby part of the front.

After the platoon commander had digested his orders and done his planning, he needed to hold his own O Group, to brief his sergeant and section leaders on what was expected of the platoon. I usually managed to assemble them just before lunch, so as not to disrupt their limited sleeping time. The latest information would be passed on and I would tell them what the task was. This was set in concrete but the method of achieving it wasn't. I would explain my basic plan and ask for comment and suggestions. This system produced good results with 'colonial troops', as we thought of ourselves. I had the final say. It was never otherwise. I would pore over our patrol book, in which was kept a record of every time each man had been on patrol, to ensure that everyone was 'getting a fair crack of the whip'. If a section corporal knew of some reason why a man should not go out on that particular night, he was expected to speak up. I can't recall an occasion when the platoon O Group broke up with anyone dissatisfied with his lot. It was a democratic platoon. It is a fact that the Australian is by nature an independent character: you cannot mess him about without getting a reaction. I, as a Kiwi, was much the same. My mate Jack Spiers, who also attended A Company's O Groups, was horrified on one occasion at the way I took on the major. He was convinced I had gone too far. I came close. I had a case but unfortunately handled my objection badly (see chapter 12).

Usually, I would manage a short sleep after lunch. Late afternoon, all would be astir. The patrol commander would brief those nominated to go with him on the fighting patrol, followed by the Bren and Owen gunners test firing their weapons on a reverse slope to satisfy all involved that none were faulty. The SMLE rifles were so reliable that we didn't need to test fire them.

Then the evening meal arrived. Dinner over, the KSC back-loaded the empty food containers and jerrycans, ammo boxes and rubbish. Soon after, it would be time for 'stand to'. Fighting trenches would be manned but with some adjustment of personnel. If a fighting patrol was sent out, it would reduce the strength left on the platoon position by nearly 50 percent. Two standing patrols of three men each would also be poised to move into position. Of course no patrols could leave our trenches until the light faded a bit. But after my experience with the Durhams, I always left our lines as early as possible, to be able to get well out into no-man's land ahead of the enemy, moving fast for the first third of the route, with less caution than I had been taught to observe. I also took advantage of the fact that some of our positions went into shadow several minutes before the Chinese ones.

If there was no incident during 'stand to', once it was completely dark the word would be passed to Company HQ to 'stand down'. Of course, if 'stand to' continued, Battalion would give an explanation. The first shift of night pickets would man their posts within our perimeter trench. They were always in pairs to keep each other awake plus, in the event of an emergency, one man could stay at the post while the other went to platoon HQ to raise the alarm. It did not always make sense to fire first and ask questions later. Either the sergeant or myself checked the pickets during the night. Our last round of the pickets was done after the patrols, other than the 'Standing' ones, were all in.

Off-duty men were asleep on their wire beds until 'stand to', 30 minutes before first light. Then another day in the line began.

– *Six* –

Tactics and Morale

Tactics in the Static Phase

After 12 months of each side grasping the initiative several times and the battle-line fluctuating from the Pusan perimeter in the south to within sight of the Yalu River in the north, the war stalemated. With the front lines half way up the peninsula, crossing the 38th parallel just north of Seoul, the fluid war had become static. Dialogue between the warring parties was opened at Panmunjom and peace talks began. Back home in the countries that had committed troops, the war was off the news. Unlike Vietnam years later, the Korean war was fought without television coverage to keep it before the public eye, so the general public quietly forgot it. But the servicemen's families did not.

Bitter local actions continued, with divisional attacks by both sides to consolidate their situation and adjust their deployment by occupying the most defensible features in their allotted sectors. 'Operation Commando', the Commonwealth Division's last big push, anchored the eastern end of the British sector on Hill 355. From then on, 3 RAR was its caretaker for quite a lot of the time.

An infantry battalion's disposition was governed by the amount of front that it was responsible for, and the nature of the terrain. A typical battalion position would be on the vital ground closest to the area it was allocated to defend. If the enemy held that particular feature, we would fight for it. Because the Chinese tended to favour enveloping attacks, it was fundamental that a battalion had all-round defence. Usually, three of the rifle companies would hold the vital ground. The fourth would be sited to give depth to the defence and be available as a counter-attack force, but not out on a limb where it would be of no use. They would all, including the reserve company, be sited within light machine-gun range of each other, to give and receive mutual support and in some cases the battalion mortars would be able to support all the rifle companies too. The situation was that the ComDiv was heavily outnumbered at 3:1 overall and, in the event of a full-scale attack on a single battalion, as much as 12:1 locally. So if a battalion deployed its companies out of small arms range of each other, it would lose them piecemeal and the whole position would eventually be over-run. The Gloucesters were in that situation. They tried to save the day by relocating companies after the battle started. It was too late.

Between battalions, larger gaps were acceptable provided they were covered by weapons with adequate range, such as medium machine-guns, field artillery and tanks, and patrolled regularly to give early warning and keep enemy patrols from carrying out close reconnaissance of our forward positions and our minefields. If a battalion had all these advantages, it was a rock.

The numerical strength of the infantry pitted against us necessitated a greater weapon scale for a battalion than was the norm for the British Army, as laid down in the training pamphlet "The Infantry Battalion in Battle" (1952), which was produced for the European scene. The following is a summary of our weapon scale, which proved to be necessary in our defence against the numbers that the Chinese fielded.

The Australian rifles were brand new, mint condition .303 short magazine Lee-Enfield No. 1 Mk 111, of World War 1 design. They were bolt action, with 10-round magazines and 18 inch bayonets. Manufactured in Lithgow in Australia, they were superior to the WW2 vintage British .303 No. 4 bolt-action rifles and the American .30 cal Garand automatic rifles. The SMLE did not jam in dusty or muddy conditions like the other two, which were too finely machined for the conditions. We also had 14 trusty 9 mm Owen guns with 12 inch (305 mm) bayonets to a platoon. Australian designed and manufactured, the Owen was without doubt a superior submachine-gun. With its magazine on top and the ejection opening directly below, it rarely if ever jammed, unlike the temperamental Sten submachine-gun, which cost so many British soldiers their lives by refusing to fire at the critical moment. However, the British Bren light machine-gun was as good as ever; we had seven to a platoon. One .30 calibre air-cooled American Browning medium machine-gun per platoon thickened up our defensive fire plan even more. There was still a 2 inch (51 mm) mortar with illuminating as well as high explosive bombs, plus one 3.5 inch rocket launcher per platoon for tank and bunker busting. We also had boxes full of the British 36 grenades. They were most useful and effective close-quarter weapons and much more deadly than the Chinese stick grenades, although a bit heavier to throw.

Besides a headquarters company for its supply and maintenance, the battalion had a support company armed with specialist weapons, which were usually deployed among the rifle companies for their own protection, although they were under battalion control. The Vickers medium machine-guns, for instance, were usually sited within a flank company's area to cover the gaps between neighbouring battalions and our own and could, on occasions, fire across the flanking battalion's front. The mortar platoon, armed with British designed 3 inch mortars, comprised three sections of two mortars each. They operated most of the time as a full platoon, but there were occasions when a section was detached to reach a specific target. On Hill 355 the mortar baseplate position was sited to cover all approaches to the front and flanks, with a mortar fire controller deployed at each end of the feature to direct the fire. When we moved to The Hook, our mortars were attached to 2 RAR to thicken their defence but were sited so they could give us support if need be.

Because of the easier access for the delivery of building material, the Assault Pioneers were based at the eastern end of Hill 355. But they swarmed all over it, supervising and assisting in the construction and repair of trenches and bunkers, etc. They also spent time in no-man's land, checking and repairing the perimeter wire around minefields. Last, but by no means least of the support platoons, was the anti-tank platoon. We did not have any tanks pitted against us after the North Koreans lost their last Russian supplied T34 tank. So our anti-tank platoon was employed as a rifle platoon. As they were stronger in numbers than a standard infantry platoon, they were usually given the task of manning the most vulnerable platoon position.

After a period of local attacks, the UNO and South Korean forces stabilised their defences on defensible features, along a possible truce line just below the 38th parallel in the west and well above it in the east. The United Nations' forces had better leadership after the change of command. The replacement of the ageing General Douglas MacArthur by General Matthew Ridgway brought a steadying influence into the directing of operations. The UNO forces dug in to stay, with the vital ground being retaken. But after the Chinese nation joined the fray, with its million soldiers in North Korea, a realistic decision was made not to attempt to go north again. Only Syngman Rhee, the sabre-rattling South Korean president, wanted an escalating war. He saw himself as president of the whole Korean Peninsula and, in his own way, was as dangerous as the communists.

Meanwhile, as there were only large casualty lists when positions were over-run or at least heavily attacked, few people back home realised that we were still steadily taking casualties in what was now a less spectacular, but no less bitter, war of attrition. With the Chinese artillery having been upgraded to equal ours, their heavy bombardments took a toll. There was also a steady flow of killed and wounded from the intensive patrolling, with clashes occurring in no-man's land somewhere along the front almost every night. Very occasionally someone was lost as a prisoner of war in a patrol clash. But night patrolling was a unit's insurance. If a battalion did not have a properly planned night patrolling program, so didn't patrol constantly with the aim of taking on the enemy patrols, the Chinese would dominate the ground between the two frontlines and what patrols the unit did send out would be overwhelmed. Sooner or later, the position would be attacked and probably over-run, for the simple reason that it could not get early warning.

The Australian battalions were strong on night operations, priding ourselves on dominating 'the valley' as we called no-man's land, because as the two sides were entrenched on the highest hills on each side, the lower hills between them were where the fighting took place at night time. Due to the disparity in numbers that could be fielded, we did not always hold the ground after a patrol clash. However, it must be said we performed better than most of our allies, with the possible exception of the Turks. It has also to be said that the Chinese infantrymen were very good at night patrolling and clashes were frequent. But although patrol casualties were a big manpower loss, we managed to deny the enemy the free run of no-man's land, thereby keeping our positions secure.

There was also a steady stream of casualties from constant artillery harassing fire and the occasional heavy bombardment. This was reduced to some extent by counter-battery fire from the NZ 16th Field Regiment and an American medium artillery regiment, both of which had

OPs high up on Hill 355.

But our best defence from artillery fire was the Australians' ability and will to dig. It is no accident that they are called 'diggers'.

Morale

Without morale, there is no will to fight. Without the will to fight, there is no way of winning or even surviving.

It should not be overlooked that from start to finish the South Koreans themselves bore the brunt of the fighting and the casualties. Despite their early disasters, the South Koreans, who are a very dogged people, were still resisting invasion by the North Koreans, who are also dogged, when bottled up with the remains of the two American divisions in the Pusan perimeter. The intervention of the UNO forces boosted the South Koreans' morale. The Americans particularly not only took a substantial amount of the burden, but also provided training and equipment for the South Korean soldiers, who learnt fast. During the subsequent static period of the war, the South Koreans were able to hold about two thirds of the 410 km front, albeit some of it on more defensible terrain at the mountainous eastern end. Although they took a hammering on the central front, right through 1952 until the ceasefire in July '53, their morale didn't falter. In fact in the last big push by the North Korean army on the central front, they hit five South Korean divisions but could not break through. The South Korean Capitol Division severed all communication with the United Nations forces for a whole week while it fought a successful defence on its own.

America, leading the political and military support for South Korea, fielded the biggest portion of the United Nations' effort, providing the commanding general and vast numbers of all the three services, including some excellent army units with a good fighting spirit and high morale. However, a few previously very good American regiments had lost their best officers and NCOs in the fluid part of the war. As a result, they suffered from poor leadership at all levels. Their reinforcements were not long service, so were not as well trained and, as a consequence, had low morale. The American infantry units were well armed and equipped, but their crack troops were still the US Marine Corps. As the poor relation of the navy, they were on a tighter budget than the army, but they had stronger discipline and higher morale, with the fighting spirit that they engender. The American technical units such as armour and artillery were of the highest order. The rest of the UNO Army was composed of contingents from 20 other countries, which had supplied forces according to their ability to maintain them in the field. The Turkish and Dutch contingents were particularly effective.

Four countries provided medical units rather than combat ones. Their contribution, however, was out of all proportion to their numbers. The highly qualified staff of the Indian FDS (Field Dressing Station) knew how to save lives, doing a great job behind the front line of the Commonwealth Division. The Norwegian NORMASH, a highly skilled and professional unit with female nurses, was only a little further back, and was the most forward medical establishment that could carry out major surgery. As in the TV program *MASH*, they were a Mobile Advanced Surgical Hospital, of which the Americans deployed many behind much of the front. The knowledge that there was a good evacuation system in place, backed by excellent hospitals, had a very positive influence on the morale of the front line soldiers.

The United Kingdom reacted quickly to the UNO call, deploying two infantry battalions from their Hong Kong garrison, as soon as they were brought up to strength in men and equipment. The Middlesex Regiment and The Argyll and Sutherlands were professional troops of the British Army, therefore their hearts were in a fight, and they were well trained and led. Teamed up with 3 RAR, they formed 27th British Commonwealth Brigade. Once it became clear that we had a major war on our hands, this initial contribution was increased with another brigade from Britain, the 29th Brigade. It comprised mostly WW2 veterans who were still on the reserve and had been recalled to the colours. Artillery, armour and large numbers of supporting specialist units followed as fast as they could be redeployed from the occupation of Germany, and the Brit contingent became the second largest after the Americans. The British troops were professional and reliable despite the fact, that as time went on, the relieving British infantry battalions' junior officers and soldiers, but not their long serving NCOs, were conscripted national servicemen aged 19 years. They were, however, well led by company commanders who had nearly all been battalion commanders at the end of WW2. The battalions' COs had commanded brigades. These experienced officers and their senior NCOs accounted for the remarkable doggedness of these fine fighting units.

Australia also, had troops close enough to Korea able to be deployed reasonably quickly. But 3 RAR, the last Australian battalion serving in the occupation force in Japan, needed to be brought back up to strength first. This was done promptly, with the re-attachment of its support company from Australia and the enlistment of volunteers, who were predominantly veterans of WW2, to swell the ranks. Before the end of September 1950, the 3rd Battalion, Royal Australian Regiment (3 RAR) joined the UNO forces in the Pusan perimeter and successfully engaged in a minor action during the breakout at the end of that month.

The Australians planned to send another battalion as soon as they could get it up to strength. They had, only a few months before the war broke out, reorganised their infantry establishment and formed the Royal Australian Regiment, with the battalion numbering system based on the Australian home states. 3 RAR had been classified as the Queensland battalion so took Queensland's number 3. However, throughout the Korean war its personnel were volunteers from all over Australia. It took another year to raise and train the Victorian battalion 1 RAR, again recruiting from all over Australia.

The Australians invited the New Zealand government to provide an infantry battalion to join with their battalions and form an ANZAC brigade. While the idea was attractive, the New Zealand government, mindful of the high proportion of casualties suffered by the country's infantry in the recent world war, opted to raise and send a field artillery regiment.

The artillery regiment, equipped with the remarkably flexible World War Two 25-pounder field guns, took six months to train. But the time was well spent, for both countries. The New Zealand 16th Field Regiment was one of the most efficient and successful units among the UNO forces. In Korea it supported 3 RAR almost all the time. The rapport between the Australians and the New Zealanders was the wonder of our other allies. The Australian battalions had almost exclusive and constant close artillery support from the Kiwi artillery and in our relationship both in and out of the line we were like brothers.

16th Field Regiment was officered at the senior level by veterans of WW2, with a few regulars in key appointments, like adjutant although even that appointment was later filled by a volunteer from the original draft. Captain Tom Channings M.B.E. was a very experienced artilleryman by the time that he was appointed adjutant.

The junior officers and the rank and file were predominantly volunteers off the street, but many of them had fought in WW2 or had served in J Force during the occupation of Japan. An Army Service Corps transport company, 10 Company, was also raised to keep the gunners supplied with ammunition and rations, etc. As it turned out, the organisation finally settled on in the Commonwealth Division was a very happy and workable arrangement. The newly formed 28th Brigade, to replace 27th Brigade, consisted of two British battalions and two Australian, and could be deployed with two battalions forward and two in reserve. They were supported by the reliable New Zealand 16th Field Regiment, which in the static half of the war was dug in on a permanent gun-line, although batteries were deployed elsewhere when necessary. The ANZACs' old foe Turkey joined in with a brigade, which, not surprisingly, soon gained a reputation for fierceness and reliability. They got on very well with the Australians and the New Zealanders.

Canada reacted quickly, with a real fighting battalion in the Princess Patricia's Canadian Light Infantry, PPCLI eventually boosting their input to a full brigade with its own field artillery and armour. I personally did not see a lot of the Canadians, other than during reliefs in the line and in hospital. They had their own 25th Brigade and never got into any trouble that they could not handle. But they gained an everlasting place for themselves in the hearts of the Korean people with the brave stand by the 1st Battalion Princess Patricia's Canadian Light Infantry at the Battle of Kapyong. For on 23–25 April 1951, the Princess Pats along with the Australian 3rd Battalion Royal Australian Regiment and the British Middlesex Regiment, supported by a company of the 72nd US Heavy Tank Battalion and the New Zealand 16th Field Artillery Regiment, plus 10 Company RNZASC, stopped a Chinese full-scale left-flanking pincer attack, which was closing on Seoul from the east. This vital battle was named 'Kapyong', after the village of Kapyong that lay within sight of the hill features on which the battle was fought. The 10th New Zealand Transport Company maintained the artillery ammunition supply.

It is not generally appreciated that the battle of Kapyong took place at the same time as the battle of the Imjin. The northern pincer of the heavy Chinese offensive, mounted to take out Seoul, overran the Gloucestershire Regiment, more commonly called the Glosters, of the British 29th Brigade. The 27th Commonwealth Brigade, with the NZ 16th Field Regiment supporting it, stopped the eastern thrust, causing the whole offensive to stall. This can be partially explained by the fact that the PPCLI and 3 RAR with the 1st Middlesex in reserve were properly deployed, whereas the British 29th Brigade's deployment was too loose. The Glosters were out on a limb and the Royal Ulster Rifles were too far back down the pass to be of any use. The 5th Fusiliers were deployed along the Imjin River also, but four to five miles (6–8 km) away to the east. In other words, they were not deployed as a brigade, but as individual battalions. The Gloster's own deployment was also pitiful. Their companies were sited too far apart to be able to give each other supporting fire, so were taken out piecemeal. To make their plight worse, the artillery regiment that was supposed to be supporting them had the responsibility of supporting several other battalions as well. So the Glosters did not enjoy the close artillery support that 3 RAR and the PPCLI did at Kapyong.

The upshot of all this was that, while the 27th Brigade, i.e. PPCLI and 3 RAR backed up by the Middlesex, stopped the Chinese thrust for Seoul from the east, the Glosters went under. Those not killed in the action became prisoners of war. But luckily sufficient time had been bought to move other units to protect Seoul from the north.

Though the Canadians were not far behind, the Australians turned out to be the lynchpin of the Commonwealth Division. They were the best infantry in the whole UN Army: superb professional soldiers to a man. Relations between the Commonwealth units were cordial, but none so much as between the Australians and the New Zealanders. This was hidden from the casual observer by a facade of good-natured verbal abuse, whenever they met. Yet they stuck together with great camaraderie, on leave and in the line. This apparent contradiction in their relationship has been extremely well interpreted and explained by Ian McGibbon in his military history, *New Zealand & The Korean War Volume II: Combat Operations.*

Morale is elusive to some people and some outfits, in any walk of life. In its simplest terms, it is faith in oneself, thinking positively, seeing difficulties as circumstances to be overcome rather than as threats which might overwhelm. In any organisation, whether civilian or military, morale is also a collective confidence in being able to handle problems successfully. This positive attitude is engendered by esprit de corps interpreted as 'spirit of fellowship, loyalty to and pride in one's group.' The leaders, respecting the people they lead, develop such spirit for the whole. Also, in war as in business and everyday life, it is essential that one can rely on one's mates. The keys to these goals are communication within the organization, and a tight but fair discipline regime imposed without fear or favour, so that each man knows where he stands. If an officer or NCO does not do his job properly, he will, in a good outfit, be replaced. That, it must be admitted, does not always happen.

The Australian servicemen are a tough breed. By that I mean, in a complimentary way, that they are the bold and robust descendants of a colonial people, some of whom survived inhuman treatment initially, but all of whom went on to conquer a large, harsh and unforgiving land. They are also democratic in their outlook. So the diggers, knowing that they were the best infantry in the theatre, invented a way to keep their feet on the ground. Typical of the inverse humour on both sides of the Tasman Sea, the 'rank and file' referred to themselves as "Baggy Arses." Quote: "I'm just a Baggy Arse." To me it made sense. The commanding officer, was referred to by both officers and men, as "The Old Man." The company commanders were called "Boss". Once he had earned the men's respect, a platoon commander was flattered to be addressed as "Skipper" by the diggers. Platoon commanders and the men referred to or spoke to the NCOs using their first names, like "Bernie". Or by a personal nickname such as "Simo". Likewise, the platoon commander and the sergeant in a happy platoon addressed each man by his Christian name or nickname and, when speaking to them collectively, as blokes or fellas. None of this "Private So and So" or "Smith!" or, "You men."

In choosing their own title, the men could not be put down or upstaged. I have heard the term "Baggy Arse" used by the men so often it was quite normal. It was a part of their vocabulary.

But I never heard anyone in authority presume to use it.

– *Seven* –

Geoff Smith's and Jack Morrison's Patrol

The pressure to capture a prisoner is, it seems, always with us. So when in mid-January, Major Jim Norrie submitted an audacious plan to snatch a prisoner by sending a deep penetration patrol from A company to the northwest of Hill 355, it was a goer. Plotting the firm bases on a map, the 1500 to 2000-odd metres didn't look all that far and was basically confined to the low ground. But on the other hand, viewed from our position, the snatch area was out of sight behind the Apostles, at the rear of Mark in fact. Of course, if you are after a prisoner it makes good sense to appear where least expected.

A Company had only one experienced platoon commander left, John Hooper. Brian Bousfield had been wounded. Geoff Smith had just been transferred to Support Company to command the machine-gun platoon. His replacement, New Zealander Lt. Robert Unsworth, had unfortunately been killed in a patrol accident. Another green Kiwi named Matthews had replaced Bob, but I was too inexperienced so early in my tour of duty. It was imperative for the security of the Company position to keep the experienced Lt. John Hooper on the hill. So Major Norrie solved the problem of patrol leader by borrowing back Lt. Geoff Smith from Support Company. Jack Morrison, A Company's most experienced sergeant, was nominated 2ic of the 3 Platoon patrol.

The plan was that Geoff Smith would lead the patrol to a checkpoint at Grid Reference 162197, then on to GR 157196, where he would establish the first firm base with 12 men. Cpl. Mackay would go a further 300 metres north across the paddy and set up the second firm base, consisting of himself and another 12 men, on a knoll at GR 157199.

Morrison was to take three men further west still, to GR 152197, to do the snatch. There he would set an ambush alongside the track, which it was reasonable to assume was frequently used by the enemy. It was approximately 400 metres west of both firm bases. These GR were given to the rest of us at the Company O Group and are in my platoon commander's notebook, which I still have. The debriefing confirmed that the plan was adhered to (see map).

Battalion maintained normal defensive patrols, but A Company kept the remainder of our men on the hill. Routine tasks such as setting pickets were carried out, and an air of expectancy kept the whole company on its toes. For myself, I moved constantly around the platoon position, looking in frequently on our platoon CP where Bernie was monitoring our radios.

For a couple of hours all was quiet. Then we heard some urgent small arms fire, away out to our left front. Submachine-guns always sound urgent, particularly the Chinese burp guns with their extraordinarily high rate of fire. Then the no-nonsense sound of the Brens reached us, soon to be partially drowned out by even more substantial Chinese artillery and mortar bombardments of their DFs, that were designed to break up attacks onto their positions. The small arms fire was so close to the Chinese positions that they would not have ruled out the possibility of a full-scale attack. However, they quickly realised the true threat and switched their artillery onto us, while their infantry patrols poured into the valley.

Once the small arms fire erupted, I went straight to Jack Spier's OP and spent some time trying to read the battle and report back to the company command post. On Hill 355, Jack had previously done this by telephone when he had time. He had two phones and two lines, one direct to the mortar line and the other on the battalion telephone loop. But I was free to report to the CP in person if need be. In actual fact I had not left my platoon position, as both the mortar OP and the company command post were within it. Yet, my whole platoon position was probably little bigger than two football fields.

Jack could not give covering fire to the patrol itself. Because of the Chinese quick and obviously heavy reaction, he had no way of knowing exactly where the three elements of the patrol were in relation to their prearranged ambush positions. He was busy advising the gunners of what he was able to observe of the Chinese artillery, while continuing to fire his own mortars onto known enemy mortar positions. I used his back-up phone to tell Jim Norrie what we could hear from the valley.

The shelling and mortaring onto our end of Hill 355 had increased dramatically. The enemy seemed quite aware of whose patrol they were chasing, and even which company position it came from.

The small arms fire in the valley was getting closer. The different weapons involved could be identified by their sounds. The sharp crack of hand grenades was testimony to the close range of the action. The Brens, Owens and burp guns rattled and zapped away with their different rates of fire. The plop of the Chinese mortars and the boom of their field guns firing from dead ground were followed by the crashes of their bombs and shells arriving at their destinations. Their collective sounds, competing with the rumble of our field guns from behind us and the sharp explosions of their shells arriving on the enemy positions, combined to produce a symphony of death. Then "the tenor" joined in Jack Morrison's easily identified voice carrying across the valley:

"Get stuck into the bastards."

"Keep together and follow me."

"Fire."

His voice dominated the fire-fight.

Hurrying off to report to Jim Norrie in person, I had just stepped from the sap into the main communication trench when a shell exploded behind me in the trench. Over I went, bowled by the concentrated blast in the confined space. The dirt was still falling as I staggered to my feet, still clutching my Owen gun. I gulped in some dust-laden air and checked myself all over. Jack, realising how close the shell had been, arrived to find out what it had done to me. Finding me still in one piece, he said a few of his customary prayers on my behalf and went back to work. I continued on to the company CP. Major Jim was so impressed about being able to hear Morrison, that he then visited the mortar OP while I went back to my regular duties. Checking the whole platoon position, I found all the men in good heart and we had no casualties from the shelling.

Jack Morrison eventually got back to Surrey Hills with eleven men. John Hooper took care of the men, while Morrison carried on to the company CP to report. When I turned up at the Coy CP, reaction had set in on him. He was in full voice, telling Major Jim and everyone else all about it.

It appears that the snatch did not go smoothly. On taking up the position, they did not have long to wait. Two Chinese soldiers came along the track and were grabbed. But in the ensuing scuffle one managed to get a shot away. Assistance arrived too quickly for the Australians to secure the prisoners. So they were both shot. Morrison reported by radio to Geoff, who called down artillery fire on the feature to cover the snatch party's withdrawal to Corporal Mackay's party.

The Chinese reaction to the fact that there were enemy in their midst was surprisingly rapid. They sent large numbers straight into the valley from their positions, effectively cutting Morrison off from Geoff Smith's firm base, which had quickly come under heavy attack. Jack did, however, manage to join up with the second firm base and took command. Meanwhile, ambushed and swamped by weight of numbers, resistance from Geoff's position finally ceased. Jack's one responsibility now was to get the remnants of the patrol back to our lines.

To extricate his party, he headed toward the enemy lines, then slipped over a ridge and, having eluded his pursuers, turned again and took off for home. Eventually, the Chinese located them once more, and things became tough. He lost two good men, who sacrificed their own lives by carrying out a counter-attack on their own initiative, giving the rest of the party a chance to make some ground. The enemy then started attacking from the other side of the ridge along which Morrison's party was moving. Jack recognised a pattern. A dozen or so of the enemy would rush to the crest of the ridge in extended line and on a command throw their grenades together, a standard Chinese practice and very effective. On arrival, the grenades exploded more or less simultaneously. The grenadiers then retired below the crest, to be replaced by a line of burp gunners. They fired a long burst each, then retired below the ridge again, as the grenadiers charged back up and repeated their act. So it went on. It was simple attrition.

Morrison's men were following him in single file. Leading his party down from the ridge he paused for a quick orders group. He told them that when he called for it, they were to rush back up the ridge and shoot the Chinese as they sky-lined themselves on the crest, but to keep moving forward in single file and follow his actions. Dropping below the ridge forced the enemy to come up to the crest to attack. As the Chinese grenadiers arrived at the top to throw, the Australians moved quickly up the slope, so that the stick grenades passed over their heads. They shot down the grenadiers, while the grenades exploded harmlessly behind the Australians. When the burp gunners re-appeared, they received the full effect of the Owen and Bren guns at close range, and the Aussies took advantage of the confusion created to move down the crest again, as they pressed on toward home. This tactic was repeated several times with no further loss to our men. There is no doubt in my mind that Jack Morrison's leadership was responsible for the extrication of the survivors of the patrol.

Jack himself had no more than flesh wounds, but he was still sweating from his exertions, and the heat of the Tilly lanterns in the stuffy CP. Fifteen survivors out of 30 was not a good score, and he was understandably upset and very hyped up. There was no proof at that stage that Smith's part of the patrol was completely wiped out, and Morrison said, "Give me some men and I will go back and find them." This was of course the reaction of an overwrought man. But I volunteered to take a patrol from my platoon, to help Jack. This was more evidence of my inexperience; it was a 'dead duck', and Major Norrie said so. No-man's land was crawling with Chinese, each one wanting to kill an Australian. They shelled our position steadily, well into the wee hours. But apart from our pickets, we were all asleep.

At approximately 1300 hrs the next day, I was called to my section position that overlooked Mildura Spur and the track leading down it into no-man's land. Three figures were waving from the bottom of the steep spur. Through my binoculars I recognised them as Australians, so knew that they must be survivors of Geoff Smith's part of the patrol action, and that they must be exhausted. The word had gone quickly around the platoon position and most of my men had come into the trench to have a look. When I called for two men to go with me to help them up the hill, there was no shortage of volunteers. Leaving our weapons behind, three of us hurried down the track. When we met up with them we found that, while they still carried their weapons, they had no boots. Relieving them of their weapons, we put our shoulders under their armpits and assisted them up the slippery ice track. I was both surprised and gratified that the Chinese did not open fire on our six-man party. They must have been watching us, as we were on the absolute forward slope of the massive hill, and at least half of A Company was aligned along the communication trench above, watching us.

These three men were the only survivors of Geoff Smith's part of the patrol to get back to our lines. I had them assisted to Company HQ and while they were receiving medical attention, they related their harrowing experience to Major Norrie.

Apart from two men taken prisoner, these three were the only survivors from Geoff's firm base. Tucked in right behind the enemy's forward positions, it was over-run as soon as the gaff was blown. Tucked in right behind the enemy's forward positions, the Chinese had responded very quickly and vigorously to Morrison's intrusion. (Both sides mostly manned the hills only. In most cases it was possible to walk between the hills by staying in the paddy-fields. It was unusual terrain with few connecting ridgelines.) We would have done the same if one of their patrols had sat itself down in the Bowling Alley, say between Anti-tank Ridge and Pt 159.

Cliff Gale was able to confirm that Lieutenant Geoff Smith had 'bought it'. He had been hit by small arms fire, but carried on fighting. When he had lost eight men, either killed or too seriously wounded to withdraw, Geoff directed the other four survivors to break off the action and escape capture, by rolling downhill like dead bodies. As Cliff and the others lay down to roll away from the scene as instructed, Cliff, believing that Geoff was coming with them, paused to check that they were all ready and was astounded to see that Geoff had turned back and was creating a diversion by counter-attacking the Chinese on his own, with a rifle that he must have picked up. He was gunned down and grenaded. 'Snowy' Gale had an excellent account of their harrowing experience published in the April 1997 edition of the Regimental Association's magazine *Old Faithful*. The fifth man, L/Cpl. Daveraux, according to his debriefing on being released from a Chinese prison camp after the truce, went back to help the wounded.

The three who got back had rolled down the hill as instructed. Having achieved that undetected, they tried to move quietly off. But, feeling hunted, they became concerned about the crunching of their footsteps on the frozen crust of the snow. Taking off their heavy winter boots that would have identified their tracks as non-Chinese, they left them booby-trapped with a 36 grenade. Their feet were in poor shape when I picked them up, but they had survived. Game blokes. At first light, an Auster spotting plane was sent over the scene of the battle. The observer reported at least 70 Chinese bodies lying in the valley. It was not, of course, possible to ascertain how they died. We considered that, while Morrison's and no doubt Smithy's men had taken their toll on the enemy, the artillery and mortars must have accounted for a great number. Of course the Chinese would have recovered a lot of their casualties during the night, as it was standard practice with them. But it is all speculation. Only they know what their problems were that night, and how they handled them.

Of all the things that happened when dawn broke, the Chinese effort was the weirdest! From more than one hilltop position, their buglers had a go at playing the British death tribute, "The Last Post". They were not very good buglers, but the tune was recognisable. Although as a bit of propaganda it was a clever attempt, it did not move us in No. 1 Platoon. We discussed whether it was a genuine tribute or a taunt, but did not come to a conclusion.

The lessons learnt were hard won and worth retaining. Some of us never forgot them, using and adapting them during the rest of the war.

The Australian survival figures picked up somewhat when four wounded prisoners of war from that action were repatriated in April '53, and three more in August in the exchange of prisoners following the truce.

Jack Morrison was promoted to Warrant Officer 2nd Class and awarded the D.C.M.. He earned a bar to his D.C.M. in Vietnam.

This map shows the directions our patrol from 3 Battalion (A Company 2 and 3PL) took on the night of 24/25 January 1953 (to obtain a prisoner). The patrol route shows the imminent dangers to be expected. It is not surprising that later it was called a suicide patrol.

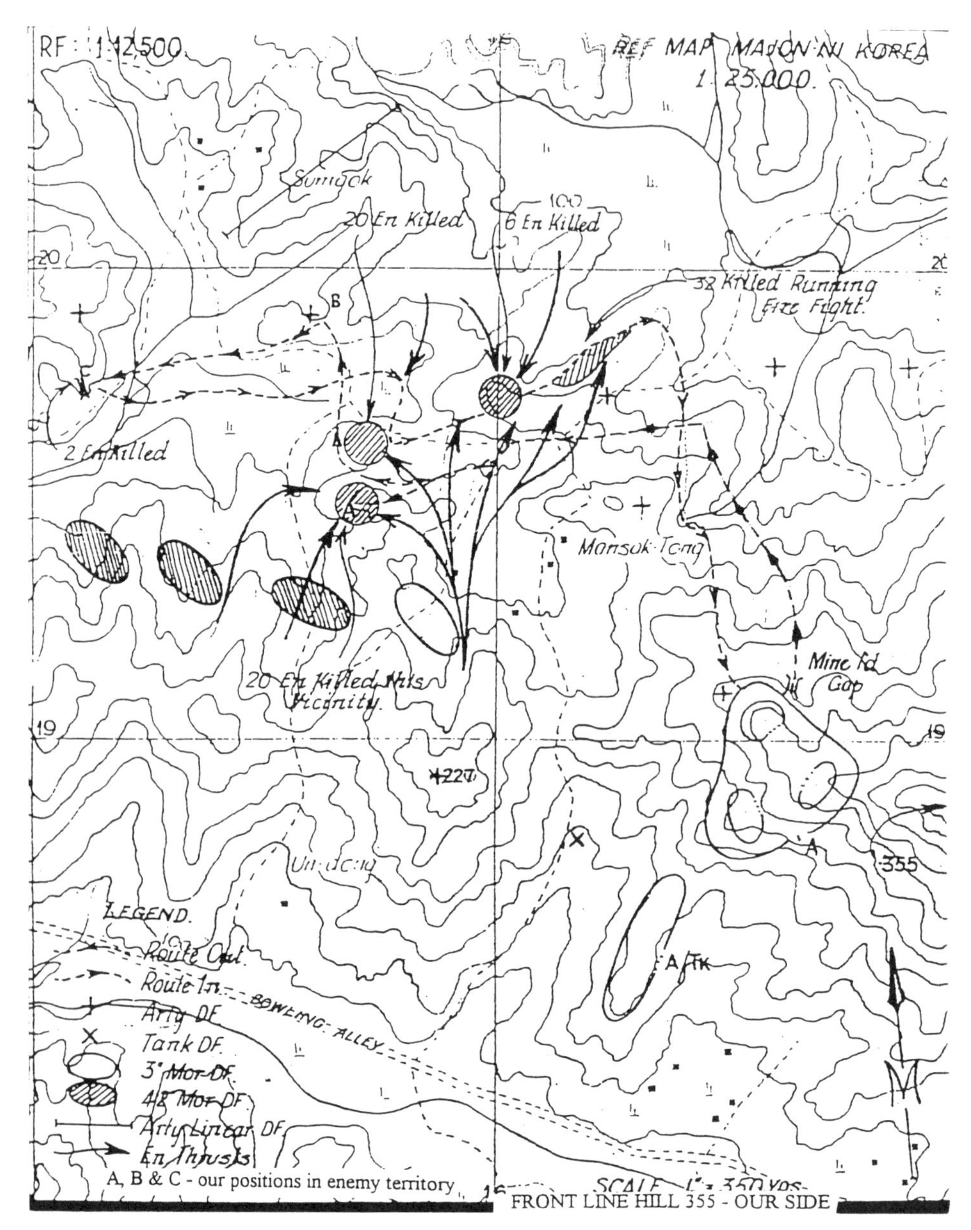

– *Eight* –
Patrolling

Policy

Eighteen months before the truce was signed, the political gap between the two Korean states was so wide that it was obvious it could not be closed in the foreseeable future. So the decision was made by the United Nations to settle the war with a demarcation line, re-establishing the status quo, the peninsula to be divided between North and South Korea again, along the line of the stalemated front line. This was logical, because the new line would, with minor adjustments, be close to the original demarcation line laid down by the United Nations Organisation. But it would be between defendable hills. It was on this proposition, pushed I believe by North Korea's ally China, that the truce talks were restarted.

It became the policy of the United Nations to fight an aggressive defence based on holding the vital ground with front line troops, thoroughly dug in and supported by adequate artillery and air support, and the domination of no-man's land to be maintained with an aggressive patrolling program. These were essential to the security of front line positions and the maintenance of morale, to avoid the development of a fortress mentality. The secondary reason for all this nocturnal activity was to deny to the enemy a free run of no-man's land at night. The aim was to keep him off balance with his own patrolling plans and stop him from concentrating large forces close to our positions. It also provided an arena in which to hone our own skills and keep an edge on our aggressiveness.

The Australians were particularly adept at the art of patrolling and every night recce and fighting patrols were sent out into no-man's land. The recces were like a boxer's straight left jabbing away, probing for weakness. The fighting and ambush patrols were like a right cross and a counter-punch. Occasionally we would let go a rip to the heart with a full raid on an enemy position, or a deep penetration patrol between his positions as an uppercut. Of course the enemy, both North Korean and Chinese, mixed it with us, but their style was more like a heavy-weight slugger. Or perhaps gangs of them.

Tactics

All patrols had an aim. The first patrols in position each evening were the standing patrols, which guarded access in and out of no-man's land. Through these, the recce and fighting patrols moved out as the light faded. The recce patrols were usually given specific objectives to investigate. Fighting patrols had the responsibility of keeping the enemy patrols well clear of our positions, and inflicting casualties on them. Sometimes, there were special patrols with a more unusual aim. The most common of these was the flying patrol. Its task was to recover the wounded from a patrol clash. To enable them to move fast with stretchers, the men carried only personal weapons, no Brens or grenades. There was one flying patrol on standby within the battalion position every night.

The fighting patrols either went to attack a definite objective or to set an ambush in a likely position. In which case they were referred to as ambush patrols and sites for an ambush were pre-chosen from the map or because of their previous history. In the winter it had to be a series of ambushes, as one could not sit or lie still in the snow for more than 30 minutes without risking frostbite. After 20–25 minutes of inactivity, one's feet became extremely cold and in need of exercise. Also the high humidity south of the 40th parallel produces a wet cold which, with the wind from Siberia adding a chill factor, is better not experienced. The trick to staying comfortable was to walk with one's fly unzipped and jacket open over the zipped up armoured vest that was an added 3 kg of weight to carry, but nobody minded. While walking we warmed up, as we each carried a weapon, at least half a dozen loaded magazines and three or four hand grenades. At the next ambush position, we zipped up again to conserve the heat generated. As mentioned, 25 minutes later we would be conscious of loss of body heat and the sweat in our boots would be frozen on top of the soles, having drained through the multi-layered plastic mesh inner soles which separated them from the two socks (a woollen one over a silk one) on each foot.

In summer we tended to stay longer in an ambush position, but sometimes instead of setting ambushes we kept on the move, sweeping areas to keep them clear. The Australians and the British also employed smaller sweep patrols, to keep the ground immediately in front of the company positions under surveillance at night. Each company was responsible for mounting its own. It was also a good way to break in new patrol leaders. One never knew when one of the section leaders would have to be moved up to sergeant, and thus become responsible for leading 40–50 % of the platoon's patrolling assignments. Routes to and from our objectives were invariably pre-planned. So a few minutes spent identifying likely ambush traps and memorising a short list of code names, were worthwhile insurance.

Patrols did not roam the valley at random. All patrols had a specific task and area, and planning was co-ordinated by the battalion intelligence officer to avoid clashes between our own patrols.

One spin-off of the Australians' and New Zealanders' ability to work together was the development of pre-registered patrol defensive fire tasks. These used the same procedures as calling for defensive fire from our main positions, except that the reference points were well out in no-man's land and their code names were marked on a separate overlay, to avoid confusion. It was important that the reference points could be easily recognised by the infantry patrols in the dark. Although the artillery officer could not see them from his observation post—and they might even be too small to be shown on the map—he would have the technical data for each code name. Once he had been briefed for a patrol, the patrol leader would place the applicable overlay on his map and commit to memory the code names of the DFs most likely to be of use that night. Apple, pear, banana, orange, might be names in one area.

Domestic animals such as cat, dog, horse, cow, donkey, were bound to be the names in another. Rose, daisy, pansy, lily, dahlia, could be on an overlay for another area. An experienced patrol leader would commit to memory only those he thought he might need. If he had a clash that he could not handle with his own resources, the drill was to break contact and pull back out of range. He would then ask his control to arrange for the artillery to put down a patrol DF, on the code name that was closest to the enemy patrol's position. His control would have a direct phone line to the artillery OP and within two minutes the ranging shells would arrive, on or near the enemy patrol. Our patrol leader would report the arrival of the shell and usually had to give a correction. The artillery fire would knock the enemy patrol about, swinging the odds more than a little in our patrol's favour and in some cases enabling it to counter-attack.

I believe that the Obo Tare (Observer to Target) method of correcting artillery fire grew out of the Korean war, but we had no knowledge of that technique at the time. However, on Hill 355, we did have an arrangement with the Kiwi gunner OP officers, enabling us to correct on a north/south line, because the mighty hill faced true north. We could not do that on The Hook because, with the targets being in different directions, it was not possible to use the north/south method of pinpointing them. However, pursuing an aggressive patrolling policy paid off, in that by striving to dominate no-man's land at night, we made it difficult for the enemy to mount a surprise attack on our positions.

The troops of the different countries fighting under the United Nations banner had different patrolling techniques. Their approach and style in handling the problems of small groups operating in no-man's land in the dark of night was, generally speaking, related to their national temperaments. For instance, the Dutch were dogged and pragmatic, the Turks totally efficient and dedicated, as were the British, Canadian, South African, New Zealand and Australian troops.

The catch-phrase was "domination of no-man's land". This implied that enemy patrols getting more than half-way across the area between the two sides would be promptly dealt with by one of our fighting patrols, possibly assisted by artillery support.

Despite Britain's gallant and quick response to the invasion of South Korea, the British infantry were woefully equipped to fight a horde army. Despite that, their spirited young national servicemen fought bravely and efficiently under the leadership of senior officers with WW2 experience and junior officers chosen from the ranks of national servicemen for their ability, instead of their social standing.

The Americans and the Turks used larger patrols, 30–40 odd, but only the Turks did as well as we did. But of course, in fairness to the British troops, they were poorly equipped with personal weapons. For example, they had badly designed bolt-action rifles, unreliable old pattern Sten guns, and an insufficient number of the best light machine-gun in the world at that time, the Bren. But they had one advantage that a lot of American conscripted soldiers did not have: guts.

Armament

In 3 RAR the accepted, though not mandatory, armament for a one and 15 fighting patrol was two Bren light machine-guns, seven Owen submachine-guns and six or seven rifles. I used to loan my issue .38 Smith and Wesson pistol and holster to the signaller, so that he could carry a weapon for his own protection while leaving both hands free to operate the radio.

The rifles were carried with their 18-inch bayonets fixed and the Owens with their 12-inch ones. Everybody except the Bren gunners and the Sig had hand grenades, but the riflemen carried the most. We found that the canvas water bottle carriers which attached to our web belts, made excellent grenade carrying bags. Sergeant Ray Simpson (later V.C.), who was a grenade enthusiast, was fond of saying, "A rifle and bayonet and a bag of bombs." He meant it too. So when he was leading a patrol out with his rifle with the bayonet fixed and a couple of water bottle bags filled with six or seven hand grenades each, it gave the new diggers a boost to their confidence in these comparatively humble, close quarter weapons.

Of some embarrassment to us was the issue of phosphorus grenades to each platoon. These were can-shaped deadly firebombs, which, when the pin was drawn and the lever released on throwing, exploded with a dense spray of white hot globules of burning phosphorus showering in all directions. This burnt straight through clothing and into the flesh. It could not be put out; not even water could smother it. It did in fact inflict a very painful death. While I was there, we just never carried them. The word had gone around the battalion that the Chinese had issued a statement that anyone they captured carrying a phos grenade would have it tied to him and the pin pulled. Mind you, I kept one in the CP in a pressed steel 2-inch mortar ammunition box in which all sensitive documents were kept, such as marked maps and overlays of our dispositions and 'Sitreps' and 'Intreps'. If the platoon position was being overrun, the signallers were expected to pull the pin, drop the grenade back in the security box and get out.

Body armour is hardly a weapon; however it had its place in our armoury. The armoured vests were the most common form. They were nylon waistcoats, with overlapping hardened aluminium alloy plates sewn in between the lining and the outer covering. Bullet-proof within reason, they would stop a 7-mm and 9-mm round at the normal range that such weapons were used and they were particularly good protection from grenade fragments. In fact, the American name for the vest was flak jacket. Initially the zip up the front was a weak spot, so an armoured flap was added and, lapping over the zip, was fastened with domes. The all up weight was 3 kg, which was no problem. Each Australian company had 40 and they were loaned each evening to the men going on patrol. The American troops had them on personal issue and they wore them all the time, even in the trenches, not, I believe, a good morale booster.

Armoured underpants were also produced and given to the Black Watch for 'user trials'. They found them so uncomfortable that they hung them on the barbed wire entanglements in front of their positions on The Hook, and used them for target practice.

– *Nine* –

Jack Spiers and Hill 355

I first met Major Jack Spiers while attending an instructional course for Territorial officers at the New Zealand Army's School of Infantry, Waiouru Military Camp. As a junior regular force infantry NCO, he was the star turn of Colonel Frank Rennie's highly successful instructional team, which often introduced the subject with a humorous skit. Jack's rise to stardom in this role was not based on his acting ability alone. At the start of the first period in the morning, one could not help but notice that his absence was delaying the play's start, causing more ad-libbing by the rest of the team than usual. When he did arrive, the officers under instruction, both senior and junior, were sitting on the edge of their seats. His cheery demeanour, but not his appearance, belied the fact that only his tough constitution had got him there at all. There was the odd stuffy senior Territorial officer under instruction, who called him wild. But to me, he was a kindred spirit.

The son of an Otago Regiment veteran who won a Military Cross in France in the First World War, and in WW2 took a company of the 20th Battalion to the Middle East with the 1st Echelon, young Spiers joined the regular force in 1949. The foundations of his military education were the instructor's course and support weapons course at the School of Infantry. There he mastered all infantry weapons, including their tactical application. His outgoing personality and his ability were noted, and he was posted to the instructional team.

Jack having been a schoolboy throughout WW2 was, with his family background, mentally prepared for combat. He was also a mortar specialist. His handling of a 3-inch mortar, our main infantry mortar, equivalent to today's 81 mm, was second to none. It was not surprising therefore that, when he volunteered for secondment to 3 RAR, he was posted to the mortar platoon.

3 RAR's mortar platoon commander Lt. Ronald Grey, a graduate of the Royal Military Collage, Duntroon, was a fine soldier. After surviving

Korea, he served in Vietnam, earning a D.S.O. while CO of 7 RAR. He later commanded the Australian Field Force, with the rank of Major General. Ron recognised a winner in the 22-year-old New Zealander, who was well educated, well trained, and had the right attitude. He made the best use of Jack's talents by appointing him his mortar fire controller.

When in November '52, the battalion relieved the 3rd Bn. Royal Canadian Regiment on Hill 355, Jack took over the OP in the left forward company position, which was the closest to the Chinese forward positions. Ron sited the mortar line behind the big hill, from where fire could be brought down, in front of each of the forward companies. Mortars are high trajectory weapons, that is, the bombs are fired high into the air, so they can go over the top of a hill. Unfortunately, their fire can't be brought in very close unless they are fired from a flank, the reason being that, although an area weapon, they have a long and narrow beaten zone; that is the pattern of the fall of shot on the ground.

We were cheek by jowl with the enemy-held position called John. Three hundred metres was the line of sight distance from our forward trenches on Hill 355 to the cleverly dug Chinese outposts. These were bunkers accessed by a tunnel system, rather than the conventional open communication trench that the Europeans favoured.

The mortar OP was not on the highest point of the big feature but overlooked the likeliest approach up Surrey Hills, the long spur running northwest from our left company position. It had the easiest gradient and was used by the Chinese when they put in a regimental strength attack against the Canadians, who saw it off by the skin of their teeth in October '52. The top of this vital spur became Jack's home away from home. He manned the OP for the next three months, mostly alone. Of course the rest of the battalion needed mortar support, so Ron and Jack trained another NCO as an MFC and established a second OP on the eastern end of the hill to cover the rest of the battalion position.

Quite early in his tour of duty, Jack distinguished himself on Hill 355. At last light, the Chinese opened up a heavy barrage onto A Company, pounding the position for hours, presumably to soften it up before attacking. The rate of bombardment was very high, being calculated at 2000 rounds an hour on the company position. Jack fought back, endeavouring to suppress the enemy mortars, but also fired at probable forming up places (FUPs) where the Chinese infantry was likely to be assembling, and likely attack routes and approaches to our positions. Eventually, about 0200 hrs, the artillery barrage died down without an attack being mounted. Jack was mentioned in despatches.

Sometime after this action, Jack had the assistance of a Kiwi signaller from 16th Field, loaned by Major Roy Spence, OC 163 Battery, who visited Jack's OP and found that he had no relief of any kind, even having to repair the breaks in his telephone line himself. Jack's new helper, a veteran of the Italian campaign of WW2, swore that in Italy he had never been in barrages as heavy as he was currently experiencing. However, Jack did not have his help for long. Once he was convinced that his new mate could do the job competently, Jack took the opportunity to go for a much-needed shower. Not having been able to leave his post to have one for over three weeks, he arrived at battalion headquarters anticipating the luxury. He was promptly informed that his offsider had been wounded and he was to get back to his post immediately. The shower would have to wait.

When we visited BHQ, most of us from A Company's position went down the long communication trench to our jeep-head, then walked back along the Bowling Alley. For Korea in those days, it was a fairly substantial road. In fact, it was the main arterial one in that area. Running east to west behind Hill 355, it carried on westward and slightly north into no-man's land, between Hill 159 to our left rear, and the Chinese-held Apostles group opposite. John, also known as Pt. 227 from its spot height on the map, completely overlooked most of the road in the Bowling Alley. On John's upper slopes a tunnel had been dug, in which a 76 mm high velocity self-propelled gun had been sited to cover the road. Therefore the prudent walked in, or close to, the ditch dug alongside the road. Being in enfilade from the Apostles made the road a bit of a trap. The following incident took place when the mortar platoon commander took his new MFC sergeant onto Hill 355 for the first time, to take over the mortar OP.

"It's too far to lug your gear; hop in the jeep, Jack. I'll run you to the jeep head," said Lt. Ron Grey. Now Ron knew that Jack was a man of great courage and that his own steady driving was nearly as good as a Sydney taxi driver's. So, as he motored up the Bowling Alley in full daylight, chatting away, glad to be able to have a yarn, he was nonplussed when his passenger, who was studying the map, appeared a bit agitated. He enquired the reason.

"We have gone too far."

"You can't read a map, Kiwi. There is Hill 355 just in front."

"Like hell it is," said Jack. "That's Pt. 227. Over your shoulder is 355."

Blaspheming, Ron swung the jeep around and put his foot down. The Chinese gunners, realising that they were not going to get a couple of prisoners after all, opened fire. Ron redeemed himself as, under direct fire from the high velocity gun, he zigzagged the jeep at full speed back to the jeep head that he had missed.

At the same end of Hill 355 where the Bowling Alley ran behind it from no-man's land, a low sausage-like spur protruded south-west from the main feature back to the road. Ideally placed to protect our rear and obscure A Company's jeep head from Pt. 227, this ridge was occupied by our 60-strong anti-tank platoon, commanded by Lt. Jack Kelly. Less than a quarter of the height of Pt. 227, it was totally overlooked and inherently vulnerable. But luckily the SP gun was crested by 227's own convex slope.

When he took over the position, Jack Kelly set to work to improve the fortifications. Working hard every night, he and his men achieved wonders. They rebuilt all the bunkers with timber frames of 200 mm square Oregon timber, spiked together with metal dogs and encased in steel mesh to hold back the soil. These 2.5-metre cube-shaped prefabricated bunkers were set 3 to 3.5 metres into the ground and then covered with earth and a bursting course of rock, to conform to the contours and explode shells and mortar bombs before they could penetrate. The barbed wire around the platoon's perimeter was thickened up as well, and it was not long before the position was a strong point. Neither did Kelly neglect his patrolling program.

Meanwhile, not happy about the Battalion's 3-inch mortars being out-ranged by the Chinese 81 mm mortars, Jack Spiers turned his frustration into positive thinking. He came up with a solution, which he tested on Major Norrie, who expressed full support. Jack then put it to Ron Grey that he would like permission to move a section of the mortars, that is two tubes, up onto the rear slopes of Hill 355. The site he had chosen was a small re-entrant in one of the large buttress-like spurs that formed the forbidding rear of the big hill. The re-entrant was deep enough to screen the muzzle flashes, but did not show up on the contours of our maps, which were from the same Japanese surveys as the Chinese used, so we could expect them to have difficulty locating it. Putting a section up on the big hill would give Jack an extra 500 metres range. Ron Grey approved the scheme and after a lot of hard digging, it was established. It achieved all that was expected of it, and must have been a source of irritation to the enemy. They used a lot of ammunition probing for it, to A Company's discomfort rather than annoyance, but Charlie Chinaman could not locate it.

Soon after the establishment of this mortar line on Hill 355 itself, the 2nd US Infantry Division relieved the Commonwealth Division and 3 RAR went into corps reserve at Camp Casey. The Americans, appreciating the importance of Anti-tank Ridge, put an infantry company on the vital position. Unfortunately, this company did not patrol thoroughly, if at all—a fatal lapse, as was soon brought home to them. About three weeks after the change over, Anti-tank Ridge was overrun.

During the nights preceding the attack, the Chinese had dug a crawl trench, or more correctly, a sap, up to and under the barbed wire to within 50 metres of the American bunkers on the ridge. With a short run in, they took the position at 2000 hrs, held it all night without much trouble, and pulled out at first light. Then most unfortunately, when the Americans moved in again, some of the South Korean soldiers attached to the American unit, having survived the night's siege holed up in a barricaded bunker, emerged and were promptly shot by mistake. At the time there seemed to be no reason for the raid, other than to establish moral ascendancy.

However, a week later, the position was lost again. This time, a counter-attack from Hill 159 was ordered. It did, however, take a fair while to organise. As was the American style, the battalion commander led the company strength counter-attack. It was not only repulsed, but the CO did not return. Another attempt to retake the position was made at first light and was successful, as the Chinese were pulling out anyway. To their amazement, the relieving force found the commanding officer alive, although wounded. A big black American soldier was standing over him. There were 17 very dead enemy, lying in a circle around the officer and his guardian. Who would guess how many wounded Chinese had crawled or been dragged away by their comrades? Once again, why did the Chinese go to all that trouble for the sake of occupying a small feature like that for 10 or so hours?

On the night of 17 March, a battalion size attack overran the left forward company on Hill 355. The New Zealand gunners did not have to be called upon—they were already firing. Captain Vern Duley harassed the Chinese all night. The 16th Field Regiment fired 4600 rounds during the night. It was on this occasion that the Americans asked 28 Brigade for the loan of a company-strong force to replace their counter-attacking company. B Coy, 3 RAR was sent. Colonel MacDonald, with his adjutant Dick Stanley-Harris, accompanied them to assess the situation in case our whole battalion had to be committed. They took Jack Spiers also, as he knew the ground intimately. Once again, after occupying the same company position for some hours, the Chinese force withdrew.

When, after a well-earned rest the COMDIV went back into its own sector, the 1st Battalion the Durham Light Infantry relieved the Americans on Hill 355 and the Royal Fusiliers relieved those on Hill 159; they had a hot time. Domination of no-man's land having been conceded in the COMDIV's absence, the DLI and the RF patrols bought a fight almost every time they went out. The Durhams were unaware of the existence of the mortar section's position high up on the rear of 355, as the Americans had not used it, if indeed they were aware of its existence. So it was not until the Australians relieved the Durhams, that the fate of Jack's hidden mortar position became known, and then only to a few. It had been systematically and thoroughly destroyed, obviously with satchel charges: mortar pits, command post, sleeping bunkers, the lot. Jack's description—"A mess!"—was the understatement of the year.

The Chinese were very innovative. Surely, locating and taking out this mortar position must have been the reason all along for the attacks on Anti-tank Ridge and the left forward company where the mortar section was positioned. Needless to say, the irrepressible Aussie mortar men, encouraged by Lt. Ron Grey and his Kiwi sergeant, set to work with a will and re-established its phantom mortarline. Try as they might, the enemy still could not locate it with counter-battery fire.

Jack battled on. During the last battle of The Hook, he manned 3 Battalion's mortar OP on Sausage, which was within 2 RAR's reserve company position and next to my position, which was 3 RAR's forward platoon position on Pt. 146, right behind 2 RAR. When 2 RAR was attacked, 3 RAR's mortars were added to 2 Battalion's defensive fire plan.

Jack's tour of duty with 3 Battalion expired the day after the truce took effect. But he was not finished with soldiering; soon after his return from Korea he was commissioned. Jack spent most of his life in the New Zealand Army, serving in Malaya with 1 NZ Regt, then in Borneo attached to HQ 17th Ghurkha Div HQ. Then he was attached to the Australians again, in the role of ground to air liaison officer, directing Canberra bombers in their ground support role in Sarawak. He finally rounded off a lifetime of soldiering as a United Nations Observer in Kashmir, where, in the event of an incident, his practical experience was of great value in assessing which side was to blame.

When Jack suddenly went down with a rare illness and died on 26 March 2001, he left behind a loyal soldier's wife and their two daughters and two sons, plus many friends in both the military and in civvy street.

His full military funeral was the biggest that I have ever attended. He was quite a soldier. And a great mate.

– *Ten* –

Artillery, Armour and Engineers

Artillery

Despite the gallantry of the respective allied infantry, the fact that the numerically stronger Chinese infantry did not wipe the floor with us I attribute to the massive build-up of artillery that they had to face. Field guns of all calibre were deployed in local defence and counter-battery roles. Having said that, it must also be conceded that the Chinese eventually brought their artillery up to equal strength. They did not, however, always have the communications to exploit the quality of their firepower.

Counter-battery fire, as the name implies, is directed against the enemy guns with the intention of knocking them out or rendering their fire ineffective, by forcing them to move their position.

Defensive fire, on the other hand, is employed against enemy attacks on front line infantry positions. Targets could include FUPs and likely start lines and, in desperate situations, right onto the positions that were being overrun. The UNO forces did this well, because of the flexibility provided by radio communications down to platoon level. Early in the static phase, the Chinese tended to plaster their whole battalion area with defensive fire, rather than just the threatened feature. But they gradually improved their communications and could, therefore, more easily correct their fire when answering requests for help from their forward positions.

But their radio comms were certainly only down to company level at best. I don't know anything about their field telephone system, but their front-line platoons and fighting patrols appeared to rely on Very light signals to call for artillery assistance. The Very pistol takes a large shotgun type of cartridge, which fires out a white, red or green flare. One night an Australian platoon commander lost his bearings in 'the valley' and called his control for help. They suggested that, if he fired some flares, they could give him a reciprocal bearing to our lines. This was agreed to and he fired red over green over green. That combination was apparently the Chinese SOS signal for that night. They immediately put down the equivalent of a divisional artillery barrage, close in front of their nearest positions.

Patrol DFs were more a specialty of the UNO forces than the Chinese. The COMDIV handled them best, because our patrols carried radios. The Americans mostly stuck with the field telephone, with the wire aerial trailing behind like an umbilical cord, vulnerable to all kinds of hazards.

All artillery can be used in harassing fire and, in our war, was. I venture the theory that in the last year the Chinese harassed us more than we did them, but we put down heavier defensive fire, in the event of being attacked.

The most successful American artillery piece was without a doubt their 8-inch howitzer. Nicknamed 'The Persuader', it was considered to be a ballistic phenomenon. Besides packing a big punch that produced a mini-earthquake when it exploded, it was remarkable for its accuracy. It could be corrected to within 5 metres of a target. Organisationally, it was corps artillery and in any other army, except perhaps the German, it would not have been on call to front-line units. Not so with the Americans. Those guns were there to be used to the best advantage, and there was none of that red tape that we had come to expect from some of our allies. I am not referring to the Kiwi gunners, who would open fire without being asked or told, if they saw the need. The New Zealanders proved time and time again in the Korean war, that a highly intelligent observation post officer under light discipline, as opposed to a rigid discipline inhibiting initiative, can influence and indeed win battles through decisive action, whether he had orders to fire or not.

The American divisional artillery was equipped with excellent 105 mm field guns and 155 mm gun/howitzers. The United Nations forces had a large supply of VT fuses available to them. These produced an airburst at a predetermined height, exploding over the heads of attacking enemy infantry, wreaking havoc. The initials VT stood for 'variable time', but were a deliberate misnomer intended to mislead the enemy. The fuse was, in fact, proximity activated by a miniature radar set built into the nose cone. It could be preset to explode at a certain height above the ground that it was approaching. On exploding, the forward momentum of the shell projected the shrapnel forward and downward, causing a far higher number of casualties than if it had exploded on the ground or for that matter, than an airburst shell with a time fuse. With the meteorological conditions on the Korean peninsula affecting their trajectories, time fuses were notoriously unreliable.

The 25-pounder gun/howitzer of the Commonwealth divisional artillery was most effective in supporting the infantry. Designed before WW2, in which it was also very successful, as well as to being able to operate as a field gun it had the ability to fire in high register. That is, the barrel could be elevated to fire the shells above 45 degrees to the horizontal, shortening the range but increasing the crest clearance. This howitzer characteristic made it, like the Persuader, ideal for the hilly terrain of Korea. In the event of an attack, the gunners, by using indirect fire controlled by an OPO or an infantry officer on the spot, could drop shells close in front of the hills occupied by our infantry. With the VT fuses available, it became even more useful and its original novel feature in the gun-carriage gave it great flexibility in traverse, enabling it to switch targets very quickly. In fact, the 25-pounder shared honours with the Persuader for the most successful artillery piece of the Korean war. Both the British field artillery regiments and the New Zealand 16th Field Regiment were equipped with 25-pounders and provided supporting fire for the infantry units, initially for 27th Brigade and then 28th and 29th Brigades.

The Kiwi's 25-pounders also had an old fashioned quick-firing system. Some of the Americans were so impressed with their rate of fire that they thought they were magazine-fed. Not so—the guns were force-fed by burly NZ gunners. Drilled almost to perfection before they left the training ranges of Waiouru Military Camp, in the hinterland of New Zealand's North Island, they achieved it on the battlefields of Korea.

It was perfectly clear that field-guns, whose primary task is to support the infantry, still have to be commanded by their own officers-in-support, not under command. However, with the close liaison between the supporting New Zealand battery commanders and the Australian battalion commanders plus the good radio comms with patrols, it was possible to provide patrol DFs which in the event of a clash could be called for by the infantry and would arrive on target within 1 to 2 minutes.

This was another example of correcting the imbalance of numbers with technology, commonsense and co-operation.

Armour

Surprisingly, at the cessation of WW2 when the British put into production the next heavy tank on their drawing board, the other powers did not.

When North Korea lunged into South Korea in 1950, it spearheaded its attack with 156 Russian T34 heavy tanks, which had been the top Russian tank at the end of WW2, and still were. They pemetrated down the few roads, pushing aside what would otherwise have been serious opposition. The South Korean Army could not easily stop them, because it did not possess anti-tank guns, let alone tanks. South Korea is not tank country in the generally accepted sense of the word, but there was a role for them.

After the siege of the Pusan perimeter, there were few T34s left. The Americans, who had defended the perimeter with a corral of Patton tanks, had knocked out most of them. In the subsequent UNO advance north, the use of tanks by the Allies was fairly minimal because of the terrain. What roads there were, threaded their way through steep mountain passes, usually with a river gorge on one side and a large hill or steep mountain on the other. The Brits brought in some WW2 Churchill tanks and the Americans still had some Pattons, but to my knowledge, once the UNO forces had passed Pyongyang, no tanks were used in the ill-fated advance to the Yalu.

During the Battle of Kapyong, a company of American Sherman tanks of the 72nd US Heavy Tank Battalion, played a vital role, particularly in covering 3 RAR while the Aussies dug in and consolidated their position under direct enemy fire. In support but not under command, the tanks' allotted task from their higher headquarters was to block the two roads to enemy vehicles. In the event, they did little of that. They were first involved in delaying the advancing Chinese infantry, giving 16th Field Regiment and the Middlesex Regiment a chance to extricate themselves from the forward positions, where they had been supporting the 6 ROK Division, which had broken under the Chinese pressure and was in full retreat. The Kiwis established a gunline in the rear of the Australians and the Canadians, who were digging in on the hills to the east and north of Kapyong village to stop the rout. Then as the battle developed, the Americans tanks gave the diggers and the Canucks much appreciated direct fire support.

The Sherman was the Americans' top tank at the close of WW2, and in Korea they used them to good effect. It was a heavily armed, reliable infantry support tank, with a main armourment of a 75-mm high velocity anti-tank gun, and a co-axial mounted .30 calibre Browning machine-gun for use against trucks and infantry. Another .30 calibre Browning, mounted in front of the co-driver, was able to engage infantry to the front. On the outside of the turret, a .50 calibre machine-gun was mounted for anti-aircraft defence, but was sometimes used with effect against worthwhile ground targets.

When 'Operation Commando' was launched in November '51, the Royal Tank Regiment was in the country, equipped with the latest model Centurion tank. This was a fighting vehicle which could do whatever was asked of it. They supported the Commonwealth infantry in their attacks in a manner similar to the original First World War application. However, because of the hills, which inhibited manoeuvre, the battles were mostly fought by infantry companies and troops of tanks instead of divisions of infantry and regiments of tanks. On occasions, during the fluid part of the war, British tanks gave the Australian infantry men a lift up the hills to meet the enemy, but they usually gave direct covering fire from the paddy fields or from 'hull down' positions on hills to the rear or flank.

'Operation Commando' was the last major offensive launched by the United Nations forces. It was a success and could have been further exploited, but lessons had been learnt. Rather than repeat the yo-yo-ing exercises of the past, which turned sour with the shortening of the enemy's supply lines, General Matthew Ridgway consolidated on the narrow waist of the Korean Peninsula. This also set the political scene.

With the front stalemated, the tanks had once again to adapt their tactics. They became mobile pillboxes of the highest order, in the front line. Large concentrations of tanks and crews were also kept just behind the front, close to obvious invasion routes. For instance, the British had a large tank park on the south side of the Imjin River at Choksong, in the middle of Gloster Valley. Some tanks from there were deployed north, to support the artillery and infantry in defending the static front line. Cheek by jowl with infantry units, they dug firing positions into the crests of the defended hills. During the day they stayed back from the crest, out of sight for maintenance and sleeping. After dark, they trundled forward a few metres into their 'hull down' position. This was a three sided hole dug into the friendly side of the ridge to fit the tank's hull, leaving its turret above ground to enable the main armourment to be brought to bear on targets in no-man's land, or the Chinese positions. Of course, they could do this in the daytime if the situation warranted.

The tanks were a source of comfort to the infantry. People might wonder why. "Didn't they 'draw the crabs' (attract hostile fire)?" they might well ask. Yes, they did. But their presence was tangible and they packed a punch. Both their main armourment and machine-guns were most effective, because they were heavier and more flexible, yet less vulnerable than our infantry weapons. The 20-pounder shells flew straight and true for 3000 metres. It was the equal of the Chinese 76 mm high velocity self-propelled gun.

Not that the tanks were invincible. Peter MacGregor, a Kiwi cobber who enlisted in Australia, was a member of our assault pioneer platoon: in fact he was Lt. Joe Quinlan's driver. Peter tells of a duel between a 76 mm SP gun and the Centurion tank next to the pioneers' position on the eastern end of Hill 355. The Brit tank was in strife because its spare ammunition was stacked above ground, too close to the tank. When hit, the ammunition became a great flare highlighting the tank to its natural enemy, with predictable results. I remember the incident well, but Peter witnessed it. I believe that the crew survived. The western end of 355, where A Company was dug in, was too steep to get a tank up onto the company position. However, there were enough tanks within range on Pt.159 to support us, although their main responsibility was to cover the Bowling Alley to protect Hill 355's rear.

The hierarchy of the COMDIV showed great foresight in concentrating the reserve armour in the Yongdong and Hook areas. As it turned out, when the weight of the final Chinese major offensive fell on that flank, the efforts of the British tanks in The Hook area tipped the balance in our favour. Their presence, right on the divisional boundary, helped the US Marines and the Turks more than somewhat, and eased the pressure on 2 RAR also. A concentration of Centurions on Yongdong, on the Allies' side of the Samichon River opposite Pt. 146 and The Hook to the west, had a commanding field of fire over the Samichon Valley. They would have savaged the Chinese had they attempted to penetrate down the valley to bypass The Hook.

New Zealand was well represented among the British tank commanders. Approximately 30 members of the Royal New Zealand Tank Regiment were at different times attached to the British armoured regiments. Jim Brown (nicknamed Dark Brown) led the way, followed by Tom Couzens. Such was the New Zealanders' reputation for enterprise that, on one occasion when out of the line, Tom Couzens, wearing his NZ badge on his khaki K Force beret, drove his Centurion past a group of Australian diggers. Their mouths dropped open. With one accord they yelled, "Kiwi—you'll never get away with it."

Bill Grupen, Jim Brown (Light Brown), Dick Pepper, Jack Brunton and Geoff Walsh commanded tanks on The Hook and its environs in the last battle. Some of them, like Bill Grupen, were actually deployed on outposts, which were little isolated front line features between the 1st Marines main position and 2 RAR, and therefore at great risk.

Geoff Walsh was the last New Zealand tankie to be wounded, just hours before the truce was signed.

Engineers

The third, but not the least, supporting arm to back us up, was the Corps of Engineers. These hardy characters with their special skills made a major contribution to the infantryman's welfare. Besides maintaining the roads and laying the large strategic minefields, they tunnelled like beavers. One example was the tunnel system on The Hook, another, the tunnel driven through the top of Hill 355 to house a 17-pounder anti-tank gun, with which 16th Field hoped to snipe the Chinese positions. As it turned out, it drew too many crabs, i.e., counter-battery fire, and the Australians forbade its use.

Having a New Zealand squadron of field engineers supporting the Australian battalions; made for a good combination. The New Zealand field engineer squadron was always well led, by such commanding officers as Mal Velvin, Keith Hall and George Butcher.

There were times when we also received help from the British engineers and they too were highly efficient. But the Kiwis, whom we saw most of, did a tremendous job. As I mentioned, tunnelling was one of their fortes. But as you will learn later, culverts were not.

Pre-cut timber for bunkers was prepared and supplied by the engineers and it saved hundreds of lives as well as making life in the front line bearable, especially in the Korean winter. Working in close conjunction with the field engineers were the battalions' own field works specialists, the assault pioneer platoon. The pioneers, in turn, trained the diggers and their officers in some of the specialist techniques, such as assembling pre-cut bunkers.

As previously mentioned, mines are an important part of the defence, not only contributing to the strength of a position, but also in closing off gaps between battalion positions to counter outflanking. However, the laying and recording of minefields is a very specialised job, so became the responsibility of the engineers.

Most pressure-activated landmines were quite small, round and flat like a dinner plate and about 75 mm or so thick. Triggered by weight, they often carried a heavy charge capable of disabling a tank, usually by blowing off a track. Others were specifically anti-personnel. In Korea both anti-tank and anti-personnel mines were used, the latter extensively, because of the large number of infantry fielded by the enemy. The most common anti-personnel mine was the American M2 that we called a jumping jack. It was activated by a trip wire which, when tripped or trodden on, pulled a pin. A bomb jumped vertically out of the short, mortar-like tube holding it, and exploded 1.2 metres above the ground, firing ball bearings in a 360 degree spread. The use of this type allowed more ground to be covered with fewer mines.

The ultimate in bloody-mindedness in anti-personnel mines was achieved with the American cluster bomb, which was first used in the Korean war. Large canisters dropped from aircraft were programmed to open up and jettison their payload at a predetermined height, disgorging great numbers of mini-mines. They were nicknamed butterfly bombs, because they had little twisted oval shaped wings attached, which made them spin and caused them to disperse over a wide area as they descended. Except for the wings, they were little different from a hand grenade in appearance and effect. They did not explode on hitting the ground; that armed them. Once armed, they were so sensitive that ground vibrations caused by someone walking within a metre or so triggered them. At the time of writing, the Americans are using cluster bombs again in Iraq.

The claymore, a cross between a mine and a scattergun, which made its debut in Vietnam, would have been very handy in Korea.

Minefields in Korea were usually about 100 metres long and 30 metres in depth. They were marked with a perimeter fence, 5 metres out from the minefield. It consisted of a single strand of barbed wire strung at waist height on steel pickets, with red coloured metal triangles hung on it at 3-metre spacing. These wires were so important to our own troops' freedom of movement in no-man's land, that we checked them regularly before dawn, each field at least twice a week. Breaks in the wire were repaired and red triangles that were missing, usually having been blown off by shellfire, were replaced. The Chinese seemed to appreciate this, as it made it safer for their patrols when probing our lines. They rarely fired on minefield checking parties still out at first light.

To save problems later, i.e. when hostilities were over or if our own forces reoccupied the ground, mines needed to be laid in a pattern, with the fields being surveyed in from a datum point and the records sent back to Army headquarters to be filed. Tragic proof of the need for this discipline has been provided in the more recent wars in South-east Asia, particularly Cambodia where, for years after the hostilities had ceased, there were hundred of civilian deaths from mines originally laid to protect them. That is not to say that the odd Korean farmer was not blown up with his ox, when his plough hit a stray mine after the war.

Once the decision had been made to contain the war by continuing to occupy key features and hold the Jamestown Line, a large number of minefields were laid before the enemy recovered and closed up again. Gaps were left between fields, to allow for our movement in and out of no-man's land. Eventually, the fields were strung right across our front; especially between battalion positions. When possible, they were sited to channel attacks into 'killing zones', where concentrated firepower could be brought to bear.

Finally and most importantly, mines, like any other defensive obstacle, are ineffective unless covered by fire, as they can be removed if the enemy has free access to them. The Chinese did sometimes in the dead of night lift a few of our mines to form a corridor through a field, for the use of their own patrols. We usually found out too late unless a character like Captain Hutchinson did some of his late night, in-depth probing in no-man's land to keep ahead of the problem.

The appointment of the battalion assault pioneer officer is a key one, in the defensive phase of a war. As commander of the assault pioneer platoon, he is a cross between a consulting engineer and a clerk of works. His main role in defence is co-ordinating the building of the battalion's earthworks and obstacles. The men of his platoon assisted the companies by laying minefields, supervising the erection of barbed wire entanglements, and supervising the construction of bunkers and command posts. It certainly was not luck that caused the best pioneer officers to be posted to us, but we were blessed by the fact that they were.

Captain John Hutchinson was a Duntroon man who, having done the extra year at the college to gain an engineering degree, was well qualified to command the assault pioneer platoon. A quiet, almost retiring chap, he was highly respected but considered a little eccentric in that, armed with nothing more lethal than a walking stick, he prowled around no-man's land on his own in the middle of the night, inspecting our minefields. Sometimes, someone made sure that an armed digger accompanied him. One night, when John was returning to our lines on his own, he strolled up as usual to an outpost in front of Hill 355. Appearing out of the snowy gloom, in front of a bloke who happened to be a New Zealander, but was nevertheless none too bright, Hutchinson was neither recognised nor challenged. Instead, he was greeted with a full magazine of submachine-gun fire. Luckily, the dumb Kiwi missed him completely.

Lt. Joe Quinlan took over from John Hutchinson at Camp Casey early in '53. Joe and I hit it off right from the start. We became good cobbers. I had a great respect for him. He was, I thought, quieter than the average Australian. No less capable for that, but he kept his cards under the table. He was a top rate companion and, with his pleasant disposition, very popular. One had the feeling with Joe, that here was a competent, self-contained, well-balanced man on whom you could rely.

One night, a covering party was positioned to intercept any enemy intrusion that might interfere with Joe's platoon while they were laying a new minefield. Joe was directing the work himself, a most meticulous job at the best of times, made more difficult by the dark and the need for silence. Work was progressing satisfactorily, when a firefight erupted from the direction of the covering patrol. Joe did not hesitate. "Our mates have bought a fight. Drop everything. Let's go."

A typical Australian reaction. They quickly adopted a fighting patrol formation, and set off with Joe leading. When he spotted an enemy soldier on the flank of the Chinese patrol, Joe opened up with his Owen and cut him down. The Chinaman must have heard or sensed their approach, because he turned and fired at the target presented in the half-light of no-man's land. Their bullets must have passed in the air. At that close range, the shot from the 8-mm bolt-action carbine went through Joe's upper left leg and straight on into his right. The Chinese soldier was probably already dead but we don't know. What we do know is that his one bullet severed the main arteries in both of Joe's legs.

The action had been joined and it is the code of the infantry, for very sound reasons, that in attack you do not stop to assist casualties. After seeing their skipper fall, Joe's men pressed home their counter-attack ferociously. With the arrival of Joe's party, the numbers were now close to being equal. The enemy did not linger. Joe may have seen them depart, but he himself did not survive. The doctor ruled that he would have bled to death in less than five minutes. Under the circumstances, tourniquets were unable to be applied in time.

On every ANZAC Day parade, it is said, "They did not die in vain." This was certainly true in Joe's case. He had, by his decisive action, achieved the ultimate. By joining up with the covering patrol he had established, for a few minutes, parity in numbers—something that we rarely had. This time the Australians were really on top and the Chinese patrol was routed with heavy casualties.

This little battle was one of many which brought no-man's land in front of 355 under control again, after our absence.

Lt. Colin Wilson replaced Joe. Once more the pioneers got the best. Colin was a great guy and became another good friend. He was very outgoing and once out of the line we enjoyed each other's company in the mess. Colin, like Joe, had extremely good man management skills, as well as knowing the practical side of pioneering.

– *Eleven* –

An Infantryman's View of the Air War

I had not been long with the battalion on Hill 355, when quite early one morning a Harvard spotter plane started to circle the Chinese positions facing us on our left flank. Training aircraft during the second world war, when used as spotters in Korea, the Harvards clocked up more flying time than the American fighters did. Their rotary engines still produced the distinctive buzzing sound. Because of this characteristic they were nicknamed 'mosquitoes' by the diggers, but were no relation to the fast British twin-engine light bomber of WW2. When we heard them buzzing around and around, we knew that an air strike was imminent. So did the Chinese.

The circling Harvard kept a respectable height, and enemy anti-aircraft fire was limited to a few slow firing heavy machine-guns. When senior divisional officers started to arrive in No. 1 Platoon's position, that confirmed that an air strike was on. Then a party of airmen turned up with microphones and loudspeakers, and set them up for the spectators' benefit. Company HQ had not warned me that my position was to be used as a grandstand.

Eventually, after about an hour and a half cruising around, identifying targets, the spotter plane dropped coloured smoke bombs on selected ones on the forward slope of Hill 227, about 300 metres across the little valley from A Company. By this time, the diggers and the brigade and divisional brass were totally integrated. They shared the same viewing positions and commented to each other without any inhibitions, enabling some of the British officers to find out for themselves that the Australian soldier was not the wild ruffian that he has so often been unfairly misrepresented as.

"Every Chinaman for miles around will be underground by now," a digger with a fair dinkum Australian drawl observed sardonically. I was sure that he was right, as the enemy were strong on tunnelling and were known to vacate most forward positions during the day, having the ability to re-man them quickly from underground galleries, similar to the German tactics in their front line positions during the trench warfare of WW1.

Suddenly, US Navy Thunder Jet ground attack aircraft roared in over the top of Hill 227. One after another, they viewed their targets, then did a circuit and returned to drop their bombs, each politely in turn. Then round again, coming in firing rockets this time. Back again with machine-guns blazing. Then back again, and again. Until their machine-gun belts were empty. Then it was the turn of the US Air Force with their Shooting Stars and Sabre jets. They turned up right on cue and went through much the same routine, but with machine-guns only, calibre unknown. But they flew faster; in fact they were very impressive. I liked the look of the Sabres.

No sooner had the ground attack and fighter aircraft done their job, than the carrier-borne fighter-bombers arrived, the big bodied, propeller driven Corsairs, with their inverted gull wings flying noticeably slower than the jets. They were armed with 500 lb (227 kg) bombs, which produced a spectacle of blown up earth but little else, which did not impress the onlookers. "The last Corsair," the commentator told us, "is going to drop a 1000 lb deep penetration bomb." We were about five hundred metres from where the bomb landed on the forward slopes of Hill 227, half-way up the spur, which protruded toward Anti-tank Ridge. We actually saw the bomb leave the aircraft and disappear into the ground. Nothing happened. Just as we began to think it was a fizzer, the spur started to tremble, then shake, as the energy in the bomb struggled to the surface for relief. Arriving in a great explosion of power, a geyser of earth and who knows what else shot about 100 feet into the air. This was more like it. I would not like to have been in a bunker in that target area.

The next planes to perform were British, carrier-borne Sea Furies, the fastest piston driven war planes in the world. They did a fly past at top speed, very impressive.

The Australian Meteor jets provided the finale, and naturally got the biggest round of applause. The pilots must have known whose position they were performing in front of and acted accordingly. How easy it is to amuse mature soldiers who have not had any entertainment for months. The show must have cost thousands of dollars, but it certainly beat stalking around in the frozen wastes of no-man's land at night. It had been quickly appreciated by the audience, that while the bombing and strafing was going on, it was safe to have your head above the parapet of the trench. We all, including the senior officers, congregated in the best places to get a good view, and commented among ourselves. Rank was forgotten.

Each Meteor did several runs, firing first rockets and then machine-guns. The diggers quickly noted the differences in the heights of the Australians' flight paths. Some wag nominated a high flying pilot as a married man. When the next plane came in so low, that we were looking down on him as he flew between the hills, there was a chorus from the diggers: "He's a single man." Then another one, making an approach at a noticeably higher altitude, was dubbed a married man. And so it went on.

New and eager, I asked the colonel why we were not going to follow the air strike with a battalion attack. Even to a young man who had only studied war, it was obvious that we ourselves could have taken Hill 227. With a little more support, say two battalions, the whole Apostle feature could have been ours—very desirable, when you look at the map. Lt. Colonel Hughes was most patient with his new ball of fire from across the Tasman. He explained that it made some sense to leave the status quo, as peace talks were in progress. Yet at the same time, one couldn't help thinking that it was a pity the Chinese and North Korean hierarchies did not see it in the same light.

In regard to our own vulnerability to air attack, we were indeed lucky that the American fighters kept the communists' first class fighter planes, the Russian built Mig 15s piloted by both Russian and Chinese, bottled up in Mig Alley over the Yalu River, which was the border between North Korea and China. The Mig was the top Russian fighter plane and had a slight edge of speed over the American Shooting Stars and Sabre jets, but the American pilots were more skilled than the Chinese. However, some Russian pilots assisting their Chinese comrades gave the Americans a run for their money. But the balance of airpower precluded any bombing or other serious air support for the communist armies, as the UNO troops enjoyed total air superiority over the battlefield.

But we were still at risk. Even in those days, the planes were so fast that identifying targets on the ground without spotter assistance was almost impossible for the pilots. The accidental napalm bombing of the Argyll and Sutherland Highlanders, earlier in the war, was a tragic example. The red and white hot, billowing rolling flames from that burning jellied petrol, engulfing everything in its path, was a terrible sight and a horrible killer, making it the most awesome of all the American pyrotechnic weapons. To be caught in its firestorm, must be one of the worst ways to die.

The answer to our identification from the air was simple and effective. Each platoon was issued with a set of air panels. Made of silk for reflection and lightness, they were 2.4 m x 800 mm rectangular sheets, coloured bright iridescent red on one side and yellow on the other. The basic code was an L or a T and was expanded with the colour code, to seven combinations, coinciding nicely with the number of days in a week. Each day's routine orders included the pattern in which the panels should be arranged on the following day (see diagram). The platoon signallers were responsible for seeing that they were laid out, but every man in the platoon was quite capable of carrying out this important task, which we took very seriously. They were pinned down or, if the ground was too rocky, held in position by a stone on each corner. They were set on the highest ground within the platoon position that was out of sight of the enemy. For a pre-planned strike, like the demonstration one put on for the brass, the spotter plane was a safer and more precise option. Incidentally, we had no anti-aircraft defences because we did not need them.

To WW2 veterans, the comparative immunity from air attack might seem like we had it easy compared with the terrible pastings that they had to endure from the German Luftwaffe and the Japanese Air Force. But, with the greatest respect, we were outnumbered on the ground to an extent unimaginable in earlier wars. There were three armies against one, and these were very strong in infantry and artillery. This was horde army stuff. Local attacks against a battalion position were never less than 9:1, that is, three regiments or brigades, of three battalions each. Or put another way, a division against a battalion.

Our division used small, high winged monoplanes called Austers for air reconnaissance. Because of their capability and the requirements of

AIR PANELS

The seven patterns in which they could be arranged to identify UN positions to our aircraft.

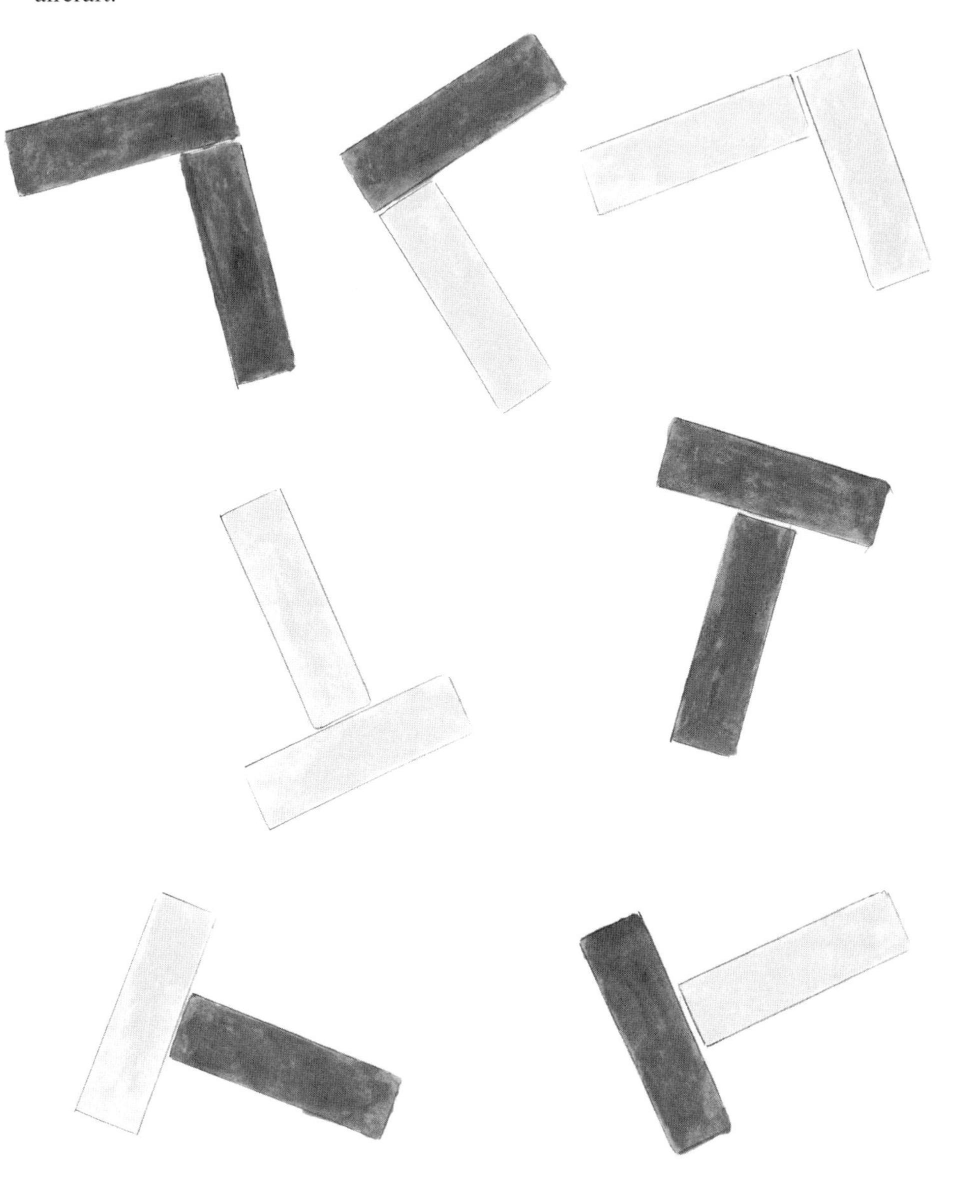

their tasks to fly very slowly without stalling, they were sitting ducks, with ground fire accounting for quite a few. But they carried out missions that no other type of aircraft in Korea could handle. The pilots were able to cut the motor and glide in quietly over the target area, and then restart it and fly out again. There were, unfortunately, occasions when both the pilot and his observer were so engrossed in the scene below that they flew into a hill. There were of course so many hills. A New Zealand gunner officer was killed like that, while piloting himself.

While it was not the first time that jet aircraft had been flown in combat—the Germans and, I believe, the British, flew a few operationally before the end of WW2—the Korean war was certainly the first time the jets had been used in large numbers by both sides, and were actually involved in aerial combat. Their performance was such that all piston-driven fighter planes became obsolete overnight. The Mustangs, the top British fighter planes in 1945, were withdrawn from Mig Corridor and put to work further south in a ground attack role. The men of the Australian 77 Squadron, who flew these excellent planes, swallowed their pride and with the usual Australian intelligence and élan, set to their new work with a vengeance. They played hell with the communist supply routes in North Korea.

Typical of their flair were the actions of the Mustang pilot who spotted an enemy train proceeding toward the front. Like New Zealand, Korea is so hilly that to run a railway, you must tunnel. Before the pilot could position himself to attack, he saw the train disappear into a hill. Locating the other end of the tunnel, he took out the engine as it reappeared. As he shot it up with machine-guns and rockets the front railway truck blew up, derailing the engine and blocking the mouth of the tunnel. Not a bad effort. He then flew back to the other end of the tunnel and bombed it until it collapsed. Effectively entombing the whole train.

Another 77 Squadron pilot, while flying alone, somewhere between Mig Corridor and the frontline, sighted a large convoy of trucks proceeding south through a river gorge. Shooting up the leading truck, he turned away and shot up the last one, totally trapping the rest on the narrow road. He then radioed his squadron and invited them to come and help him finish the job. They responded, and the loads on those trucks never made the front.

The aircraft that is not really a plane made its operational debut in the Korean war. The helicopters were not armed, in those days of their early development. So the gunship concept was not part of the Korean scene. But the choppers were used in the limited role of flying VIPs around and the unlimited one of flying out the seriously wounded. It was a common sight to see a procession of Bell 60 helicopters flying through the valleys in the morning, after heavy gunfire all night had indicated another test of strength further along the front. With a stretcher in each pod, just above the skid on each side of the flimsy looking fuselage, they could carry two casualties back to a MASH in, say, 20 minutes. This had been unheard of previously. Any other method of evacuation in that terrain could sometimes take up to a whole day. It also meant that these casualties went directly to a mobile advanced surgical hospital, rather than first to a field dressing station and then to a casualty clearing station, and then on to a MASH. The major benefit of flying them out was that, in spite of the large number of casualties suffered, the United Nations' wounded had a higher survival rate than the Allies' wounded had in World War 2.

Strategic bombing by B52 Super Fortresses flying from bases on Okinawa was used against North Korea's industrial targets and the bridges over the Yalu and other rivers, to slow the flow of Chinese reinforcements. We never saw these planes, but they played their part in keeping the pressure on the enemy.

There were many planes shot down by both sides in North Korea, but the American and Australian pilots were flying over enemy occupied territory and the population was more than hostile. So a search and rescue co-ordinating unit was set up to direct the rescue operations. Helicopters flying off Allied occupied islands and Navy aircraft carriers, played a vital role in recovering downed pilots. The choppers flew anywhere to pick up airmen who had been forced to ditch. With better communications than ever before, the pilot in trouble would put out a Mayday call on the SOS channel, giving his present position and stating where he expected to come down. He then endeavoured to fly or glide as far as he could toward help, before having to bail out. The heavy jets had to glide at a high speed to stay airborne, and the bunds made the paddies unsuitable for fast landings. However, many pilots managed to glide long distances, as the dogfights over North Korea took place at very high altitudes, between 20,000 and 35,000 feet. With the density of the North Korean population, plus their army, there was not much time or safety for rescue attempts. Yet the men in the choppers pulled off some amazing ones. Sometimes, the downed pilot's squadron buddies would close on him and shoot up anyone pursuing him on the ground or otherwise trying to interfere with the rescue. The lives of many pilots were saved in this manner and the practice was carried over into the Vietnam war. There, bigger helicopters had crews who were specially trained and equipped for such emergencies. They were nicknamed the 'Jolly Green Giants'.

Some pilots had no option but to ditch in the sea. All going well, they could still be rescued if the navy had ships in the area, but their chances were drastically reduced in winter. A man might live for 15 minutes in the freezing water, because of his insulated clothing. That was a considerable improvement over the five minutes survival time during the Russian convoys of WW2, where the winter water temperatures were about the same. But it still wasn't very long.

– *Twelve* –

Relief in the Line

After three months in the line, our battalion was due for a rest. The men were holding up well, but keeping us at a high pitch for too long would eventually result in mistakes and cause unnecessary casualties. This was, of course, true of the whole Commonwealth Division, which had occupied this sector since the Jamestown Line was established nineteen months before.

So at the end of February 1953, the 2nd US Infantry Division replaced the COMDIV in the line, as there was no other British division in the country. The 2nd Div had fought hard in Korea since the start of the war but now, having been grievously drained of its best men, it was no longer in the top flight of the US Army. 28 Brigade was relieved by the 9th Infantry Regiment, which was under a cloud for a breach of security, with the result that they were forbidden to wear unit identity. It was most unusual to see Americans without the flashes and paraphernalia that they so love to sport. To add insult to injury, they had been told that they were heading for Koje Island to guard prisoners of war—a subterfuge that might have helped their security, but didn't do much for their morale when they ended up on Hill 355 and Pt. 159.

During the week before the relief was to take place, the American platoon commanders, each with his four sergeants, were attached to Australian platoons to familiarise them with the positions and the situation in the valley. It was an eye opener to witness the sergeants arguing with their officer as to who was to go out on patrol with us. They were, in fact, there to do just that, but were disinclined to risk their necks.

I took the whole five that were attached to No. 1 Platoon, out on a full fighting patrol to start with. They came as supernumeraries, so that I would still have my own organisation intact if we had a contact. As it happened it was uneventful, but the Americans should have gained an insight into serious infantry work. However, when we laid an ambush, a couple of the sergeants bitched about having to sit on the snow.

Once we knew when the relief was to take place, preparations were made for the change-over. As the Americans had different calibre weapons from us, we had to remove all our reserve ammunition, except the boxes of belted 30 calibre for the Brownings. We also had to take our reserve rations. These were American C rations, one day's meals for one man, packed individually in little cardboard boxes, that had in turn been packed inside bigger ones measuring 300 x 300 x 400 mm and strapped both ways with tough plastic. We had a pallet full of them in a recess dug into the side of the communication trench, presumably as a reserve. They had certainly been there before our current occupation, and we had never had occasion to broach them. When we went to move them, we were astounded to find how light the first box was. The whole pallet of boxes had been plundered. The bottoms had been cut out and the contents removed, without removing the strapping. They had been stacked up again, so you couldn't tell the difference. We blamed the poor old Korean Service Corps people who carried our supplies, but it could have been anyone. However, one thing that I am quite sure of is that it was not our own men, because they were not only well fed, but they were all volunteers who took the war very seriously and would never dream of weakening the position like that.

On the morning of the relief, when I attended our last O Group in the Company CP, I was astounded to be told that Bernie Cocks was to be sent out at 1800 hrs with six picked men, to cover the relief. Nothing wrong with that, except that with the change-over being timed for 0300 hrs, they were to stay out until 0200 hrs. I couldn't believe it. February is the coldest month in the Korean winter, when the temperature drops to –20 degrees Fahrenheit at night. To put men out there in the open for eight hours in the coldest part of the year was, I believed at the time, inhuman. It was of course, for the protection of the rest of us. We had to do the relief without losing the position. But I couldn't accept eight hours and I told the company commander so. He refused to relieve them halfway through. Major Norrie did not take too kindly to me telling him his business and chopped me down. Jack Spiers was present and has often said since that he thought I had gone too far. Well, I had. I have been ever grateful to Jim that he did not dump me. My 'blue' was that I had overlooked the presence of the American officer. Had I had sense enough to accept what the OC said at the O Group and then approached him afterwards, I am sure that he would have altered the order. But I didn't and Bernie and the boys had to suffer. I am conscious of a certain irony in this, as I was critical of the American sergeants arguing with their officer about going on patrol. But I was battling for my men, not myself.

The time passed more quickly for me than it would have for the seven men freezing in 'the valley'. I had to do all the last minute supervision of clearing the gear off the hill and maintain the security of the position at the same time, without my right hand man. The Americans had no direct responsibility, even for security, until 0300 hrs. Eventually, everything that to go was on the trucks at the bottom of the hill, except for the radios and telephones and personal weapons, which of course we still needed. I also had the water bottle with the platoon's rum ration.

Finally, Bernie and his patrol returned, frozen almost senseless and out on their feet. I offered them their well-deserved rum ration and some self-heating cans of chocolate malted milk. The young soldiers, without exception, refused the rum, saying, "No thanks, Skipper. I'll just have a chocolate malted milk. Must get some sleep." They were bushed. I lit the cans' wicks for them. The self-heating cans were a great innovation of those times. I have never seen them since, but I have a faint recollection that they were of Canadian manufacture. Ripping off the lid by its tag, you lit the wick of a cartridge that ran down the middle of the can. The cartridge burning fiercely with a few splutters and sparks quickly heated the surrounding contents.

The boys' mates took them over and helped them rest up for what little time was left before we moved. Then they assisted them down the hill, and did a second trip to get their own gear.

Bernie, on the other hand, replying to my offer of a nip of rum in his West Australian drawl, said, "Don't mind if I do, Skipper. I like a bit of the old tom thumb."

I remembered that Bernie had been in sight of the Yalu on his first tour with the battalion and went right through the bitterly cold winter of 1950. Maybe that was why, out of the whole company, Jim Norrie had chosen him for this vital patrol that he had just carried out. He had proved that he could handle the cold. I offered to top up his mug of rum. "Don't mind if I do, Skipper. Don't mind a bit of the old tom thumb." A little later: "By the way Skipper, don't worry about the phones. I'll carry them down the hill."

"There is no need for you to do that, Bernie. The Sigs have got it in hand. Would you like another rum?"

"Yeh. Thanks. Don't mind a bit of the old tom thumb, Skipper. I'll take the phones down the hill, though."

"Fine, Bernie, we'll be moving soon."

I had organised a couple of blokes to assist Bernie down the hill and onto the truck. A third carried his gear, including his Owen and a fourth the phones, which had to stay to the end. The Sigs of course lugged the radios. Bernie did not feel a thing. Everything went well. No one tripped over in the dark, and the Chinaman did not interfere.

We travelled south in the American trucks that had brought their troops up. We crawled at about 2 miles per hour in the pitch dark, each driver following 2 metres behind the truck in front, with nothing to help him but a white spot painted on its tailboard. The NZ 10 Company had given the matter more thought. They had painted their differentials white and rigged a little light over them. As a result, they were able to travel faster, with less stress on the drivers. After 20 minutes or so I became aware of my feet being even colder from a draught, the source of which, despite shifting my pack around the floor of the cab, I could not locate. I was therefore unable to take the catnap that I craved, because I was so cold. After passing the 'Light line' headlights were switched on; the drivers increased speed. The further back we got, the faster they drove and the colder their cargoes became. We arrived at Camp Casey just after first light.

We were now in corps reserve. The whole Commonwealth Division, with the exception of the New Zealand Gunner Regiment, was out of the 'line' for the first time since the division was formed.

Our New Zealand gunners had a well-established gun position and field quarters, about 4 km south of Hill 355 and NE of The Hook. But they did not get a break and were to be frequently called upon to provide close support for the Yanks, because of the flexibility of their 25 pounders and the speed with which they could put rounds on the ground.

The American High Command had shrewdly made 16th Field's retention in the line and availability to provide support, a condition of their supplying a division to relieve the rest of us.

– *Thirteen* –

Camp Casey

3 Battalion quickly settled into a less stressful life style in the winterised tents of Camp Casey. Winterised meant that besides wooden floors, the tents had board walls inside the canvas to a height of 1.2 m, and the savage drop in temperature at night was combated by the installation of diesel fuelled pot-bellied stoves.

Our primary aims were to rest and retrain. They knew where to find us in an emergency. Camp Casey was a large complex of battalion size camps about 5 km directly east of the main supply route. On a small plain, with rolling hills to the south and protected from the north wind by a steep wooded range 500–600 metres high, the Camp Casey valley had only a few paddies and they were dry. Most of the plain was drained by enchanting little streams, which were totally frozen over when we took up residence. It was a beautiful place in early spring, when it finally arrived. I have vivid memories of our stay there, ranging across almost the full spectrum of life.

First of the worst was our first battalion parade. On the morning of our arrival at our new quarters, on this wind-swept snow-covered plain, dress for parade was laid down as combat trousers and jacket, which were wind-proof. We wore no headdress, as our slouch hats had not yet caught us up, but our woollen balaclavas, rolled up of course, would have been quite satisfactory. Even our steel helmets would have been better than nothing. There had not been any sign of winter ending and we stood there in a bitterly cold wind for a good ten minutes before Colonel Hughes's jeep pulled up and he climbed onto its warm bonnet. His outer clothing was a big parka with the hood up; ours were back in our tents. He also had the 'sit down flap' buttoned up between his legs. With his back to the biting wind—we of course were facing it—he stood us at ease. A few diggers unconsciously stamped their feet, to keep the circulation going. "Stand still," rapped out the colonel, "it's not cold. You only think it's cold." Unfortunately, his attempt at a bit of lighthearted humour fell rather flat on the suffering troops. No one laughed. As was only right and proper, Colonel Hughes then made it clear that we were not on holiday. Although we were to be rested from the demands of the frontline, he stressed the need for ongoing training. "There is always room for improvement," he said. Then he related the incident of Captain Hutchison's close shave, when our able assault pioneer platoon commander, returning from no-man's land late one night, was mistakenly fired on at close range by one of our own men. The CO concluded with the statement: "Not challenging and lack of fire control were bad enough. But the most serious weakness was the fact that the soldier did not hit the captain at all. That was inexcusable at 3 metres range." No one laughed at that, either. But it was taken to heart, and any complacency anyone had from serving in a famous battalion was replaced by a resolve to maintain the standards that had made it so.

Our first and most pleasant experience was our visit, by companies, to the Americans' shower unit. Unlike the British Army's old-fashioned open air shower units, there was no feeling of being rushed through, no pressure on the troops to get it over and done with and move on out. For once we could take our time, scrubbing off more than two months of grime, with ample hot water. Meanwhile our clothes were being laundered and our 'under dunkers' discarded. In the drying off area, we were issued with brand new underwear.

There were Korean villages in the vicinity of the camp, out of sight in re-entrants and valleys to the south. Occasionally, we saw a funeral party heading off north across the paddy bunds to a hidden site. It was strange to see them returning a couple of hours later, in small groups of two or three, hanging on each others' shoulders and staggering all over the place, obviously full of some sort of strong liquor. More joyous sights, which it was my privilege to observe, were little children skating on the frozen surface of the beautiful streams that drained that part of the Camp Casey plain. Their skates consisted of oblong pieces of wood the length and width of their feet, with two cleats nailed across the underside. Loosely plaited dried grass loops held them on their feet. The sight was peaceful and civilised, and therefore good for one's soul.

The thaw produced a few topics of conversation. Before its onset, it was recognised that what was currently a solid strip of ice in a depression in the main road was the bed of a fairly large stream that went through the centre of the camp and separated A and B company areas and would, with the thaw, revert to quite a deep ford. The OC of the New Zealand Field Engineer Squadron, Major George Butcher was called in. His men set vigorously to work putting in a culvert, a credible effort as we soon had a level road over the stream, and life went on as usual. The Kiwi engineer officers were invited to our mess for drinks on Sundays and everything was palsie-walsie, that is until the thaw, when the capacity of the culvert proved inadequate.

The stream banked up, flooded the front of B Company's compound and poured over the road into A Company. But of course, field engineers can destroy as easily as they can build. So back they came with beehive charges, so named because they are a parabola shape like a traditional beehive, which concentrates the force of the explosion. Within seconds of the detonation, high flung rocks were landing on A Company's cookhouse, like an artillery barrage. The pent up water was starting to flow freely, so was the language of A Company's cooks and fatigues.

"You mugs might have killed somebody."

"Look at the bloody great holes in our tin roof. You bloody great galahs."

The Kiwis responded, saying, "She'll be right, sport. Next time we'll put in a pipe as big as your mouth."

"You won't get the contract next time, yer bludgers. Go and blow up some Chinese."

I was watching, but kept out of it. However, I inspected the damaged cookhouse, to show where my loyalties lay. To be fair, the roof was like a sieve and you could have put your fist through some of the holes not to mention one sheet of corrugated iron on the side of the building that was peeled back by the blast and flapping in the breeze. The New Zealanders did of course come back and rectified the drainage problem, using concrete pipes at least three times the diameter of the original ones.

Activity for the first week or so in Casey was confined to making the camp more comfortable, having inoculations brought up to date, tracking down mates in other companies, and generally unwinding. After that the aim was to employ the men gainfully, but just sufficiently to keep them out of trouble while they recovered from the stresses of the front-line and regained their mental and physical strength. That applied to the officers also, although their responsibility toward the men was the first priority on their agenda. Torn or worn uniforms were replaced; boots also. Pay was brought up to date, and the establishment of a wet canteen, a sergeants' mess and an officers' mess soon proved beneficial. Everyone gradually got the stress out of their system and was able to relax again. Later, we got down to serious training and worked six days a week and three nights. Sunday was a complete stand down, with church services held on Sunday mornings but not compulsory.

The men of each platoon were quartered in two large squad tents. The company sergeant-major and the sergeants shared a squad tent, the OC and his officers likewise. The diesel-burning choofers in the tents were kept going all night. As the junior in our tent, it was my job to be first out of bed in the morning, to light the Tilley lamps and turn up the stove. I also put on a brew and made some toast. The bread, which was of better quality than you can get in New Zealand today, was placed on old Bren gun magazine springs on top of the almost red hot choofer. The thick browned slices, with their white zigzag patterns where they had laid on the springs, were considered a delicacy, especially by the tall and lean company 2IC, Captain Colin Brown. We had plenty of canned butter and jam.

Each company had its own wet canteen, where the diggers could relax in the evenings. The gaps in our ranks were steadily filled with new faces, some of them quite colourful characters, all with something to contribute. Both messes were happy ones.

Colonel Hughes knew the value of getting to know the people that we had to work with. He had the 2IC arrange midday parties in the mess on selected Sundays. These were of a high standard of organisation, catering and behaviour. Despite the difficulty of travelling in the severe winter conditions that we were still experiencing, they attracted the cream of the high ranking officers of the divisional and brigade headquarters and the CO's fellow battalion commanders. A few American officers were invited, including representatives of a helicopter squadron, who appropriately flew in, although we had no airfield. Officers of the New Zealand 16th Field Regiment were of course represented and made most welcome, due to our special relationship. Those of the RNZE Field Squadron were also on the 'must invite list', their slip up with the culvert forgiven and forgotten.

We junior officers were detailed to direct the parking, open the vehicle doors, escort the guests into the mess tent, and introduce them to Colonel Hughes. We then returned to face the elements. The warmth in the marquee, produced by big diesel choofers made from 44-gallon drums, was a lifesaver. Unfortunately for us, the arrivals spread over one and a half hours, during which time we had to stand out in the open in the freezing wind. Eventually we were free to join the party, and thawing out started. Our outsides were warmed by the choofers, while our insides responded to some food. Plus, of course, a tot or two of whatever poison we fancied. Toward the end of the party, we had to go outside again to organise the guests' vehicles, and open the jeep doors for them. But it was a great experience to converse with men who were holding senior appointments in the Commonwealth Division, yet were capable of relaxing when given the opportunity. Everyone that I assisted thanked me graciously. These were men who could, to quote Kipling: "walk with kings—nor lose the common touch."

We had not been long in Camp Casey when the MO reported a dramatic increase in VD cases. This was a serious matter, as most of Korea had four different armies through it during the previous two years. That is not just an unfortunate choice of words. Investigation revealed that some of our men were 'going over the fence', and the favoured village was soon identified. After considerable discussion at all levels, no solution was found. Then Sergeant-major Jack Morrison solved the problem. He started a rumour that the MO had sent blood specimens back to the experts. Laboratory tests had isolated a new and incurable strain of syphilis, which had originated in this particular village. Because of its obvious characteristics, the medical powers that be had named it "The Green Drip". The rumour spread, at the speed that rumours do. Absence without leave stopped overnight, and the pressure came off the Regimental Aid Post.

Sunday afternoons at Casey were free time and a good release for all ranks. The first Sunday, some of the boys and I climbed the big hill to our north, across the little plain. It was 550 m high but no big deal, as we went up a reasonably gentle ridgeline—by our standards anyway—at its western end. From the top, it was a great view. We also found some old foxholes and a bit of a cave, which had served as cover for some unknown but obviously very young and uneducated GI. There were empty 30 calibre carbine cartridge cases and other bits and pieces of rotting equipment lying around. I found a half written letter to his 'Mom'. It portrayed confusion and instability. I wondered how anyone could be sent to war so mentally unprepared.

On another Sunday, three of the men made up a party and asked me if they could go pheasant shooting. As they intended to take only rifles I could not see a problem, so gave the expedition my blessing. At the end of the day they returned rather chastened. One bloke, who shall go unnamed, got onto a low flying cock pheasant. Traversing his weapon quickly to get a lead, he fired and nearly blew the head off another member of the party. Good soldier he might have been, but hunter? Hunting expeditions were never suggested again.

Bernie Cocks and I had become an efficient combination and firm friends. One day in Casey, he invited me to the sergeants' mess for drinks before their formal dinner. This was a great privilege indeed, not accorded all officers. I duly reported at the appointed time with a few other invited guests, including the other New Zealand officer, Captain Dick Stanley-Harris. At that time, Dick was 2IC of D Company. Bernie escorted me into the big marquee and introduced me to the RSM, as is the protocol. After this formality, he said, "There is someone else I want you to meet, Skipper."

Out of the corner of my eye, I had noticed that the RSM had not moved far away, but was watching with interest. I knew Jack Spiers well, and shook his hand heartily. He of course belonged to this mess. But who was this other New Zealand sergeant, who had just appeared? Tom Couzens, no less. I had last seen Tom in Waiouru, where he had been a regular force corporal in the Royal New Zealand Armoured Corps. Unaware that he had been sent to Korea to serve with the British tanks, I was very pleased to see him again. A fine man and a good soldier, he was now sporting three stripes, for which I congratulated him sincerely. My congratulations were graciously accepted with a straight face. Then the whole bunch cracked up. They had sewn the extra stripe on, so that Tom could gain entrance to the mess and attend the dinner. Obviously, the RSM had given his consent, as he was laughing too. Tom did well with the British tanks. When they were reposted to Egypt, the Brits approached the New Zealand Army and requested that Tom be allowed to accompany them. But our army turned them down, and Tom was posted to 16th Field Artillery Regiment to finish his time in Korea. He was commissioned soon after the war ended. Tragically, Tom lost his life in an unavoidable Snowcat accident at Cape Selbourne in Antarctica in 1959. However, that was well into the future. This evening, we were four young men relaxing together over a few drinks, before going into battle again. Just the same, being an invited guest I was most careful to behave myself and treated my special invitation and the sergeants' mess with the dignity and respect that they deserved.

A lot of changes had taken place in the battalion since coming out of the line. Sadly, the CO, Lt. Col. Hughes, had to go home on compassionate grounds. The well-respected 2IC Major Bill Henderson, was appointed administration officer of the battalion, until the new CO arrived. When Lt. Col. A.L. MacDonald, also a Duntroon graduate and veteran of the New Guinea Campaign of WW2, took command, one of his first moves that I certainly applauded, was to replace the Scottish adjutant. Captain Dick Stanley-Harris was given the key appointment which, unfortunately, he did not appreciate as he and the new CO did not see eye to eye.

The men in No. 1 Platoon were extra good. The platoon had a high morale and I made a point of having a few drinks with the fellas once a week, in the company wet canteen, and I always bought them a couple of crates of beer. This was appreciated, and contrary to some military thinking, I gained rather than lost respect by doing so. Unfortunately, the winter hung on. As the roads were designated RED, meaning essential military traffic only, I could not get to the New Zealand pay office. The shortage of ready cash did not matter in the mess, because we all ran mess bills. Where it did matter was in the men's canteen. I missed a Friday night get-together with the platoon, because I could no longer afford to shout the crates. This did not go unnoticed. The following Thursday, I was approached by 'Honest Roy' and 'Square Deal George'. "You didn't make it to the canteen last Friday night, Skipper. Will you be there tomorrow night?"

I tried to give a convincing explanation of why I would not be, without stating the real reason.

"Well", said Roy, stepping forward, "we think that you have not been paid."

With that he shoved some notes into my breast pocket. "See you tomorrow night."

I accepted the gesture graciously. The following night we had our usual enjoyable time in the canteen. Not a word was said about the handout the day before. The next week, the gunners' pay office got around to fixing me up, and I paid Roy and George back. They were the salt of the earth and had become my permanent forward scouts early in the piece, on Hill 355. It was a good arrangement, as they were used to working together and did a mighty job.

Quick witted and real hard cases, they were inseparable. While in Camp Casey, company HQ received a signal asking for any men with sewing experience to be sent to the RQMS's store to modify the cloth bandoleers that our .303 rifle ammunition arrived in. The idea was to unpick them and sew two together, to form a harness with pockets for carrying Owen gun magazines across the chest. They turned out to be very useful, too. When I put the request for help to the platoon, on our morning parade, Roy promptly volunteered the information that he used to be employed making saddles. George professed to some experience as a cutter in a shirt factory. No one else in the platoon volunteered, so the two departed for the regimental Q store, with my naive blessing. By the time they turned up for dinner, I'd had a chance to think. At the men's mess parade, I asked them in front of the rest of the platoon, if they had enjoyed a restful day, lounging around the camp. They grinned hugely and the 'game was up'. We all had a good laugh at my expense. The interesting thing was, that was better for the platoon spirit than if I had done my block. When the battalion went back into the line on Hill 355, Roy lost an eye in a patrol clash.

A Company was still short of a platoon commander. To make matters worse from Jim Norrie's point of view, with Jack Kelly having gone back to Support Company with his A/T Platoon, A Company had only three Duntroon graduates. These were Norrie himself, Colin Brown the 2IC and John Hooper, who was the only graduate platoon commander and was due for promotion. A rifle company's establishment was three platoon commanders. In addition to John and myself, WO2 Jack Morrison, now the CSM, was again being employed as platoon commander of No. 3 Platoon. Well, it is fair to say that there was not a surplus of graduates in the battalion anyway.

It was common knowledge that Charlie Yacoppeti in D Company

was having a little difficulty settling in: minor hiccups, probably through trying too hard. Major Jim saw an opportunity to gain a boy from the 'old school', and at the same time assist Charlie to find his feet. Jim, the most aggressive company commander in the unit, always had the CO's ear. The new colonel was persuaded and the transfer effected. The first cadet of Italian birth to graduate from the Australian Royal Military College, Charlie Yacoppeti was an honest striver and an RC, with all the strength of character that implies. He also had his own way of doing things. If they happened to coincide with the Army's way, well and good. Charlie quickly settled into the friendly atmosphere of A Company's officers' squad tent. He and I got along just fine, in the short time that we worked together. I had been wounded and evacuated before the battalion went back into the line, when he was shot up and taken prisoner. At the time we thought he was dead.

Training in Camp Casey was not totally restricted to weapon training and tactics; one period a week was designated CO's Hour. An appropriately qualified person, usually the MO, lectured each company. His subjects included: first aid, field hygiene, sexual hygiene and the dangers of, and prevention of, VD. Other speakers covered such subjects as treatment of prisoners, and correct behaviour and attitude toward our allies, all useful and important themes.

One morning, the battalion officers moved out en bloc to a large building near the main supply route, for a lecture laid on for all the officers of the British and Commonwealth units and their logistic support units. These specialised units made the ComDiv a self-supporting, heavy weight division. In excess of 100 officers were present.

Various intelligence officers gave us a series of short lectures, covering such topics as: the overall strategic situation, variations noted in Chinese and North Korean tactics, tricks to watch for in no-man's land, and several other useful subjects. They forced their message home with a report that has stuck in my gullet all these years—an execution of ten North Korean prisoners, carried out by personnel of the Republic of Korea's Army.

The ROK soldiers marched their prisoners into a dry paddy field. They then smashed their spines with rifle butts and left them there to die, in their own time. From the audible intake of breath followed by an incredulous hush that came over the audience, I don't think that I was the only one who was wondering if we were on the right side.

This unpleasantness aside, it was a real privilege to attend a lecture in the company of the cream of the British Commonwealth's military forces.

Digger Jacky Peel with Bren gun in a battered communication trench on the forward slopes of Hill 355.

Above: An airstrike on enemy feature 'John' as seen from Hill 355.
Below: A rear bunker overlooking the 'Mad Mile' of road leading into The Hook positions.

Above: WO2 Jack Morrison DCM & Bar enjoying a midday meal with a couple of other A Company men.
Left: A relaxed Kiwi gunner officer.

Above: At Kimpo Airport, November 1952. Three 'Poms' (English) to the left, and three Aussies to the right (changed hats). Max Kieseker is on the right, Vic Dey is next to him.

Below: A road leading into the rear of The Hook positions. The camouflaged 'Mad Mile' starts just around the corner.

Jack Coyle.

Above: Geoff Laurens, Bill Kenneally, Ken Lynch.
Below: 'C' rations.

Pat Jones at Puckapunyal.

Above: New Zealand gunner officers reconnoitring for new gun positions.
Below: Lt. Geoff Smith (killed in action 25 January 1953) and an unidentified sergeant.

Bert Haines and Jack Philpot.

The entrance to a bunker.

A casualty is evacuated.

Above: A casualty is evacuated on the flying fox rigged at the rear of Hill 355.
Right: Max Kieseker (Bodgie).

Above: Back row: Snowy Woodcock, Dick Avery, Ken Goudie, George Foenando.
Front: Lofty Cahill, Tommy Wallace (killed in action), Curley Curtis, John Smith, unknown Scot, Colin 'Peanuts' Kappler.
Right: Dick Avery and Larry Francisco.

Left to right: Bob Cozens, Larry Francisco, Vic Dey, Kevin Griffiths.
Front: Bill Kennelly

A scene on the front line the morning after the ceasefire, 28 July 1953, during dismantling of a bunker, Bluey Broderick facing the camera. The Samichon River is in the background.

Above: The morning after the truce, during the dismantling of the bunkers. Major Jim Norrie with the baseball bat, the author using binoculars.
Below: Two Australian infantrymen meet their Chinese opposite numbers in no-man's land, the morning after the truce.

Above: From left to right: Bruce Matthews, Jack Spiers and Jack Brunton leaving the pagoda at Panmunjom (present day North/South Korean border).
Below: Bruce looking at the North Korean DMZ (demilitarised zone) from check-point 5 in 1988.

– *Fourteen* –

Sojourn at Rear Div

While we were at Camp Casey, battalion sent No.1 Platoon to the Ordinance field park at Rear Div in Gloster Valley for a ten day stint. Our task was to unload winter stores, which were being back loaded from the division's units, and stack them into three big marquees. As we were also responsible for their security, we took our personal weapons and ammunition with us.

Two young English Ordinance Corps officers met us. The two pipper was possibly a regular, but the one pipper was certainly a national serviceman. The snobbish demeanour of the senior one, and his attitude toward the men in my platoon, reminded me of the Duke of Wellington's famous statement about his troops: "I don't know what they do to the enemy, but by God they frighten me." I don't think for a moment that the general meant it, but the Brit lieutenant did. He was obviously in awe, of what he no doubt would have termed colonial troops.

"Do you think you can keep your men under control?" he asked me, looking down his nose with his head cocked up. I ask you? From a Pom lieutenant. Apparently, even in 1953, the reputation of the Australian soldiers was still not all that good with some Brits. Even though in every war that they had been involved in, the Australians had shown themselves to be superior to all other countries' soldiers, except for New Zealand's, with whom they are on a par.

It seemed that I, as an officer, was above suspicion, or was I not suspect because I wore unmistakable brash, white on black New Zealand flashes on my epaulettes as well as the beautifully embroidered Royal Australian Regiment's white on red brassard on my left arm? To be fair to the poor, ignorant but arrogant bloke, he was responsible for the receipt, storage and guarding of winter stores, which had been issued to the Commonwealth Division's units to ensure the survival of the troops during the bitterly cold winter. In today's terms, they would have been worth close to $2 million. But should I have felt both humble and flattered about our employment at Rear Div? I think not. I saw my responsibilities as being the lives, fighting efficiency, deployment, employment, comfort, welfare and physical and mental health of 35 fine young Australian soldiers. In addition to doing the specified job properly, we were there to carry out any assignment asked of us, but this jumped up snob was peering down his nose asking "Can you keep them under control?" I was so annoyed at the insult to my men, that I was having a problem keeping myself under control. I did, and it paid off. The job was really a perk. We provided the labour to unload the trucks, store the gear and guard it. Bernie and I carried out any supervision required, but the section leaders directed their own men.

When I suggested to Bernie that he and I share a tent so that we could function as a command post, he agreed and it proved to be a good arrangement. We had two days' grace before the stores were due to start arriving, so we put the men to work repairing the concertina perimeter wire, and sat down to plan how we were going to tackle the job. Interestingly, we had not been given the responsibility for counting and recording the deliveries. No paper work. Maybe the lieutenant thought we colonials couldn't read or write.

Talking it over and doing some figuring on paper, Bernie and I concluded that we had more men than the job required. We drew up a 12-hour roster, assigning one section to unloading the trucks and stowing the gear away in the big squad tents. Another section was allotted guard duties for the night; the third was in reserve. We gave the reserve section men the whole 12 hours to themselves. So long as they stayed within call, they were free to sleep, sunbathe (the weather was becoming warmer), write letters, and otherwise totally relax—the sorts of things they were usually only able to do on Sunday afternoons when out of the line. The platoon Sigs had it easier still. They were not rostered to work, but were on call to run the odd message if required. A good spell wasn't going to do them any harm.

With some firm talking, I was able to make arrangements for our men to use the wet canteen. Bernie had been invited to become a member of the sergeants' mess and I the officers'. Had there been any trouble, it would have been in the men's canteen. However, an amazing thing happened. In comparison with the under-paid British soldiers, the Australians were flush; in the pay scale, they rated third after the Americans.

The Canadians were first, which did not please the Yanks. Anyway, the Brit canteen was stocked to the roof with crates of beer, which the underpaid national service soldiers could not afford to buy. Well, the diggers decided that they could buy for everyone. It was an ideal solution which, I am pleased to be able to report, they all had sense enough not to spoil.

I found the officers' mess a congenial if slightly stuffy venue in a respectable permanent wooden building with its ante-room overlooking the back garden of a Korean house. Life for the elderly couple living there appeared to be going on regardless.

Bernie was happy and relaxed on this independent assignment, and we had long discussions about his experiences up by the Yalu. He actually got within sight of the mighty river while on a deep penetration patrol. But his memory was scarred with other things that he had seen. The worst of them was the plight of a young North Korean woman who had been so badly treated by the rabble of both warring sides, that she had become fly-blown between her legs and could not put them together enough to walk. How can you grade atrocities?

Bernie had also fought with the battalion at Kapyong. He told me how, when the retreating soldiers of the 6 ROK Division and Korean civilian refugees were running down the road in a state of panic, there were Chinese soldiers running in amongst them. A brave effort and smart, but the Australians quickly picked it, and shot most of them. They also grabbed what South Korean soldiers they could, bundled them into the trenches and handed them rifles, making them stand and fight alongside the Aussies. But he preferred to talk about his dream of buying an orange orchard outside Perth, when he finally went home. Korea was to be his 'swan song' after years of fighting for his country. His mother was waiting in Perth. I listened intently; he deserved a good audience.

He was, however, still a keen soldier. Having more time at Rear Div, he devoured Erich Remarque's *All Quiet on the Western Front*. He was impressed with the Germans' use of sharpened shovels in the trench fighting. They found them easier to handle than a rifle and bayonet in the confines of a trench. He suggested to me that we sharpen our shovels as an addition to our armoury in the event of the enemy getting into our trenches, quite a common occurrence in the Korean War. I agreed.

Files were acquired, and the shovels sharpened enthusiastically. The need for us to use our shovels in a lethal role did not arise, but they would have been handy for the Black Watch and the Duke of Wellington's on The Hook.

Security of the stores was most important, because Rear Div was south of the 'civilian no go line'. A substantial area behind the battle-line, it was out of bounds to the civilian population, for obvious reasons. In the Commonwealth divisional sector, the Imjin River defined it. Rear Div was at Choksong, just down the road from the hills, where the Glosters made their famous last stand. The British tank park was in that area also. It appears that these stores that we were receiving back after the winter had, before being issued to the units in the previous autumn, been guarded by a British platoon similar to mine. One morning, the Brit sergeant, rising early, stepped outside his tent to shave in a better light. To his professional eye, a Korean male with a stack of grey army blankets on his head, running out through a gap that had not been in the perimeter wire the night before, must be doing the wrong thing. As the thief jogged away, the sergeant ducked back into the tent for his .303 rifle and, with one shot, killed the miscreant at 400 metres. Good shooting and sound judgement.

While the platoon upgraded the perimeter wire around the storage tents, the question arose of how to close off the compound's exit. The entrance typically had a counter-weighted pole, so dear to the military mind. Its function was really only as a vehicle check. The exit, however, was a wider gap of 4.5 m. Further away from the main activity, it required something more secure than a pole. It needed to be deliberately opened by a person on foot rather than be able to be ducked under, yet allow the trucks to depart without undue delay. I took a working party with me to sort out the exit and issue the necessary instructions at the same time. Explaining the requirement to the working party, I realised that the answer was so obvious that I simply stated that we would build a Taranaki gate. To my amazement, there was almost a mutiny.

"No, no, Skipper," said the diggers in unison, "what we should do is build a bush gate."

"No," I replied, "I want a Taranaki gate."

They started to plead. They obviously had never seen such a simple device as a Taranaki gate, invented in New Zealand's pioneering days and named after one of its provinces. So, picking up a stick, I started to draw in the dust on the road, thinking that I would soon win their co-operation.

"You lay down timber battens like this," I said, drawing a series of vertical parallel lines. "Then you run five or seven strands of barbed wire across them and staple them, where they cross the battens." I looked up, to see if I was impressing them. I sure was. Their mouths were hanging open with wonderment. So I described how one end of the contraption was then fixed to one post and the rest stretched across the gap, with the batten at the other end being placed in wire loops, top and bottom, on the opposite post. The upper loop was to be above the top wire, to enable it to be lifted clear of the batten, to open the gate at that end. "And that," I emphasised, "is a Taranaki gate."

"No," they all yelled, "that's a bush gate!"

We laughed long and heartily at our contrasting vernacular. Our New Zealand Taranaki/Australian bush gate was a great success, and the wonder of our allies from the Northern Hemisphere.

I wanted to have a look at the wet canteen, to see how my blokes were being treated. I was determined to take the two British subalterns with me. After nearly a week without incident, they had mellowed toward the Australians, but no way would the senior of the two, who was probably my age, be seen inside the men's canteen. However the younger one, against his better judgement, agreed to accompany me. I was determined to go on my own if necessary. We were made very welcome, especially by the Australians, who were obviously pleased that I had brought the Brit officer along. To show off, my boys suggested a cock-fight. The Tommies, forgetting for a while their aversion to officers, joined in enthusiastically and for a few minutes there was bedlam. After they got that out of their system, I bought two 2-dozen crates of beer and they all settled down to some serious drinking. After a bottle of Asahi beer each and a chat with some of the men of both nationalities, we discreetly took our leave. I don't know what it did for British army discipline, but it gave a few people a better understanding of their colonial cousins.

There was another thing in our stay that we thoroughly enjoyed; the meals at Rear Div, perhaps not surprisingly, were superb.

However, our ten-day stint in this backwater, but no less important part of the army, soon passed. We in No. 1 Platoon returned to our unit refreshed and with an even stronger bond between us.

– *Fifteen* –
Honing Skills

After 1 Platoon's sojourn at Rear Div, 3 RAR's platoon and company training got into full swing.

As training intensified, I was very much in my element because of my Instructor's background. This also gave me an affinity with another subaltern, Lt. Ray Burnard. Ray had a flair for planning exercises and training in general. We had a lot of stimulating discussions, which I found most helpful in my efforts to produce the best trained platoon.

This was not because I was trying to win a competition, but because the best trained and led platoon should be the most effective, and hopefully have the best chance of survival in action. Night patrolling was our most demanding task in the line, requiring all the disciplines, from navigation, pre-planned drills and formations, to tactical sense, night vision and fire control—but most important was stealth.

One day, after having done my homework, I announced that each section would be tested in patrolling that night. During the day, I took the section leaders to view the ground, and then briefed them individually. Each had his own objective and code-names for certain topographical features along the route, to report his patrol's progress from. I went to some pains to give the impression that the sections were to be tested successively, then sent the leaders on their way to brief their men. They had been given different start lines, but were not aware of it. Two sections had a platoon signaller attached and the third and numerically strongest one was given an 88 set, but had to find their own operator.

They would be told by radio when it was their turn to start. What I had not told them was that I had allocated a different radio channel to each section nor that they each had the same start time and the same objective. Bernie and I then moved to a feature with a commanding view of the exercise area to ensure clear radio communication. We had sufficient 88 sets to be able to use three frequencies at the same time. I had also brought along the more powerful platoon HQ's 31 set in case our control 88 set played up, not an unusual occurrence with 88s.

It was a very dark night. To be able to use our torches to read the map, without giving the patrols a beacon to assist their sense of direction, Bernie and I sat back from the crest of the hill, which dominated the training area. Having got the section-strong patrols moving, we plotted their movements as the reports came in. By ordering the setting of an ambush by one of the patrols, and then sending them off again after a few minutes, we were able to regulate their progress relative to one another, so that after an hour or so, the three patrols arrived in front of us all at the same time, without having had a clash. As the reports showed them converging, the tension at Control mounted. Suddenly, the three sets burst into life, each with the same message.

"Enemy in front. Am attacking."

Shouts and cheers erupted. There were no blanks in the theatre, for obvious reasons, and live ammunition would have been a bit over the top. So I blew the whistle quickly before they took to each other with rifle butts. A white Very pistol flare showed the patrols frozen stationary, almost at each other's throats. Bernie and I charged down the hill and held a collective debriefing there and then, with top marks awarded to all. Each of the section leaders gained a lot of confidence from this hands-on control. I also believe that the men got a better appreciation of the burden of responsibility that is carried by a patrol leader. Bernie was a great help in setting up and controlling the exercise and, like me, he enjoyed listening to the situation develop.

One morning A Company marched away in anti-aircraft formation, that is, in single file along the sides of the road, with large gaps between sections and platoons.

We headed west toward the Main Supply Route, for about 4 km, then turned north and marched along paddy bunds for about the same distance. Leaving the paddy, we headed west again for another kilometre, over flat dry ground with sparse undergrowth and clumps of young blue gum type trees, not unlike the Australian outback, to a rough, hilly area that was ideal for field training. John Hooper, who was now 2IC of the company, led us, and the major turned up by jeep. We had a very good morning of training exercises run by John. Jim Norrie was good like that. He went out of his way to give his junior officers a chance to develop their skills. After a break for lunch, I was put in charge of running the training.

At about 1400 hrs, the major was informed by radio that the whole battalion had to attend a demonstration at the Royal Fusiliers' area in Camp Casey at 1530 hrs. A ROK team was going to show off the merits of a recoilless gun in attack. Now, Jim Norrie never allowed A Company to get behind the eight ball. He instructed me to get the company back to our lines as fast as possible. No ifs, no buts; we were not to be late. He then took John Hooper with him in the jeep, and I had the whole company, including the other two platoon commanders, under my command.

I gathered the men and their officers around me, and explained the situation.

"For the reputation of A Company, we can't afford to be late," I said. "We have got to make the best possible time. I will lead, and to stop me breaking into a gallop I will carry two Bren guns. OK?" There was general assent, and I took the Brens off the two smallest Bren gunners in the company. Then off we went along the bush track, toward the paddy bunds. I set a cracking pace, as we were all superbly fit. After a few minutes, the track took the turn at its junction with the bund. I had not gone more than 12 paces along the bund, when I heard a voice from behind call out, "Bruce!" I reacted automatically on hearing my name. No one in the battalion, except Jack Spiers and the commanding officer called me Bruce. Not even Jim Norrie. I was always addressed as Kiwi, Matthews or Skipper and we had no other Bruce in the company. Without thinking and without slackening pace, I turned my head and stepped into space. Then dropped feet first into a 44-gallon drum, which had been buried flush with the ground by the Korean farmer as a holding tank for his night soil manure. You could describe it as a super-honey pot. It was about half-full, but the tidal wave of displaced water drenched me in shit from the chest down. Standing thigh deep in the stuff (luckily it was well diluted) I started to laugh. It was really funny. But the diggers couldn't believe it; they thought I was acting. Once they were convinced that I was genuinely amused, they all joined in the laughter.

"OK, who was the son of a gun that called out?" I enquired, without any malice in my tone of voice. Then Roy Stewart—who else?—owned up to calling out my name. When he had assisted me out of the drum, he said that he had spotted it set in the side of the bund, on our way out in the morning. Great stuff for the morale and again it had no negative effect on discipline. The platoon was becoming a family. The rest of the march dried off my uniform, and we made the demo on time. So the major was happy. If he noticed stains on my uniform or an unusual aroma, he never mentioned it.

With an OC of Jim Norrie's personality and experience, company and battalion exercises were no trouble to A Company. For our company test we went north of the 'civilian no go line', so that we could have live firing support, although our own weapons would be empty. All was going fine until No. 1 platoon had to lead the final assault, supported by Vickers medium machine-guns firing live across our front, from our right. Traversing ahead of us at a safe distance, about 6 metres, they were not under my command, but in support. The MMGs were firing steadily, two sections firing their long bursts alternately, so that the supporting fire was continuous.

Having travelled along the top of an approximately 45-metre-high hill, we moved purposely over the crest and could then see the village that we had to clear, in the valley below. I glanced down to make sure of my footing, before calling for the charge. One metre in front of me the earth was being churned up, like fat splattering on a hot plate. I held up my hand and bellowed, "Halt!" I called the signaller forward and asked him what he saw.

"Cripes! Bloody machine-gun bullets."

"Right. Call Sunray and tell him that they are too close."

We all stood fast, so there could be no argument. It didn't come to that; Jim Norrie had the situation under control very quickly. It was no big deal, but it could have been. The thing is, that the same sorts of slip-ups occur in action, due to tiredness or lack of experience, all too frequently ending in tragedy. Once we got going again, we cleared the village in the approved manner. There wasn't much left of the village—only one house was still in a habitable condition. It was a good size house and had obviously been evacuated in a hurry, as it appeared that most of the peoples' belongings were still in place. A child's doll lying on the floor spoke volumes, figuratively speaking. It was difficult to maintain a dry eye.

Our next challenge was the battalion exercise, on ground just south of Gloster Crossing. That is the ford that enabled the Chinese army to pour across the Imjin River to attack the Gloster's position earlier in the war. Later a wooden bridge named Teal was built upstream of the ford and then after it had been swept away by seasonal flooding, a concrete one replaced it. On our approach march, in single file along the side of the road to the assembly area, A Company came under a real attack, from smiling aggressive Kiwi truckies of 10 NZ Transport Company. The driver's mate on each truck had a ready supply of fire extinguishers filled with water. These were squirted at the marching Australian infantrymen, as a tangible sign of the friendly rivalry that existed between the troops of the two ANZAC countries. My New Zealand flashes did not save me from coming under fire. However, the Australians didn't cower in a ditch. We resourcefully grabbed any lumps of dirt that we could lay our hands on, and of course the water they had squirted had wet it, so it stuck. When the trucks finally passed by, they were all badly in need of a wash. So honour was saved.

The 36-hour battalion exercise, umpired by the officers of the 1st Battalion, the Black Watch from 29 Brigade, went like a charm. Our deployment drills were smooth and when we officers passed the assembly area on our way forward from the orders group to do our recces, I was heartened to observe Bernie chatting to the men, and putting them in the picture. The tactics for the attack phase were based on the British training pamphlet "The Infantry Battalion in Battle 1952", adapted to suit the situation in Korea. The Commonwealth forces had learnt about dealing with mass infantry, the hard way. The Black Watch umpires were up with the play, and very good fellows they were. Easy to get along with, they have for a long time been one of Britain's ready-reaction battalions, and have a history of being involved in dealing with trouble spots. In fact, they are probably the best known of Britain's fire-brigade battalions.

In my opposite number in the famous old regiment, I found a new friend. 2nd Lt. Alex Rattray M.C. was a very fine young man and we hit it off from the start. Our friendship was strengthened when 3 RAR umpired them, and I umpired Alex's platoon. He was a most personable fellow who handled his men well, tough little battlers that they were. One found it hard to believe that the junior officers and NCOs had only been in the army 12 months when sent to Korea, and that they were conscripted national servicemen like their troops.

When the Chinese tried to overrun the Black Watch and capture The Hook feature from the COMDIV the first time, in November 1952, Alex earned his M.C. for the key role he and his platoon played in stopping them. The Watch also repulsed the next attack against The Hook in May 1953, but it cost many Scottish lives and Alex's was one of them. We had been friends for only one month. At the time, I knew nothing of his decoration of the Military Cross for his gallantry in the previous attack on The Hook. I read about it in his regiment's battle log, years later.

The briefing of the umpires took place on Castle Hill. Marked on the map as a castle site, spot height 148 m, it is well-known for its part in the Gloster Regiment's last stand. Perhaps not so well known is the fact that Castle Hill was not just any old hill in Korea. It owes its name to Kublai Khan, who conquered Korea in the 13th century. Because of its strategic position on the main route south, he turned the hill into a fortress from which his cavalry could attack any bandits who attempted to plunder his camel trains, and could themselves plunder any that were not his. The Korean peninsula under his tutelage became a link in his trading with Japan. His Mongol troops dug into the sides of Hill 148, forming a spiral road to the top. The precipitous inner face was then faced with smooth rock, dressed and laid with very tight joints, to form an unclimbable surface. A few resolute men could then defend the road, keeping the top inviolate, as no one could scale the sides. When a caravan passed, the Mongols quickly intercepted it by charging their horses down the spiral road. Castle Hill, and others also marked on the map as castle sites, no doubt played a big role in keeping the country under Kublai Khan's subjection. Historic ground indeed!—and still playing a similar role seven centuries later.

While we were in reserve, the opportunity was taken to hold a brigade parade and march past for Brigadier Tom L. Daly. The well-respected Australian commander of 28th Brigade had a knightly aura about him. He was a man who could lead troops without bias or bluster. The four battalions on parade, two British and two Australian, were an impressive sight. The Royal Fusiliers especially, put on an impeccable display of marching. However, there were a few light moments at the rehearsal a day or two before.

The drill for a ceremonial 'march past' by heavy infantry was with their rifles carried at the slope. That is, the butt of the rifle was held in the left hand with the forearm parallel with the ground and the stock rested on the left shoulder at an angle of about 60 degrees to the forearm. To salute the inspecting senior officer reviewing the parade, as the battalion marched past, the battalion's commanding officer gave the order, "In succession, eyes right." Each company commander, as his company approached the saluting base where the dignitary stood, would order "…. Company. Eyes right!" The officers would turn their heads and eyes to the right and salute. The rest of the company would not salute, but would respond to the eyes right, with the exception of the right marker of each platoon, who would continue looking straight ahead to ensure that the platoon kept marching in a straight line. But the light infantry had an entirely different style of marching past.

British light infantry regiments such as the Durhams traditionally march at 140 paces to the minute, instead of the 120 paces required of heavy infantry. The Durhams also march with their rifles at the trail. However, for a 'march past' they double at 170 paces to the minute, with their rifles at the short trail, and their left arms held at their sides. They are a sight to behold, particularly the officers, when the order 'Eyes right' is given. Doubling with their left arms not swinging and with their right hands at the salute caused their bodies to incline forward at such an angle that they looked about to fall over. The Australians had just got over that when the next Durham company commander gave the order, "Eyes right!" He was wearing a denture and as he beefed out the 'right', it shot out of his mouth, not for the first time, I would wager. For, as quick as a flash, his right hand diverted from its trip to his forelock, reached out in front of him and gathered in his wayward teeth, which were then expertly popped back in, on the way back to the salute. Almost the same arm movement as saluting with a sword in a march pass. There were several muffled hoots in our ranks.

A week or so later, in the company of our two sister battalions, we paraded before Brigadier Daly again—an historic occasion. 2 Battalion, Royal Australian Regiment, had arrived from Australia to relieve 1 Battalion; this was the formal hand over ceremony. The Brigadier bade farewell to 1 RAR and welcomed 2 RAR, correctly prophesying that they would do their duty as well as 1 RAR had. Then he finished off by addressing 3 RAR, calling the battalion 'Old Faithful', that was sent in first and was still there doing its job. This remark struck a chord in the hearts of the 3 Battalion men. It was seized upon, eventually becoming part of the unit history and 'Old Faithful' becoming our official nickname.

3 Battalion had been rested and reinforced, so was refreshed and up to strength when we moved from Camp Casey to Area 6 as brigade reserve. This was rather a good set up with companies camped in their own re-entrants, tucked in under the southern side of the Wyoming Line. But it was a shock to the system when we arrived. The previous tenant had been a Thai battalion. In A Company, we were appalled at their lack of field hygiene. Sheer filth. Everyone set to work clearing the paths of human waste. I dropped a phosphorus grenade down the platoon toilet, had it filled in and another one dug.

We had not been there long when the Chinese overran the Americans on Anti-tank Ridge, at the western end of Hill 355. For the second time since we left the front line, B Company was sent up to cover for the American counter-attacking company. Unfortunately, in the dark without its lights on, one of the trucks left the road, and a digger was killed.

When the division went into the line again, 29th Brigade went back to the left flank of the Div sector, putting the Black Watch on The Hook. 28th Brigade took over the other flank, with the Royal Fusiliers on Hill 159 and the Durham Light Infantry on Hill 355. The two Australian battalions remained out of the line as brigade reserve. Things had become a bit hectic up front, as control of no-man's land had been lost in the COMDIV's absence. There were patrol clashes every night in front of Hill 355 and Hill 159, while another attack against The Hook looked imminent.

We had not been long settled in Area 6, when it was decided that as things had hotted up and as the Australians had a lot of platoon commanders fresh from Australia, the junior officers would be sent up to the two Brit battalions for familiarisation with the front line situation. Specifically, of course, no-man's land.

2 RAR sent personnel to the Royal Fusiliers and 3 RARs to the Durhams: two batches from each battalion. Why Alec Weaver and I were sent in the first batch, when we were both experienced patrollers, was at the time beyond me. However, age has granted me some wisdom, and I now believe that it was so the experienced patrollers could assess the change in the situation in the valley. It was however, a privilege to serve with the Durham Light Infantry for seven days.

– *Sixteen* –

The 1st Battalion, the Durham Light Infantry

For some unaccountable reason, I arrived at the DLI battalion headquarters alone, and presumably first. Why, I still do not know. Our other companies must have acted independently, or perhaps A Company did. After a very warm welcome by Colonel Jeffries, the Durham's commanding officer, he took me to their officers' mess where he ordered a large glass of scotch each. The colonel had a short chat, finished his drink then went back to work, while a hearty meal was laid on for me about two hours before their evening meal was due. Then a DLI jeep took me up the Bowling Alley to Hill 355.

On such a full stomach, I had no hope of lugging my pack, Owen gun and loaded magazines up the long, steep communication trench and keep pace with the young Geordie light infantry rifleman who had been detailed to be my guide. He was only carrying a rifle and was used to marching at 140 paces to the minute, compared with the 120 that we of the heavy infantry marched at. But I knew this trench well anyway, as B Company of the DLI was holding the same left forward position that our A Company had occupied. So I just plodded on, and he disappeared around a bend in the trench.

When I reached the company position, I could not believe my eyes. The forward trench had, every 30 metres or so, sprouted sandbagged pillboxes. Great cube shaped mounds, 3 to 4 metres wide and projecting about 1 to 2 metres above the natural ground contours. These had housed the American 9th Infantry Regiment's machine-guns. Some of these edifices were already looking unstable and the DLI had no intention of using them, except perhaps as decoys to draw fire, to help them locate the well camouflaged and deeply dug Chinese bunkers.

B Company's commander welcomed me, introducing me to his HQ staff and Second Lieutenant Pat Woodbridge, the commander of No. 5

Platoon that I was to live and operate with for the next week. I had complete run of the company area, with no responsibility. I was free to sit in on the company orders groups. Indeed, I was encouraged to do so. I could pick and choose which patrols I went on, from the whole company programme, not just those allotted to Pat's platoon. A fairer deal could not have been imagined. In the event, I managed two patrols per night, although some were only standing patrols. That did not matter to me, because it is good experience in itself and also gave me a chance to analyse the function of a standing patrol. For the men involved in guarding an entrance into a company position, it is a boring non-event most of the time. Further, if an attack is mounted against the position, it can be a death trap, but their warning shots will alert the company. A platoon commander never has time to sit out half the night, manning a fixed position in the company defences. That is not his function, but the men all had to take their turn. So I learnt firsthand what a boring job the men had to put up with.

Volunteering for whatever was going, I had a feast of night patrols. None were very ambitious, neither were there any clashes until the end of the week. To start with, the fighting patrols that I went on with Pat or his sergeant, were one and nine strong—or weak? They were easy to control and operated with one scout and in single file formation. We investigated the 'Mungandi Diggings' and, generally speaking, concentrated on the immediate environs of Hill 355, not straying too far afield. For the first four days, there was no reaction to B Company's conservative efforts.

Late one moonlight night, I did a second patrol after midnight. I went with Pat's sergeant to recce the narrow valley between Hill 355 and Pt. 227. It was the type of patrol that the Americans should have mounted on a regular basis to gain warning of any threat to the anti-tank position. I found it interesting, not having been along the bottom of that little valley before, with 355 towering over it on the one side and 227 being right alongside on the other. Half-way through the valley, I spotted a Chinaman lying in a rocky area between 355 and us. I told the sergeant to cover me while I took a closer look. Fine. I closed in slowly, my Owen at the ready. Eventually identifying a very Chinese looking rock, which the moon had highlighted, I turned to go back and found that the sergeant had followed me. He was only about 10 paces behind, and covering me a bit closer than I had expected. By 'cover me', I had meant 'be ready to give me covering fire if I get into trouble'. But I suppose he felt responsible for me and, after all, I had given an ambiguous order. Then I spotted the trip-wire of an anti-personnel mine. This was for real. There had been no sign of any minefield wire fences, with the red triangles on them. Presumably, rust and shelling had taken their toll. But the trip-wire was still anchored to the mine. It was an American jumping jack. Looking around, I saw more primed American mines and trip wires and indicated their presence to the sergeant. We withdrew with some caution, being very careful where we placed our feet, as the tripwires overlapped one another. On the way out I picked up a silk parachute from what had been an illuminating flare. It is just under a metre across and has since been donated to the NZ Army Museum in Waiouru, along with some other souvenirs I brought back from the war.

So it went on. Every night. Out in no-man's land sitting in an ambush position listening to the seductive female Chinese voice with an American accent, broadcasting through those powerful loudspeakers positioned on top of the Apostles, telling the British soldiers what the depot RSM was doing with their wives back home, while they were here fighting an imperialist war for the Wall Street gangsters. Apparently her scriptwriter didn't know that the national servicemen she was addressing had been conscripted at the age of 18. In Korea at the age of 19 they were paid a mere pittance so were most unlikely to be married.

I had been operating with B Company for about five days when, at the daily O Group we learned that BHQ had ordered a special fighting unit of a sergeant and nine men. The sergeant was a tough old regular and they were to be out for eight hours. Battalion had briefed them, so it must have been either an important mission or a very risky one, possibly both. Surprisingly I was ordered to take two men, armed with a Bren and a Sten respectively, and establish a standing patrol on Somerset. That was the outpost beyond the end of Surrey Hills, which we in 3 Bn called Alice Springs, but the DLI had not been manning it every night like we had. My orders were to stay out until the sergeant's patrol came in through us at 0200 hrs. No problem in April, with the weather getting warmer. Unfortunately, that night a late seasonal blizzard swept in, bringing a cold snap. The temperature plummeted well below freezing point, causing a fall of heavy snow. It was dark when we left the company position, going out through Surrey Hills at 1800 hrs. I had no idea where the sergeant's patrol enterered no-man's land, nor what his task was.

But I was annoyed with the Americans when I saw the condition of the Alice Springs outpost. The three fighting pits which the Australians had dug were now half full of rusting C ration cans. It was an adverse commentary on how alert the American patrols must have been, sitting there munching C rations. Because of the noisy rattling of several empty cans if we as much as touched one, we had no option but to stay in the crawl trench connecting the fighting pits. Positioning the Bren gunner on the western side of the knoll and the Sten gunner on the eastern, I spent 15-20 minutes with each one alternately, throughout our stay. The hours dragged on. The cold got colder.

It was approaching midnight and still snowing. I was with the Bren gunner on the west side of the knoll when I heard a faint shuffling sound. The noise increased steadily, but very slowly. Somebody was approaching, but it was two hours before the Durham's patrol was due. I told the Bren gunner not to take any action of his own, that I would only be a few seconds getting his mate. All was quiet on the other side of the knoll. So I brought the Sten gunner around to give a hand. The noise was now loud enough to tell me that there was a party approaching from the the direction of the rear of the Apostles feature. The question was, who? It was too early for the DLI patrol to be returning, but it could be. Equally the Chinese had been playing hell during the last two months, so it could just as easily be an enemy party. The British battalions had a very basic weapon scale compared with ours. They were also light on radios and field telephones. Only fighting patrols were equipped with 88 sets. Standing patrols? Not even a field telephone, although permanent outpost positions like Alice Springs had line laid to them. That meant that if it was the patrol that we were awaiting, we could not be warned that they were coming in sooner than expected.

I instructed my two men to be ready to fire, but on no account to do so until I did, as we could not afford to make a mistake. We waited. A blurry line of figures gradually materialised through the falling snowflakes. I thought, this is it, the chips are down, safety sleeve off, Owen up to the shoulder. What will be the roll of the dice? So far, there was no indication that the approaching party knew that they were coming up to an outpost. So they must be enemy. If they were the Geordie patrol, we should by now be hearing "The Bladon Races". The Durhams had a system, which I subsequently adopted, of whistling their regimental march when approaching their own positions in the dark. This was a great idea and worked especially well with "The Bladon Races", a most distinctive tune. But there was no signature tune to be heard right now.

I was immensely impressed with the steadiness of my two offsiders. The unidentified party was now close enough to look like shadows through the snow; their images blurred by snowflakes, flickered like an old fashioned black and white movie. Neither their gait nor smudgy outlines gave anything away. I could not delay challenging much longer, without risking being overrun. Then light from some gun flashes enabled me to see that their weapons were slung. I breathed out and challenged. The exhausted sergeant, who was leading his weary men to safety while they could still walk, grunted out the countersign. Distressed by the freezing cold, they were completely done in. They must also been very hungry. The DLI, having established their cook-houses within the company positions on the feature, favoured giving their patrols the main meal of the day when they returned, instead of before going out. That may be fine for short duration patrols; in theory the men are supposed to stay more alert. Even that is debatable. But this patrol was of too long a duration in low temperatures for them to have been sent out without a meal. I neither questioned the sergeant nor reported that he had come in two hours early. I just lived with the fact that I had come very close to pulling the trigger on ten of our own men.

In view of the activity reported before sending Australian personnel to the DLI, it had been a quiet week. The next day, though, Charlie Chinaman was upset about something. He shelled and mortared B Company's position all morning. Having been out late and also having had a late dinner, I skipped breakfast. Sleeping on the top bunk of a tier of three, in the hutchie I shared just below the crest on the reverse slope, I woke up to the sound and vibration of exploding shells. One of the Geordies came back to get his steel helmet. They loved their woollen caps comforters and normally wore them on the position, instead of steel helmets. He told me that there was no sign of enemy infantry activity.

I checked my Owen gun and spare magazines and took a walk around B Company's position to assess the severity of the shelling, which was quite heavy. Then I went back to bed—I needed my sleep. My job was in no-man's land, not being a target for field and medium artillery. I knew that should an attack develop I would be alerted in time to play a part. I also knew that if a medium shell landed on the roof of the dug-out, the bursting course would not stop it. Bursting courses of rock were built into the roofs to explode the contact fuse of field artillery shells before they could penetrate, but medium artillery is in a different league. As it turned out, the rate of fire was about 25 rounds per minute. 1500 rounds per hour was considered quite a heavy bombardment onto a single company position.

The barrage was severe enough to upset the rats. As I was in a top bunk, I awoke again when a particularly close shell shook the bunker like an earthquake, and dirt from the shaking roof rained down on me. The rats even came out of their nests, and they did not look happy. They were obviously shell-shocked. When I moved, they scuttled back behind the steel mesh that held back the dirt, between the timber frame of the bunker and the sides of the hole that it was buried in. Worst off, and most dazed and wild-eyed, were those who lived on top of the timbers that held up the roof. They were in a far less stable area and closer to the explosions. After coming out of their holes, they were trying to keep a footing on the 8 mm steel rods of the 150 mm square mesh that lay across the timber beams holding up the clay roof. They looked mad, snarling and baring their teeth only 600 mm above me, and I was in grave danger of them dropping on me.

However, I went off to sleep again and when after four hours the shelling stopped, there was not much physical damage of importance to show for it. As the men had been kept under cover in the bunkers and fighting pits, there were, as far as I know, no casualties. But the bombardment achieved two positive things: it made the Geordies more bloody-minded, and the stupid and vulnerable towers that the US 2nd Division had built above the perimeter trench were gone. Those sandbag monstrosities that had made the position look like a medieval castle proved no match for modern gunfire. The Geordies, being the hard toilers that they are, had in fact already cleaned out and brought back into service, most of the real fighting bunkers and built several new ones, long before this barrage.

The weather improved again, and my last day with the Durhams arrived. It was the 24th of April 1953, the day before ANZAC Day. I learned many years later that, on that day, Major Henderson, 3 RAR's highly respected Battalion 2IC, sent a bottle of Scotch to the Australian subalterns on Hill 355. But I never saw any of it. The reason is as follows.

At the DLI's B Company O Group, we were told that C Company was to send a fighting patrol of one and 15 out through B Company to Summerset, the Durhams' nickname for Cloncurry. As B Company had nothing interesting going on that night, I asked to join the fighting patrol and was granted permission. The patrol was not as well briefed or prepared as the ones that I had accompanied with B Company. C Company Commander's orders were very short but, I suppose, to the point: 'set an ambush on Summerset.' When the Patrol Commander, 2nd Lt. Hall, a 21-year-old national serviceman, invited me to accompany him while he organised it, I found that he had to go to the artillery OPO and ask for DFs for the patrol. As the Brit artillery had not pre-registered patrol DFs, there were no overlays available to the company. In fact, I couldn't make out why we were being supported by the British 45th Field Artillery Regt. anyway, instead of the NZ 16th Field. The DLI were, after all, a part of 28th Brigade.

By 3 RAR standards we were late leaving the company position. The patrol did not assemble until it was dark, and then the young officer decided to brief the men while we all huddled together in a forward trench. The briefing covered little more than the objective and the formation to be used. The diamond formation was straight out of the Infantry Training Manual 1952. I started to have doubts. Theoretically sound for giving all-round protection, and possibly suitable for the meadows of northern Europe, it was not a good formation for the broken and hilly terrain of Korea. In the paddy fields, it was a ludicrous formation to use, because it was not compatible with moving over bunds. Even worse, the patrol commander did not employ scouts. Instead, he moved half of the patrol forward 30 or so metres and then waved up the rear half. Splitting a complex formation like that made it too cumbersome to control. That in turn reduced the rate of progress to a snail's pace. As we had already been too late leaving our lines, I was becoming concerned. This stupid manoeuvre was repeated again and again. I couldn't believe it. But I would not remonstrate with the patrol commander in front of his men. Anyway, I was only an armed observer. For all practical purposes I was just an extra submachine-gunner. I had no authority in another officer's patrol, although I would have taken command had he become a casualty. This was different from the 'Alice Springs' standing patrol, when B Company's Commander had nominated me the leader.

As the point of the patrol paused at the foot of Cloncurry, to allow the rear half with the command element to close up, I noted that the time was just after 2100 hrs. We were at least two hours too late. Hall then took the lead and the whole patrol moved up the little hill. I was still in the right rear as we quietly approached the top. The crest was clear as Hall stepped over it, and the men surged forward. It is a natural thing to do, to keep the leader in sight, and momentum tends to develop as an objective is closed on.

'Brerrr__et!' there was a long burst of burp gun fire and Hall came flying back over the crest, landing a few paces in front of me, as I too had closed up. As he rushed past me, he shouted, "They're here first! We'll have to pull back!"

The Chinese had been just over the crest, and he had almost walked over them. As it took them a little while to bring all their firepower into action, it is probable that they had been watching in a different direction and did not hear our stealthy approach. They appeared to have been as surprised as Hall was. Although amazed that we were not going to carry out the drill, which was to rush the ambush, I still knew my place in the scheme of things. He was in command. I could not argue with him in front of his men. Also, we had already lost the initiative. I answered, "I will cover you." I did not hear his reply, as he moved off to organise a withdrawal because the Chinese were firing now and so was I. Afterwards, I could not remember shifting the safety slide on my Owen gun. But it was probably when we started to move up the hill.

Pausing after a couple of bursts, I noted that two men had not followed him back down the slope. The three of us stood our ground. About 40 paces to my left, the one with the Bren was firing controlled bursts from the hip. The other Geordie was firing away with his Sten gun, about the same distance out to my right. With the noise from the small arms fire, both these game young men were too far away to co-ordinate by voice. We did not speak the same dialect of the English language anyway. But they seemed happy enough to stay with someone who was prepared to stand and fight. The Chinese small arms fire had started like a platoon firepower demonstration, with all their weapons blazing away. However, as they had concentrated on the retreating patrol, that went over our heads. My own shooting settled down after my reactionary burst, and I started to pick targets, now silhouetted on the crest of the hill. Firing double taps with an occasional three or four round burst, I shot down a few. Standing on the skyline disadvantaged the Chinese. Although they held the high ground, they would have done better firing from the prone position. But they didn't. There did not seem to be too much to worry about. We three, keeping up a controlled and accurate fire, were definitely out-shooting the Chinese.

But once the rest of the Brit patrol was out of range, the Chinese took more interest in us. However, as we were so dispersed, they had to spread their firepower and most of it was still too high. After I had shot a few more burp gunners and my two mates had between them almost certainly accounted for even more, the Chinese fire eased noticeably. Our Bren was the only light machine-gun in the action and I am confident that it, coupled with the fact that they were sky-lined and we weren't, were the factors that kept the Chinese in check.

Then the enemy changed their tactics. The burp gunners were pulled back from the crest and were replaced with grenadiers—similar to what happened to Jack Morrison. Their throwing was a bit haphazard for a start, before they started to synchronise it. The exploding grenades increased the amount of light on the little battleground, so our fire became even more effective, but the grenades kept coming. Then the Chinese started throwing their grenades together, also like they did in Morrison's fighting retreat. For the record, it is a quite devastating technique. Most exploded in the air with a bright light, but it was the concussion that came with the sharp crack of the explosions that worried me. I thought, 'if another one explodes close to my head I will pass out'. It didn't occur to me at the time, but I realised later that they were stun grenades. The blast on my ears was unbearable. Shrapnel-wise, they were not as deadly as the British 36 grenade or the more orthodox Chinese fragmentation grenade, but they were becoming a bit of a worry.

In the heat of the battle, I did not feel anything hit me. When my Owen gun felt slippery I thought: 'I'm sweating. It's hot work all right, but interesting.' Then I realised that I was in danger of dropping the gun. The slipperiness was caused by blood running down my arms, from what turned out to be a bullet in my right forearm and grenade shrapnel in my left upper arm. Passing the sling over my shoulder so that I couldn't drop my Owen, I continued firing. The muzzle flashes from the burp guns, and the light shining back onto the grenadiers from their own grenades, made them easy targets. Mind you, it must have worked both ways. Remarkably, it did not affect my night vision. My two mates and I continued to take our toll of the Chinese grenadiers. Although it was only a short time in the scheme of things—our private fire-fight with the enemy patrols was probably no more than ten minutes—it seemed to be going on interminably.

Second Lt. Hall eventually reorganised the rest of the patrol and friendly fire opened up from about 200 metres behind us. That was too far away for their Sten submachine-guns to be effective and we had their only Bren, but it was our signal to break off the action. My remaining two mates, or 'muckers' as the Geordies would say, looked at me. I acknowledged and started to walk backwards, still firing short bursts. They followed my example, although we were close to running out of ammunition. But I still had five primed 36 grenades in the water bottle pouch, which I carried on the web belt on my waist. I had of course been unable to throw them uphill.

When we three started to retreat, the Chinese made no move to come down the hill after us. But I was concerned that if we turned our backs, they would. Had their burp gunners instead of their grenadiers been still on the crest, it might have been a different story. Out of range eventually, we turned around and continued back another 100 or so metres, to meet up with the rest of our patrol. I was so hyped up that I did not realise the extent of my wounds. I reported to Hall and suggested asking for artillery fire onto the feature. Not only would that cause casualties among the enemy, we might even be able to assault after the barrage, take the ground and possibly pick up a wounded prisoner. He thought it a good idea and got on the radio. However, he got little sense out of his artillery. Eventually, having ascertained that we had three walking wounded, besides me (although I don't think that he had realised that I was wounded), he asked for a stretcher party and headed for home.

After the excitement, Lt. Hall was not sure of the way home. Aware that I knew the ground from patrolling it earlier in the year, he asked me to lead the patrol back. I managed this, although I was by now having difficulty walking. When we arrived at the bottom of Mildura Spur, the company had three stretcher parties waiting. Very good of them, but four would have been better. This was when I made my second mistake. I was so concerned, as a good officer should be, for the welfare of the men who stayed and fought with me, that I insisted that the other three wounded be carried. Unfortunately, I did not tell Hall that I, too, had received a hammering from the Chinese, and he did not ask. So nobody realised that I also needed help. Labouring up 300 metres of Mildura's steep slope on my own, I pumped away more blood that I could spare, thereby hindering my recovery.

Having fallen well behind, I entered the communication trench on my own, through the gap at the top of Mildura Ridge. I was rolling like a drunk due to loss of blood and a knee that was jammed stiff, with what turned out to be a large piece of grenade lodged between the knee and the ligaments. I collided with a Korean, who was working with the British engineers repairing the trench. I would have fallen, had I not been able to grab the parapet of the trench. To my everlasting shame, I told him where to go. He probably knew little English, but the hostility in my voice was obvious. I still deeply regret the outburst, the more so because I have a very high regard for the Korean people.

Once inside B Company's command post, I was in the hands of a team of professional soldiers, overseen by their company commander of WW2 experience. They wanted answers to be able to deal with the future. Not wanting to criticise the young national service platoon commander, I didn't have much to say, other than that I estimated that we had clashed with a 40-strong Chinese patrol, but that it wasn't an ambush in the true sense of the word. Their automatic firepower was superior to a full British platoon's and they also had grenadiers. The quality of the leadership of our so-called fighting patrol was not brought up and I did not make an issue of it. By this time I was too far gone to express any criticism of the handling of the action, let alone go into detail. In fact, I eventually passed out. The company headquarters team, under the direction of WO 2 R.W. Hawksworth, revived me somewhat, with the best hot cocoa that I have ever tasted. With a sharp knife they sliced my armoured vest down from each armhole and lifted it away, thereby relieving me of considerable weight. I was interested in what the vest had stopped, but was too tired to ask. Conscious of my shirt being cut off and shell dressings being applied, which stanched the flow of blood from most of the six different grenade and gunshot wounds, I must have passed out again. My next recollection is of being on a stretcher in a covered trench that I knew so well adjoining B Company's command post on Hill 355.

There was the hot exchange of artillery fire that usually followed a patrol clash. So the casualties were kept under cover in this trench, at the top of the evacuation route, until the barrage eased. Then strapped on a stretcher carried by four men, I was on my way, straight down the steep rear slope of Hill 355, to the ambulance jeep waiting at the jeep head. It was harder going for the stretcher party than the communication trench would have been, but faster for my survival. We arrived at the bottom with the minimum of discomfort for me, but what must have been the maximum for them. I am still very grateful.

The end of my involvement with the men of this famous British battalion was in their best tradition. B Company's Sergeant-Major Hawksworth sent all my gear back to 3 RAR: personal kit, pistol, Owen gun and bayonet. Damned decent of them, when you consider that the Owen used the same 9 mm parabellum ammunition as the Sten. A less honest unit could have acquired a superior submachine-gun by merely reporting that I had not brought it back.

When I returned to 3 RAR after hospitalisation, there was a letter waiting from Warrant Officer Hawksworth, that truly professional CSM of B Company, the 1st Battalion the DLI. It expressed his personal regret that I had been wounded. He also said that I would be welcome in B Company any time.

– *Seventeen* –

Evacuation

I lost consciousness again in the stretcher jeep. These were reconditioned WW2 American Willys Jeeps adapted to carry two stretchers. Being low to the ground, with a four-wheel drive giving them a good cross-country performance, they were most suitable for the short runs back from the forward positions to the Regimental Aid Post.

I came-to in the Indian field dressing station, hearing Major Norrie's concerned voice enquiring how I felt, then his welcome face appeared through a haze. Re-surfacing next on the operating table of the 8055 Norwegian Mobile Advanced Surgical Hospital, I just had time to comment on their beautiful Nordic blond hair and blue eyes, to the two sisters leaning over me, when in went the needle. Of the comparatively small number of women serving in Korea, the nursing sisters working in the MASHes across the country were without doubt the closest to the front line. I have no idea what repair work the Norwegians did but it must have been good.

I awoke in a tented ward. That was quite an experience in itself. I felt quite with it, though more than a little disconcerted to find my arms strapped across my chest. We were on stretcher beds, with gaps of about one and a half metres between them and approximately 20 down each side of a long tent. There was a mixture of nationalities, but no other Commonwealth personnel. Surprisingly, I felt lonely among all these foreigners. Then a commotion erupted three beds to my left. A Turk, realising that the very sick man next to him was a Chinaman, struggled out of his own bed to finish him off with his bare hands. Luckily, the orderlies got the situation under control smartly. Soon after that, a bloke opposite me, who perhaps had just come to, started to scream.

"I'm blind. Oh God. I'm blind. Help me somebody. Help me. I'm blind." He was an American, and he ran through his lines again and again, until his compatriots, who made up the bulk of the casualties in the tent, got stuck in.

"Shut up, you son of a bitch. You're not the only one with troubles."

He didn't get the message.

"Cut the crap, Mac! Or I'll deal with you myself," stated a strong looking character in the bed next to him, with convincing earnestness. The first two speakers having shown a lead, the whole tent full joined in until there was absolute bedlam. Eventually, an orderly sedated him and the ward quietened down again. It was all a little bit hard to follow while lying on my back, trussed up like a fowl prepared for the oven. With both arms strapped across my chest, I could quite easily have been in a strait-jacket in a mental asylum. There were more blank spaces. When I woke up in Brit Com General Zee Hospital in Seoul, I felt that I was home. Staffed by Australian nurses, sisters and doctors, it was a fully appointed hospital in a permanent building. A cheerful nurse cleaned me up with a much needed shave.

They X-rayed me at Seoul, to assess whether I could be patched up there, or should be sent to Japan. Japan won. A convoy of army ambulances, the big square ones that could carry four stretcher cases, took a group of us to Kimpo airbase. We flew out on a DC 3. The stretchers were hung on brackets, three or four tiers of them down each side, for the usable length of the fuselage. Ambulances waiting at Iwakuni Airbase in Japan took us to a hospital train, which ran alongside the Inland Sea to Kure. All in a bit of a haze, as vision was limited and it was so easy to doze. However, I still remember the snobbish rudeness to the Commonwealth soldiers, of an obviously much sought after American nursing aide in her glamorous, tailor-made, greenie khaki uniform. If it was not her war, it certainly was her opportunity. But, as she obviously disliked foreigners, I didn't try to talk to her.

Brit Com General Hospital Kure was a large two storied building, purpose designed and built by the Japanese, presumably prior to or during WW2. I don't know what our medical people thought of it but it seemed to me to have all the facilities that a first class hospital should have, such as well appointed operating theatres and spacious wards with high ceilings. It was set in beautiful grounds, with well-kept gardens and lawns, not jammed in between industrial buildings, as it might well have been in crowded Japan. When army ambulances delivered us from the railway station, our stretchers were laid out in two long rows on the lawn alongside the driveway. I estimated, from my lowly position on a stretcher on the ground, at least 30 men to a row. The majority were from the 1st Battalion, the Black Watch. It was only then that I heard of the third battle of The Hook. Unfortunately, there were a number of that famous regiment who did not survive the battle.

The matron of the hospital was an Australian. Walking behind the stretchers, reading the attached cardboard labels with our details on them, she spotted the name of my unit and stopped behind me.

"Hello, Lieutenant. 3 RAR, eh? Which state are you from?"

"Well Mam," I replied politely, "actually, I am a New Zealander."

"Huh!" She grunted and stalked off, avoiding the next two stretchers altogether. I couldn't believe it. I guessed that a Kiwi must have turned her down, somewhere along the way. But after all these years, I am not so harsh in my judgement. She ran a good hospital and may well have been sick and tired of the few ill-disciplined New Zealanders she'd had through her wards. There were quite a lot of Kiwis, who had been living in Australia and had enlisted in the Australian infantry, some of them quite wild. I hope that my friends in 16th Field Regiment and 10th Transport Company will forgive me mentioning it, but some of them were not too well behaved away from the front either. However, my welcome in the officers' ward was much warmer. That's right. Segregation.

The biggest boost to my morale was the arrival of a letter from the boys of No.1 Platoon. It had originally been addressed to the NORMASH, dated 26/4/53, two days after the action. Honest Roy Stewart wrote in a better hand than mine, thus proving that there was a lot more to that young man than his clowning. Some of his mates in the platoon added their comments. Bodgie Kieseker apparently wrote his in the canteen of the Royal Fusiliers. Honest Roy finished it off, with Square Deal George and Stan Hubbard beyond the blood alcohol level for being in charge of a pen. They were still out of the line having what, as in a lot of cases in A Company, proved to be their final fling. I was pretty groggy when the letter was read to me. It is very precious and humbling. So much so, that I have no intention of publishing it. However, Ray Kellehear and Kenneth McKenzie (Mac) caught me up because of the delays in my evacuation. They were so seriously wounded that they were sent straight to Japan. My letter to the blokes in the platoon came home with me, without ever getting posted. On the other hand, I eventually 'returned to unit.'

The New Zealand K Force padre, Major Percy Smith of the Salvation Army, visited the New Zealanders in the wards. His visits were most welcome and very comforting. A great man, he had gone to no end of trouble after coming to see me at the casualty clearing post. Collecting my toilet gear from the Durhams, he took it to Seoul hospital where, having missed me, he handed it to the wonderful Sister Smith, who was leaving for Kure. He also posted a letter to me to let me know what was happening.

The commandant of the Brit Com General Hospital was a colonel in the British Army 'Medical Corps' and as pompous and rank-conscious as hell. It is a fact that he expected the men to sit to 'Attention' in their beds when he entered the wards. I crossed swords with him on my first attempt to walk on my wounded leg. It was 8 o'clock in the morning and I was limping around the precincts of my bed with my dressing gown over my pyjamas to test my leg, when he turned up.

"Attention!" he ordered. This order not only applied to those out of bed, but the men in the beds were expected to sit to attention. When he reached me, he ripped into me. "What are you doing out of bed in a state of undress?" he demanded. I explained that I was trying out my wounded leg for the first time.

"If you can get out of bed, you can get dressed," he snapped. It appeared to me that nothing had changed in the British Army Medical Service since 1914. I didn't even know where my uniform was.

The ward was full and, as you would expect with the war now static, we were mostly subalterns, but there were at least two majors. One, an Englishman, had a lump of shell in his guts and another, a Kiwi, was an ordinance officer who had been blinded and had lost the fingers of both hands. He had been dismantling a new type of Chinese shell fuse to find out how it worked, and it exploded.

The only patient that could move around the ward with ease was a Brit captain, who was in fact a malingerer. He had been in charge of a detachment of guards in a prison camp on Koje Island. When he was posted to a frontline unit, he mysteriously developed a stomach ulcer. It certainly did not stop him drinking like a fish. In fact, heavy drinking was the likely reason for his reposting north.

Another unusual casualty was a South African fighter pilot. He had shot himself in the foot because he did not want to serve his government, as he disagreed with its apartheid policy. This back in 1953? That was his story, anyway. More honourable wounds, though hardly more credible, were those of a Canadian lieutenant who took a burst from a burp gun in a patrol firefight. One round went into his stomach. Another shot away the lobe of an ear. The third went under his helmet and skidded around the inside over the top of his head, emerging from the rear of the helmet to penetrate his shoulder. He was a good bloke and a game little battler.

A tall well-built French Canadian lieutenant named Jacques, with whom I later became a drinking mate, had five .45-inch calibre Tommy gun bullets removed from his breadbasket. I'm sure that a smaller or less tough man, would have been cut in half. As it was, the stitches running diagonally up from his waist toward his armpit would have done Frankenstein proud. His experience was that, during his recce of a forward position prior to relieving the American platoon on it, the sentry on the rear entry to the perimeter was changed while Jacques was inspecting the reserve ammunition dump. This naturally was sited on the reverse slope but, unnaturally, outside the barbed wire—a stupid place for it. Returning in the gathering dusk to re-enter the gap in the wire, he was challenged and then shot down. At the Court of Enquiry, the American GI responsible, on being asked the obvious question, replied, "Oh yes. He answered the password OK. But he spoke with a funny accent."

I was only in Brit Com General one day or so when Pat Woodbridge, my mate in the DLI, joined me. The night after the fiasco in which I was involved with the Durhams, they had another one. B Company's commander had led his whole company out into the valley in front of the barbed wire entanglements on its northern face. He then fanned out patrols to intercept any enemy ones and force a showdown. He intended using the patrols like chessmen, with the idea of reacting quickly to any Chinese activity across his company's front. The idea itself had merit, in that such a concentration of numbers would be a most unusual situation for an enemy patrol to encounter. But the major established a HQ group comprising only himself and his signaller, in front of the re-entrant between the two spurs, Surrey Hills and Mildura. These large spurs running down from each end of the left company's position had tracks down their spines with minefields on each side of them, and across the re-entrant between them. They were the access to no-man's land from B Company's position. From a control point of view, the siting of his HQ was adequate, but with minefields on both sides and behind him, there was no escape route. Also, he had overlooked providing local protection for his mini-HQ. He would have been better off to have set up his HQ at the end of Surrey Hills with a covering party on Alice Springs. Later in the night, when Pat went back to this tiny HQ element to report to his OC, a lone Chinese soldier followed him. Pat, noticing the Chinaman's presence, advanced to deal with him. But the hunted had now become the hunter, and opened fire on them killing the company commander, wounding his signaller, and giving Pat a good hosing down with his burp gun. Pat, returning the fire, killed the game Chinaman. Thanks to his armoured vest, Pat's only serious wound was to his right arm. As time went on and his other wounds started to heal up, the arm, instead of gaining strength, began to wither. It became so serious that he was promptly evacuated back to the UK, but not before he and I had a couple of afternoons together in the bar of the Kure Officers' Club.

But the saddest case was that of a brave young platoon commander from the Duke of Wellington's Regiment. A sliver of steel from a Chinese mortar bomb had lodged in his left eye. The matron was very sensitive towards his case. She put another bed in for him, between Pat Woodbridge's and mine, and asked us to befriend him and keep him informed of what was going on around him. She told us that they had bandaged both his eyes because, had he been allowed to use the right eye, the damaged one would have automatically followed any movement by it to its detriment and accompanied by excruciating pain. He was to be sent back to England, and the bandages were to be kept on for six months to let the eye settle down before removing the shard. I hope that it all came right for him, because he was so game. No one ever heard him complain. He was also a gentleman.

One day, soon after arriving in Brit Com General Kure, I was X-rayed in the morning and visited in the afternoon by a young English doctor who was doing his National Service.

"Strange business about these X-rays," he said. "Front on, there is a lump of metal in the middle of your right knee, but it does not show up in the X-ray taken from the side. I can't explain it."

"I can," I replied. "The radiologist told me to lie on my side, with the left leg behind the right. He obviously must have X-rayed the left leg instead of the right."

"By Jove! You're right. We'll have to do it again."

Once that large bit of grenade fragment and another smaller one in my left calf were removed, I healed up pretty quickly. Four bits, that were too difficult to probe for without doing more damage, were left in, although in the case of the 5 x 5 mm piece in my left upper arm, which still gives me some discomfort, they tried cutting in from another angle, but without success, because they didn't want to damage the muscle. A small jagged shard about 15 mm long is still 10–15 mm from my spine, just below the belt level; deep in the calf of my right leg is a piece about the size of a .22 bullet. My right forearm still carries a 7 mm burp gun bullet.

I found life in the hospital most congenial. We were each issued with a tin of 50 Woodbine cigarettes per week. Well known to the British Empire soldiers of WW1 and WW2, they were still packed in round tins. As a non-smoker, I regularly traded mine with the Japanese flower sellers, who were permitted to visit the wards. The nurses were only too pleased to put the flowers into vases, so the ward was always that little bit brighter. It didn't cost me a dime and the flower sellers were able to make a bigger profit.

Surprisingly, one thing that the British Army Medical Corps was up with the play with was a liquor ration. The troops, both officers and men, received an issue of one quart bottle of Melbourne Bitter between two patients, every afternoon. In the officers' ward, in addition to the pint of beer, we were also given an ounce of whisky each. The nurses in Brit Com General Kure were all Australian, but the sisters seemed to me to be from all over the British Isles. One afternoon on the change of shift, we got a new sister in the ward. A charming but naive Irish lass, she went efficiently about her work. Then out of the blue, about an hour before the usual drinkies time of four o'clock, she announced to the whole ward in her lilting brogue, "Oi've been told that you get a liquor ration. I doon't know much about it, but Oi have a key here. Where is the liquor locker?"

Like a shot out of a gun, the Pommie captain from Koje was on his feet, stomach ulcer and all. "Sister, I could help you," he said with an accentuated suave accent.

"Oh weel. If you know all about it, Oi'll leave you to it then. I've plenty of work still to dooo." With that, she gave him the key and left the ward.

It was a great party, just what we needed. But next morning retribution was visited on me: and me alone. In strode Matron like an avenging angel, making a bee-line for me.

"What do you think you were doing last night? Why did you not stop the debauchery? As an Australian, you knew better. Didn't you?"

I thought that was a good one. Knowing the Aussies like I did.

"Of course you did. But you let it go on. Why?"

She conveniently overlooked that I was in fact, if not in spirit, a New Zealander. Also, she chose to ignore another salient fact. That was that I was only a second lieutenant, in a ward where the ranks ranged up to major, and all had participated. I had sense enough to keep my mouth shut, and there were no further repercussions. So we got off lightly. There was a bit of a token penalty, when we were told that evening:

"That is it. There is no liquor ration available. You have drunk it all." But things returned to normal surprisingly quickly.

Before Pat Woodbridge left for home, he and I were given afternoon leave and we headed for the Kure Officers' Club, where I found that Tom Collins was my favourite drink at that time, and that it is full of Dutch courage. On our second day out at the club, Pat and I were five minutes late arriving back. The hospital's practice was to lock the front door at 7 pm and any patient locked out was admitted on knocking, but his name was taken, which after my previous run in with the commandant, I wished to avoid.

As it was the middle of spring in Japan, whose seasons are a month ahead of Korea's, it was still quite light. I did a recce around the back of the building, my intention being to get in through a window and then let Pat in the front door. A silly idea in hindsight. The ground floor windows were barred, but a fire escape ran down the wall from our ward on the second floor. I dragged myself up it, game leg and all, and attracted the attention of the sister on duty, a delightful little Scottish lass, a really lovely girl. She opened the window with some trepidation. More, I thought, than was warranted. Then she pointed out two salient facts. The first was that the mosquito screens were fixed, so could not be opened for me to climb through. Secondly, the commandant of the hospital was lying in the swimming pool after a hard day, watching my antics. A quick glance confirmed this state of affairs. I retreated quickly but carefully, keeping my face pointing away from the direction of the pool. Amazingly, although the damage must have been done, my Australian uniform being easily recognisable, there was no repercussion. The Scottish sister opened the front door for us. So our names were not taken.

– *Eighteen* –
Convalescence

"How can you expect the men to behave when their officers play up?" So spoke the Commandant of Cassel's Camp, a convalescent establishment designed to get sick and wounded men physically and mentally fit again to a level that enabled them to be sent back into action. The camp was named after the much-respected first commander of the Commonwealth Division. As you would expect, it was well run and a credit to General Cassel's famous name. However, before I got as far as the convalescent camp, three noteworthy events occurred.

Firstly, as my mental health improved along with my physical, I eased up on the drinking. Secondly, when I was given a clearance at the hospital, I thought that I should repay the blood bank for my transfusions. I therefore sought out the bank and gave them back a pint. That was the start of a lifetime habit of donating blood.

The third significant thing happened before leaving the hospital. I was introduced to a very nice young English nursing sister. Quite out of the blue, a couple of sisters on our ward, deciding that it was a good idea for us to meet, told me to get dressed, then took me to the ward where she was on duty. I was impressed. She was a very lovely, personable and good-looking young lady, with a lot of character. She was a little younger than I was. But as a lieutenant in the Queen Alexander's Royal Nursing Corps, the QARANC, she actually at the time outranked me. Not that that mattered to us, but you have to watch these things with the British Army. We started dating. In the interests of propriety, I have lost a lot of sleep trying to decide whether to name her, as we got to know one another rather well. She was such an important part of my recovery that I feel that she should be named, but, as we finally went our different ways, I would not want to embarrass her. I have therefore decided to refer to her as Leslie. I hope that she does not mind.

It was immediately after this meeting that I was discharged from hospital and, with the alcoholic English captain, sent to Miyajima to recuperate amid the beautiful and restful surroundings of that sacred Japanese island. Dedicated to the Emperor of Japan and the worship of Shintoism, it is south of Kure in the Inland Sea. In those days one travelled by rail to Miyajimaguchi then crossed by ferry to the island, on which the Japanese would allow no one to die, nor a baby to be born. Pregnant women were sent to the mainland as their time approached. Even the night soil, collected in the traditional wooden 'honey buckets', was shipped to the mainland for disposal over the paddies. Spindly trees and sparseness of grass were testimony to the lack of manure on the island itself.

Despite the ratification of the 1952 peace treaty which restored Japan's sovereignty—it had been suspended at the end of WW2—an Australian run army rest centre established during the occupation was still functioning on Miyajima. The little hotel, with its excellent food and friendly atmosphere, accommodated the recuperating officers. There were no Australian or New Zealand 'other ranks' on the island, but the British troops had their own separate recuperation establishments and there were no problems. For the first time in their military life, the British troops were free to come and go as they liked. That is, until 2200 hrs. The only drawback to the idyllic lifestyle was the presence of the feared Pommy Red Caps, who came out of their holes at 2200 hrs. The provosts were ignorant, ruthless, loathsome bastards. They were scum themselves, with too much power; they bullied the British soldiers as if they were criminals when, in fact, they were young martyrs for their country. Although I never personally tangled with the provost in Japan, Korea after the truce was a different story.

The town, where the ferry berthed, had become a tourist attraction. Built around the shores of the only deepwater cove, it was about a kilometre from the officers' rest centre. There were few shops but plenty of brothels. The small industrial area behind the town was, however, full of craftsmen who produced hand-made souvenirs of a very high quality. They sold their wares in their workshops. It was an interesting walk to the village, as there were plenty of things of a different culture to observe, but by Japanese standards it was a bit of a sleepy hollow. That is, until there was a school visit. The arrival of a ferryboat full of school children was a great sight to witness. They poured ashore with their school bags and drawing boards. Little girls in navy gym-frocks, their straight black hair cut exactly level, just above their collars with a fringe across their foreheads. The boys were in navy tunics and long trousers, wearing navy blue peaked caps over their GI haircuts. Each child headed off to a vantage point from which to paint the multitiered pagoda.

One could even take a short cut to town through the big Shinto temple, which was built upon piles over the shallow waters of a wide bay, around the corner from the village and its ferry landing. The temple had the largest torii in Japan, protruding from the mud flats about 400 metres beyond the temple on the seaward side. When the tide came in, it became a gateway for ceremonial processions of small boats manned by Shinto priests, a most impressive sight.

Within the temple, other things of interest to the tourists were sacred platforms supporting tombs, particularly Emperor Hirohito's. There was also an elaborate stable and stall for Hirohito's sacred white horse. Japanese pilgrims arriving to pay their respects and sightseeing foreign tourists could buy cubes of sugar to feed to the horse. Tiny receipts accompanied the cubes, with the donor's name written on them by an attendant monk, as proof of the pilgrimage.

For the first few days I had the hard case captain in tow, because we shared a room. However, he was quite good company and professed to know a bit about sailing, so we hired the only yacht available, a hard-chine 14-footer. He elected himself helmsman, explaining that he was familiar with sailing. I couldn't have cared less, as I was still only about 80 percent fit. I didn't bother to tell him that I had skippered our own yacht *Red Shadow* to a win in the cruising 18-footers' race in the annual Auckland Anniversary regatta on 29 January the year before. It was the biggest one-day regatta in the world in those days. My young brother Stewart took the cup again while I was in Korea. However, both the hired boat and the Brit captain sailed quite well and it was just the thing for my damaged muscles. When I did take a turn on the tiller, I sailed her across to the mainland and we had the unusual experience, for those early days in their development, of witnessing the tending of a cultured pearl oyster farm. The divers were women, wearing nothing but the pearls in their hands.

Suddenly, things changed dramatically for the captain. He overstepped the mark by getting caught boozing with other ranks, after their curfew. He was promptly bundled off, hopefully to the front, which until then he had so skilfully avoided.

After a month on night shift, the nursing sisters in Kure Military Hospital were entitled to five days rest at Miyajima. Leslie arrived on the island a few days after I did, and it was the beginning of a torrid romance. We were together all the time. When she went back onto day shift, I took a train to Kure every afternoon and we spent most of the night in a hotel. After seeing her back to the hospital in the early morning, I would catch the workers' train to Miyajimaguchi, then the ferry across to the island, and would still be in time for breakfast.

Following the convalescence on Miyajima, I was, as previously mentioned, sent to Cassel's Camp to be brought back to a state of fitness for return to unit. Once again, I enjoyed the privileges of an English officer, being only required to join in the muscle re-building exercises in the mornings, and was then free to leave camp. The men were kept at playing team games into the afternoon, presumably to keep them occupied. On arrival, the commandant interviewed me. A doctor and a fine, sensible man, whose job was not the sinecure it may have first appeared. I told him that in my opinion I was ready to go back, and asked to be released to rejoin my battalion. At the time my plea went unheeded. However, it must have been noticed that I spent little time in the camp. I never had an evening meal in that establishment.

Leslie and I spent many afternoons in our favourite bar, in downtown Kure. A narrow little place called Maxine's, it was not patronised by any other military personnel while we were there possibly because it was more expensive than the beer halls, which were more like pubs where a soldier could meet a friendly Japanese girl. While they were most congenial, the beer halls were no place to take a lady commissioned officer. Drinking little—well, not too much—we talked and talked and listened to soothing music while we got to know one another. Teresa Brewer singing 'Til I waltz again with you' was one of our favourites and 'It takes two to tango' another. 'The Darling of The Forces' of the early '50s, Petula Clarke, charmed me with 'I'll walk alone.' Maybe I listened too much and got brainwashed. When we felt hungry, the management would have our order of steak and eggs, or a fish dish, or whatever, delivered from a nearby food shop.

When Leslie was not on night duty, we usually ended up in each other's arms in a hotel. I could not propose, as no one knew how long the 'war of attrition' was going to drag on. The potential life span of a platoon commander, during the static phase, was approaching WW1 figures. By my count, A Company 3 RAR had lost 13 junior officers killed, wounded or missing in nine months. So without putting too fine a point on it, as people tend to do in major wars, we had a close relationship without commitment.

Three weeks after we met, we arranged to attend the celebration of the coronation of Queen Elizabeth at the Kure Officers' Club. During that afternoon, I met up with Sergeant Mick O'Donnell as I was leaving Kure House, where the New Zealand Army pay office was housed. After greetings and my enquiry about the state of his burnt back, he remarked,

"It's a pity about Bernie Cocks."

"What is?" I enquired innocently.

"He was killed the other day."

"Oh no." I was devastated. Dropping my gaze to hide my grief, I saw that my hands were shaking. Bernie had been like a brother. When I looked up again, Mick was gone.

Bernie was my best friend. He never called me anything other than Skipper. I always referred to him as the Sergeant to the troops, but addressed him as Bernie, whether in front of the men or not. We were great mates. Both dedicated soldiers, with a similar management style. I had a great respect for him and I can still say that he was one of the finest men that I have ever met. My reaction to Bernie's death bore out the old axiom that one should not become too close to anyone in a war situation. But I still don't go along with that philosophy. Mateship is the backbone of the Australian army, indeed of the nation. I had been away from the battalion a little under five weeks, and had not expected it to be sent into the line again quite so soon, as the Com Div had been promised a long break. The only explanation, I believe, is that the pressure being applied on Hill 355 was of concern to the hierarchy, so the Australian battalion, with the best record in 28th Brigade, was sent back on to it as a sensible precaution. I went to the hospital and enquired about recent admissions of Australian personnel. There were more than there should have been. They were mostly from A Company, including my own platoon. It was like a bad dream to see Kevin McKenzie with his right shoulder shattered by the same salvo of mortar bombs that had killed Bernie.

At the age when most young men in those days started experimenting with smoking, I hadn't. I figured out, quite correctly, that the time when a soldier's nerves are most stretched and he thinks he needs a cigarette is usually when he must not smoke. However, right then I thought that it would not endanger anybody, and might just steady me up. So I went back into the American PX and bought a packet of 20 Lucky Strike. Leslie was very supportive at the Officers' Club that night, making sure that we joined in all the activities, to keep my mind off my personal tragedy. We even played housie; it was the only acceptable gambling game under British army regulations. Leslie won a game and chose as a prize a whisky flask, which she presented to me. This was a loving gesture and it gave me some flexibility by acting as a reserve. In action I always carried with me the silver flask that my father had given me. He had filled it with good whisky to take to the war. I had vowed to myself to only broach it in a last stand situation. However, my experiences were never so bad that my own fighting spirit could not cope. As it turned out, I survived to bring it home and drink it with dear old Dad.

Leslie and I were both in good nick when we left the club. After taking her back to the nurses' quarters at the hospital, I returned to the convalescent camp. I had smoked one and a half cigarettes during the evening and given two away. On arriving at my billet, consisting of no more than a bunk and a mosquito net, I started to fret about Bernie again. I threw back the 'mozzie net' and, most unwisely, lit up. When the packet was finished, I crashed.

On the program for the next morning, about which we had not been warned, was a seven mile (11.2 km) forced march, presumably ordered by a sadist. 'Forced' meant that we had to march at a pace much faster than is normal for a route march and there were to be no stops. In addition to that, our finishing line, one might call it, was the top of a very steep mini-mountain, 200 metres high. To make our plight worse, we were carrying no water. I had no trouble with the forced march, but my mouth was very dry. When the hill climb got under way, I knew that I had a problem because of the cigarettes. I was dehydrated. I would have been better off not to have touched them. As we all laboured up at our best speed, I passed a lot of young soldiers who were probably as unused to the liquor that they had consumed in the coronation celebrations as I was to smokes. They were falling by the wayside, emptying the contents of their stomachs. I was going strong, but tiring because of my breathing. The peak was in sight, almost within reach. I could hear heavy footfalls and heavy breathing getting louder: someone was catching up. Ten paces and a little more effort would see me there first. I gave it all I had. Then a Brit staff sergeant rushed past me, beating me by a couple of strides. Damn, I thought, it's all over, I have come second. It was not a race, but pride had brought out my competitiveness. Then I realised that the staff sergeant was Ordinance Corps, so was almost certainly working for the doctor.

This was borne out the next day when I was summoned to the commandant's office. Our fitness levels must have been under scrutiny, and mine had shown up well.

"Why are you not behaving yourself, Matthews?"

I replied that I was not conscious of misbehaving.

"Well, you are not setting a good example to the troops."

"With respect, sir, these troops are not mine. The men in my platoon need me, I want to go back."

"All you colonials say that." (This in 1953). He went on, "Even the men. And you all play up to try and achieve it." He was most gentlemanly in the way that he said this. He did not bluster, the way that the colonel commandant of Kure Hospital had.

"Sir, we are all volunteers and we feel that we should get back to our unit, as soon as is reasonably possible. I believe that I am getting around fairly well."

"So do I," he replied with a twinkle in his eye, which I didn't miss. "Look, Lieutenant, I will make an exception and do a deal with you. If I post you back now, will you undertake to pass the word to your colonial troops, that they must co-operate if they end up here?"

I tried not to show elation, and soberly promised to do so. I did of course thank him for giving me a fair go. If he ever reads this, I hope that he will forgive me for not fulfilling my side of the bargain. Things had hotted up all right, and to say to my troops, 'If you are wounded etc.', would have been the height of folly from a morale point of view.

Leslie was very upset and tearful at the jetty, where I boarded the launch which would take me south down the Inland Sea to Iwakuni airbase. I hoped to see her again and maybe marry her, but I could not read the future. Once back with A Company, the letter writing started. We wrote to each other almost every day. How I did it with my workload, I do not know. The diggers soon cottoned on at mail call that I was receiving mail regularly from Kure. In accordance with army regulations, the sender was required to put his or her name and address on the back of the envelope. I became a sort of folk hero.

"A nursing sister, eh? Nothing queer about our skipper."

But the day came. The truce had been signed and the fighting had ceased about a month before. I had still not proposed. I got my 'Dear John' letter.

– *Nineteen* –

3 RAR Back on Little Gibraltar

As I have already mentioned, I was still convalescing when 3 RAR went back into action on our old home, Hill 355. But for the sake of continuity, I will report what was told to me by my colleagues when I returned to the unit despite the fact that I mostly heard about the defeats rather than the successes, of which there were a few. These usually resulted in our patrol conceding the ground, but inflicting more casualties on the enemy than he was prepared to accept, so there was no follow up. We just did not have the manpower to send out patrols equal in numbers to the Chinese ones. The Americans did. Their patrols were usually 40 or so strong, but their tactical handling did not make for impressive results. The Chinese patrols, also of at least 40 men, were strong in grenadiers and submachine gunners as I have previously described, and much more effectively led than the American ones. Their tactical handling was excellent.

Once back on Hill 355, the priority for 3 Battalion was to continue the work put in by the Durhams to regain control of no-man's land. They had made a reasonable start, but they did not have the weapon scale for the task that we had, nor the manpower. The enemy, in turn, doubled their efforts in an attempt to prevent the Australians from achieving that aim. The fighting in the valley became even more hectic. The casualty list published in "Australian Operations on Jamestown line" records that in the month of May, 3 RAR took 79 casualties out of a total of 143 in the four-battalion-strong 28 Brigade.

The demolition raid on Hill 355's forward mortar base during the battalion's absence would have given the enemy an opportunity to assess the strengths and weaknesses of the big hill, giving them some confidence about taking it. But they had to defeat us decisively in no-man's land first. Despite some setbacks, the battalion denied them that total domination they needed. The reason lay in the Australian attitude. Neither battalion on returning to the front line had recommenced patrolling by probing tentatively outside their wire. The fact that the enemy was coming so far across 'the valley' that he had been perceived to be knocking on the COMDIV's door carried no weight with the battle-experienced Australian units. The platoon commanders and their men, whether of 1 RAR or 3 RAR old soldiers by Korea standards—or the newly arrived men of 2 RAR—appreciated that getting well across no-man's land and taking on the enemy where and when you could find him should take the pressure off our positions. And so it proved. The enemy could hardly harass our local defences if they lost half their strength getting there. Using our superiority in communications and the flexible and readily available artillery support of NZ 16th Field Regiment, Australian patrols were often able to even the odds. Even if we were not always able to hold the ground in the event of a patrol clash, the Chinese plans were frustrated and our outposts alerted. Our own patrolling program would continue as usual the next night, but with the ambushes in different positions.

Pre-dawn minefield checking was another form of patrolling. It was generally less hazardous, but no less important, as shellfire frequently destroyed the single marker wire. It was therefore unfortunate that Lt. Ray Burnard, my talented associate, who was as efficient in action as he had been in training, was one morning caught out by the arrival of daylight while on a minefield check, with regrettable results. While not A Company's responsibility for checking, the particular field was nevertheless well within our area of interest from a defensive point of view. So when in the half-light of dawn, one of our diggers who had exceptional eyesight spotted three figures on our side of the field, he called his section leader. The NCO referred the sighting to platoon HQ, which confirmed to the best of its ability that the minefield in question was not listed for checking by anyone that morning. It was therefore considered safe to assume that the three distant figures were enemy, and fair game for the Bren gunner. He set his sights at 700 yards and fired one short burst, laying his chosen target low. Unbeknown to him, his target was a battalion officer.

Through the efforts of Alec Weaver, I have recently made contact with Ray (now a retired brigadier). The following is his reply to my letter: "You are the first person to ask about the incident on 16/17 May

'53. An event still pretty vivid in my mind. This is what I recall.

"The checking party comprised a sapper from the British Field Squadron, my signaller and me. We had a late start time, probably to avoid clashing with other patrols. From memory it was about midnight when I phoned Bruce Trennery the Company Commander that I was leaving. We had no problem with the inner fence but the outer fence was a bit of a mess. We had located and recorded a couple of breaks and were heading for the minefield gap to go home. Suddenly the sapper, who was leading stopped, turned and whispered. 'I think we are in a bloody minefield.'

"He got down on his hands and knees and began feeling and prodding his way toward the inner fence with the two of us treading carefully after him. I can't remember how long it took, but it seemed like eternity. Dawn was breaking as we reached the fence and the mist, which had pervaded throughout the night, lifted quite suddenly.

"No sooner had we crossed the fence than we were fired upon by, I gather, a Bren gun from A Company. I was shot in the base of the throat with the bullet leaving a rather large exit hole in my back. Unfortunately, although I was wearing a 'flak jacket' I hadn't zipped it right up. I can still remember the strange sucking sound coming from my back! My signaller [I think Pte White] gave me a shot of morphine and I was out to it.

"Ray had taken a plunging shot through his throat. The .303 bullet proceeded down into his chest, clipped the top of one lung and passed out through his back. It left a hole that you might have been able to cover with your outspread hand. If you had a big hand."

Ray taking up the story again:

"I gather the Sig radioed for help [or did they return to get it?]. In any event a stretcher party from A Coy led by the CSM, that great old warrior Jack Morrison, came down under a white flag to get me. Some years later when Jack was serving with me in Vietnam, he said it was the most eerie experience he had known. He said it was deathly quiet and he knew a thousand pairs of eyes were watching them—and half of them were slanty eyed bastards. I was very sad to hear later that Bernie Cocks had been killed when they mortared A Company after the party came in.

"Anyway, I was carted off to the RAP where I must have been semiconscious for a while, as I clearly remember someone saying 'I don't think he is going to make it.' How wrong he was. I was flown off to the Norwegian Mash in one of those helicopters with pods on the side."

When Ray arrived at the MASH, there happened to be one of America's top plastic surgeons visiting from Stateside. The medical team not only saved him but the visitor, with incredible skill, ensured that he was not disfigured.

Ray continues: "When I awoke a day or so later [after surgery which obviously saved my life], I remember the shock when the first person I saw was a Chinese in the opposite bed! A nurse reassured me that I was not 'in the bag' and that the chap was a POW. I then disappeared into the American evacuation system via 121 Evac Hosp in Seoul [a horrifying experience as for some reason I was put in the burns ward]. Then on a giant Globemaster to Tokyo Army Hospital, which became 'home' for the next four months.

"By this time my bride of eight months was frantic. She had been told that I was on the 'dangerously ill' list. Unfortunately the Aust Army had lost contact with me but after a couple of weeks the international Red Cross came to the rescue with updates on my progress.

"I was the only Commonwealth officer in the hospital, with a dozen or so British and Canadian soldiers. We were given an allowance of $US1 a day [as our Brit currency was unacceptable]. They even tried to give me a 'Purple Heart', which I diplomatically declined. We were treated very well indeed and toward the end of my stay I was allowed to recuperate at Ebisou between operations. This was not such a good idea as I got caught up with my mates on R&R and returned to the hospital a bit the worse for wear. One amusing incident was when the ladies of the Canadian Embassy invited the Commonwealth patients to an afternoon's entertainment. We all arrived in our pyjamas and striped dressing gowns and to our horror found that we had to sit through a two-hour recital of chamber music by a string quartet. The Scots, Geordies and French Canadians were not amused and one by one went outside for a smoke. At the end, only three of us were left and I had the job of thanking the ladies and saying how much we enjoyed the recital.

"Anyway after four months in hospital, I was asked if I wanted to go home or return to the battalion. Much as I very much wanted to see my wife, I realised that as a professional soldier there was only one answer."

I was back with the unit myself when Ray returned from his convalescence. Like the rest of the mess, I was astounded but delighted at his amazing recovery. The only indication of the entry of the bullet was a thin scar-line in the centre of his throat, which a necktie would have hidden. His back of course was a different story. But to return after such an experience was something in itself, and we were all pleased for him. To give him a chance of seeing out his tour of duty, the CO put him on the staff of BHQ, where Ray's remarkable talents were better employed in any case.

Unfortunately, as Ray mentioned, Bernie Cocks had not been so lucky. I never considered the possibility of such an experienced, war-worn veteran not surviving. It hit me hard. We had been great friends, leading a great team. Bernie's death was totally unnecessary. Kevin McKenzie told me when I visited him in hospital that someone had decided that the Mungindi Diggings should be reoccupied during the day, to lure the Chinese into sending a patrol to investigate. Apparently, the theory was that we would have an ambush waiting for them. Mungindi, which had been established by the Canadians on a little spur in the narrow valley between Hill 355 and John, was about 300 metres from Dog outpost, a strong Chinese bunker facing us on the upper slopes of John. Dog outpost totally dominated Mungindi 100 metres below it. Had I been still with A Company, instead of in hospital, I would have put up a strong case against the ambush. Months before, Mungindi had proved too costly to hold and had been abandoned as a site for an ambush patrol. However, No. 1 Platoon got the job of being a decoy for another ambush. Not surprisingly, the plan went wrong. Instead of waiting until dark and sending a patrol into an obvious ambush situation, the Chinaman took the cost effective action, which had caused the outpost to be abandoned in the first place: he mortared it. Casualties were suffered and Bernie Cocks, who had been lightly wounded the day before, and had returned to the company after treatment, was the first to reach the wounded. These were L/Cpl. Lyons, Pte. McGee, Pte. Ralston and Pte. Smart, all my original 1 Platoon men. Bernie was dragging them under cover when joined by Charlie Yacopetti, Corporal Kevin McKenzie and another great digger, Bodgie Kiesecker, No.1 Platoon's stretcher-bearer.

The *Sydney Daily Mirror* staff reporter in Korea was quoted in the 22 May 1953 edition as saying, "Lieut. Charlie Yacopetti told me that when the mortar bombs landed within 10 metres, as they were trying to pull men out, he told Sergeant Cocks to take cover in the pits. Bernie replied, quote 'I'm all right, sir. We have got to get the wounded back.'

According to the same report, two seconds later Bernie and Kevin were hit and Charlie, who was only a metre away from Bernie, was sent sprawling on his neck. Kevin McKenzie told me when I visited him in hospital that the 81 mm mortar bomb landed about a metre in front of Bernie and exploded upwards, blowing his lungs out through his back. According to the *Daily Mirror*, Bodgie Kiesecker and Charlie Yacopetti brought Bernie's body back to our lines, when more help arrived.

As soon as I had got my thoughts into some sort of order, I wrote to Mrs Cocks, the mother whom Bernie had loved so dearly. I received a sad but brave reply, written for her by another son, whom I had not known existed. Bernie had not got around to telling me that he had a brother. His mother was his main focus in the bachelor soldier's life. Mrs Cocks picked up the fact that my regimental number was different from the Australians' and asked me to write again and give her some details of myself. To my everlasting shame, I did not write again. I was personally so upset that I felt that I was not up to the task. That was a bad weakness, for which I have never forgiven myself. However, the hurt I had felt all those years, for not being there when he was killed, was somewhat alleviated when in 1988 I returned to Korea and visited Bernie's grave in the beautiful Pusan war cemetery.

How Lieutenant Alec Weaver came to be in the Australian Army I did not know at the time, despite the fact that he and I were great friends. We still are. Four years after the war, Alec and his bride Margaret visited my wife Annette and myself when they were in New Zealand on their honeymoon. Alec was still in the army awaiting a posting to a training unit, having spent the post-Korea war period as commander of Miyajima Island's R and R and Convalescent Centre. He was also aide-de-camp to the Commander-in-chief of BCFK, which involved him in doing interpreting work for the general, who was busily engaged in negotiations and diplomatic involvement with the Japanese. (Alec, a natural linguist, had learnt the language after the surrender by the Japanese in 1945 and his posting to intelligence operations during the occupation of Japan.) A thorough gentleman and a born soldier, Alec announced on his arrival in the battalion that he had been born in

Sudetenland, but vol II of *Australia in The Korean War* says he was Polish. He has since confided to me that he was actually born in Berlin, Germany. He and his parents spent some time with relations in Sudetenland in 1937, before heading for Kenya, where his parents remained and were eventually interned by the British authorities. Alec had gone on to Australia alone, where he joined the AIF during WW2, claiming Polish nationality, which was readily accepted by overworked recruiting staff at that time. His real nationality was eventually found out. But the CO of his battalion in New Guinea saw to it that he was accepted and initiated naturalisation procedures for him. Anyway, he was a popular member of our mess, a good soldier and a great mate. Not a big man, he nevertheless had a presence. With jet-black hair, rather than the blond hair of the stereotype German, he spoke clipped but excellent English. When out of the line, he would rarely be in the mess early, but would enter when nearly all were assembled. Striding up to the colonel, Alec would halt in front of him, click his heels together and bow his head slightly. In a loud voice he would say the traditional, "Good evening, sir." But it came out as "Good evening, Saar!" The real entertainment was the Colonel's reaction. We used to wait for it. Colonel MacDonald always contrived to appear to be surprised. Night after night, with a straight face, he would exclaim, "For God's sake, Weaver, stop clicking your heels." The merriment that this engendered among the rest of us set the tone for a cheerful evening.

The night following Bernie's death, Charlie Yacopetti, who now had command of No. 1 Platoon, my old platoon, took out a fighting patrol. Alec wanted to get to know the ground in that area, so volunteered to go along as a supernumerary submachine-gunner. The following is Alec's account of the action:

"The patrol took up a position on a forward slope some distance forward of the minefield on the extreme left flank of Hill 355. And, after a while of quietness was assaulted by a large force of Chinese troops throwing grenades and firing their weapons. It was a full moon that night and they had been able to easily observe the patrol's movement from the top of the hill.

"Charlie ordered 'grenades' which was Standard Operational Procedure, instead of disclosing our exact position by firing our weapons early in the encounter. A vicious close quarter battle ensued as our small patrol of two officers and 15 diggers became severely mauled. Charlie managed to say to Alec, "Alec, I can't walk and no one could help me."

"He would not accept any help and asked Alec to get the diggers out as best he could. Then Alec was crippled in both arms and hit by a stun grenade. He got Private 'Chalky' White M.M. to take his grenades, which White used to good effect, but in the confusion of the battle, and amidst screams of pain in Australian as well as Chinese voices, it became impossible to tell friend from foe.

"Luckily Alec knew the way back through the minefield at the distant right flank of Hill 355 and was able to shepherd the walking wounded as far as his own position on the hill, where he collapsed in the arms of his waiting platoon sergeant.

"Charlie Yacopetti had been completely immobilised with apparently severe gunshot wounds to his legs, as was the case with his trusty signalman. They were rapidly snatched by the enemy who were keen to get prisoners, hence the use of stun grenades as well as fragmentation grenades. In the absence of the signalman, Alec and the rest of the survivors had no opportunity of calling for artillery or mortar support to cover their withdrawal. Luckily they passed a standing patrol position from where the badly needed interdiction fire could be brought down, preventing the enemy from effectively pursuing the battered remnants of the patrol. This was of course of no help to Yacopetti and his signalman, and no help in retrieving the bodies of their mates who had been killed in the action. Alec recommended White for a bar to his M.M. in acknowledgement of his excellent and steadfast conduct under fire. This was later awarded."

When I eventually returned to A Company, the general opinion was that Charlie was dead. Some diggers were still muttering to their mates, "Poor Charlie. He was a good bloke." What really happened to him came to light when Charlie was released in the prisoner exchange after the truce. The following is, as near as I can remember, his account of the patrol clash, given to our representative who debriefed him.

After the first action there was a lull around Charlie, as the enemy harried the withdrawal of the rest of the patrol. Charlie gave himself a shot of morphine, to ease the pain. Patrol commanders carried small tubes, with the attached needle protected by a glass cover, to relieve any severely wounded member. Charlie went out like a light. Unfortunately, his bad luck continued. When he came-to, the Chinese had returned and were souveniring his webbing and searching his pockets. They had obviously thought him dead. Once they realised their mistake, he was unceremoniously hauled to his feet and promptly collapsed again. So they carried him. Then his ordeal really began. This was May 1953 and being a POW for four months may not sound long, but he was a prisoner of the fanatical communists.

For the first few weeks, he was kept under guard in a front-line position, directly opposite Hill 355. The only medical treatment available for his legs, which were full of burp gun bullets, was boiling water—no antiseptics or antibiotics whatsoever. Nothing. He stated that the Chinese wounded got no better. Whenever our artillery shelled the area in which he was held, he was bundled at the point of a bayonet out into an exposed trench. Covered by his escorts, he was forced to endure our bombardment in the comparative open. When the shelling stopped, the interrogation began again.

They did not wish him any harm. But, he could only be taken out of danger if he co-operated. Where were the weak spots in Hill 355's defences? Which were the best approaches? What sort of weapons could be brought to bear, in the case of a full scale attack?

But they could not have had a tougher minded prisoner to work on. Eventually they gave up and he was sent to a POW camp, where his wounds healed to some degree. North Korean guards, who were notoriously ruthless, ran these camps. In that dreadful environment began Charlie's 'finest hour'. He was a devout RC. I am not, but I like to think of his efforts as a struggle between communism and catholicism. The communists could not do a bloody thing with him. He bucked all their systems and quickly became the leader of the British prisoners.

As the date of Queen Elizabeth's coronation approached, Charlie, with the assistance of 'old hands' in the camp, organised the acquisition of a small quantity of rice wine by devious means, such as bribing the guards with cigarettes and sweets from the food parcels that had finally got through to them. Carefully hidden, there was eventually enough saved for a nip in each Commonwealth prisoner's mug.

At the appropriate time on the great day, 21 June 1953, this game Australian officer formed up the British troops. Quickly sharing out the wine, he proposed the loyal toast.

"To Her Majesty, Queen Elizabeth the Second."

The guards belatedly caught on when he called for three rousing cheers for her Majesty. He had pulled it off. But the parade was savagely broken up, with the application of rifle butts by very angry guards whose loss of face made them more severe than usual.

Charlie's guts had finally changed his luck. He was released in the exchange of prisoners in the month following the truce. After the Commonwealth troops from the camp were debriefed, his name went forward for recognition. He was decorated with a Military Cross for his conduct of the patrol action and subsequent behaviour in captivity.

A nice finale to the story was that Alec Weaver, because of his special language skills, was posted as liaison officer to operation "Big Switch" at Panmunjom, where the prisoner exchange took place. He was one of the first United Nations officers to welcome Charlie Yacopetti back to freedom, and the first Australian to do so.

– *Twenty* –
Return to the Battalion

When I rejoined A Company the battalion was out of the line in Area 6. I found that quite a few changes had taken place as a result of the recent casualties.

Lt. Dick Witton had replaced me in No. 1 Platoon so I was given command of Charlie Yacopetti's No. 3 Platoon, who were also first class blokes. I was still mates with the diggers of No. 1 Platoon, although quite a few had been evacuated wounded, and Bernie was dead.

I had little time to get to know my new platoon before we went in the line to relieve the Royal Fusiliers on Hill 159. The platoon sergeant Ray Simpson, whom I already knew, was another second tour of duty man. He had been running 3 Platoon until I rejoined the unit. In Ray, I inherited one of the characters of the battalion. He had become a very good soldier since being given rank and the responsibility that goes with it and—dare I say it of a Victoria Cross winner?—once he had learnt to fit into the army system. He was a colourful figure. Game all right, though not quite as capable a platoon sergeant as Bernie Cocks had been. Simmo was rougher but not tougher. He did, however, have the leadership attributes required of a good platoon sergeant. Definitely a nonconformist, he had learnt his man management skills as a tram conductor on the Bondi run, the roughest tram-run in Sydney, in the immediate post WW2 days. He had a reputation of being wild, and it was correct. But he was no fool, just an honest man whose profession was soldiering. He was blessed with great courage, including utter fearlessness in the face of the military hierarchy, as well as the Chinese enemy. Possibly because we both cared for the men's welfare, Simmo and I got on very well, although we didn't have the time to build quite the same bond as had existed between Bernie and me.

I counted myself lucky to be able to return to Jim Norrie's A Company. The majority of the men having been in the company for some time, we were not total strangers. The men in No. 3 Platoon were typical

Australian soldiers, just the same as my wonderful No.1 Platoon men. In a very short time, we were a close-knit and cohesive sub-unit. I was a very lucky man.

The battalion officers had a cosy mess tent set up in Area 6 to which, on my first day back, I was taken rather earlier that one would normally attend for the evening meal. One after another, the members of the mess bought me drinks and I was not allowed to shout at all. Overwhelmed by the enthusiasm of my welcome, I joined in heartily. It was not surprising, therefore, that I was a bit in my cups and became careless.

A tall gangling figure, with angular chiselled features, set off by a five o'clock shadow, and wearing New Zealand flashes, walked in. I had met Captain Joe Manning a week earlier in Japan, on his way to join the battalion. We'd had a few drinks together. He had struck me as a heavy drinker, a heavy serious one. Anyway, someone brought him over and said, "Kiwi, do you know Captain Joe Manning?"

Without stopping to think where I was, I carelessly answered, "Yes, I know my old mate Joe," and shook hands. Joe was happy to see me. He was, after all, brand new in the unit. But a little while later, the Battalion 2IC, Major Bill Henderson, took me to one side and told me that the CO was disappointed at my reference to a more senior officer in the terms which I had just used. I was very contrite and rather disappointed, because I had summed Manning up in Japan and had no intention of teaming up with him. He was too heavy a drinker for my liking. In retrospect, I can see that Colonel MacDonald either knew of Joe's reputation or had himself assessed him. He was warning me not to associate too closely with him. Especially as, John Hooper having completed his time, Joe was taking over as A Company's 2IC, two facts of which I was unaware, having just arrived back.

Now that I was back, my priority was to get to know the 3 Platoon men, and to familiarise them with the patrol formations and tactics that I had devised in hospital. We practiced them, I discussed my ideas with them, and we honed them to what we thought were the best and most flexible formations. In other words, I did not ram my ideas down their throats, rather I told them what I thought we could achieve with them. All were involved, and some contributed a point of view or experience gained in a patrol clash. By the time we moved out of reserve, Ray and I had the platoon in good nick for whatever was ahead. Rough he may have been, but he knew as much as I did about running the platoon, having been required to command it every time it lost an officer. The main thing was that we both had the good of the men at heart. We were both aggressive in our soldiering and, most importantly, we respected one another.

There was no trouble moving into the Hill 159 position. The whole platoon soon settled down to trench warfare and living in holes in the ground again. We re-adjusted to going on patrol every second night, plus all the other duties associated with defending a position. The reinforcements were absorbed and learnt the finer points quickly. The dispositions were three companies forward, with C on the left, A in the middle and B on the right. To add to our comfort, 2 RAR personnel were given their chance on Hill 355. They had a fairly serious assault put in against them early in their tenure, and saw it off with little fuss, thus showing the Chinese that the new Australian battalion was as formidable as the other two.

The Bowling Alley, running between the Apostles and Hill 159, was the big hill's Achilles heel. Only the Anti-tank Ridge position could bring effective fire to bear on it from Hill 355 and was itself the most vulnerable position on that feature. Therefore Hill 159, which had been heavily attacked some months before, was vital to 355's defence because it covered the Bowling Alley from Anti-tank Ridge westward.

The enemy did not at first do anything to acknowledge our return. There were the usual propaganda broadcasts over the valley, which duly welcomed us back. After a week or so, he started to tickle us up with shelling from medium guns. His first success against us on Hill 159 was a fluke shot, which hit a Centurion tank between turret and hull, jamming the turret's traversing gear. We did not hear of any casualties so, as the Brits had plenty more tanks at Gloster Valley, there was no real harm done, especially as the Chinese did not know of their success. A day or two later, a round was lobbed over the crest and into a basin area on top of Hill 159, in which C Company was enjoying a collective midday meal. It did much more damage. The casualties included the company commander, Major Warmsley, a very fine man. Luckily, he was not seriously hurt and was able to carry on.

For a start the weather was great. A real Korean spring, it was clear and fresh, but no longer cold. The hillsides had regrown their scrub very quickly and it was an amazing variety of shrubs, all growing higgledy-piggledy together. There were no acres of flowering manuka as we have in New Zealand. But just as good were the many hillsides covered with the prime shrub of the temperate climes, azalea. I believe that the beautiful purple flowers of the azalea are the crowning glory of the harsh Korean landscape. It is one of the most uplifting and beautiful sights that I have ever seen. Unfortunately shellfire makes a mess of them.

As summer developed, humidity came with the heat. Then it started to rain with an intensity that I had never experienced. There was no wind driving it. It just came down. Trenches started to run with torrents of water. Then their sides slipped, unless they were revetted where there was no rock or root system to reinforce them. Eventually, after days of continuous heavy rain, the river systems could no longer cope and the result was widespread flooding and impassable rivers. We were air-supplied for three days because the bridges across the Imjin could not be used. This coincided with a request to the troops for donations to help the people flooded out of their homes in England. I saw some irony in this, as we were digging men out of their collapsed bunkers. Luckily we did not lose anyone that way, but we did donate to the 'Old Country.'

It was on Hill 159 that my suspicions of Joe Manning were vindicated. As A Company's 2IC he was based at A Echelon, a couple of kilometres behind the line, where expendable stores were held for the battalion's resupply and our meals were cooked. One night, he accompanied the rations onto the feature, which, as company 2IC, was something he should have been doing regularly to keep in touch with the situation up front, in case anything happened to the company commander. Not navigating the trench system very well, he ambled into a section position and was challenged. He was recognised and his drunken condition assessed, even in the dark. After months of operating at night, most of us had night eyes like a cat. He apparently did not know the password, or could not remember it. Instead of identifying himself and admitting that he had forgotten it, he turned tail and scarpered. The sentry was disgusted and was tempted to fire a shot over Joe's head. But the sentry was 'Hawk-eye', so nicknamed, because it was he who fired the fateful burst at Ray Bernard's minefield checking party. He was, of course, in no position to teach the drunken officer a lesson.

But Hawk-eye, although not in my platoon, reported the incident to me but to no other officer. Joe himself was hardly likely to report it and as far as I am aware knowledge of the incident did not go any further until now.

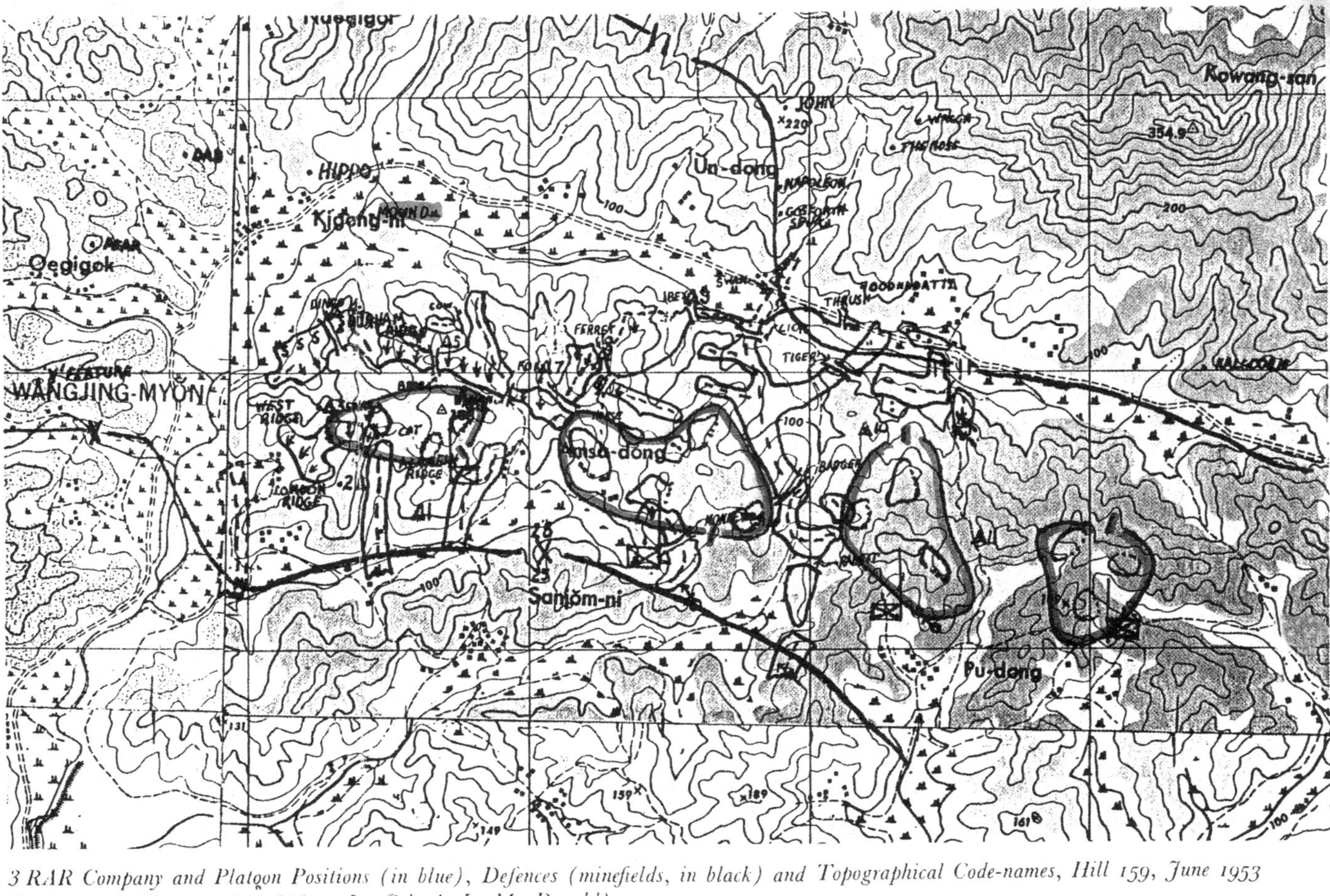

3 RAR Company and Platoon Positions (in blue), Defences (minefields, in black) and Topographical Code-names, Hill 159, June 1953 (battle-map of Commanding Officer, Lt. Col. A. L. MacDonald)

– *Twentyone* –

A Company's Cross

Close in front of the Chinese positions, 1000 metres across the valley from 3 Battalion's C Company on Hill 159, was a lone, steep-sided knoll at grid ref. 145186. Shaped like a loaf of bread, it stood about 80 metres above the surrounding flat land and paddies, with one end pointing toward the Chinese lines and the other toward the United Nations' lines. This little hill, nicknamed 'the Mound', was destined to become A Company's cross.

Situated on a ridgeline running north from Hill 159 was A Company's left forward outpost position called Fox. So named because its contours show up on the map in the shape of a fox's head. With its two ears pointing north and its snout north-west, one could not draw a better looking fox head than its contours on the 1:25,000 map of Majon-ni NE. A track led out to the outpost established on the middle of its head and continued on along the snout, then over a series of knolls and saddles, directly toward the Mound. On both sides of the string of knolls were paddies full of water, contained by fairly level bunds. The knolls ended about 150 metres short of the little hill's steep sides; from there on the ground was flat and dry.

The forward slopes of Hill 159 were not particularly steep, and some had quite high bush covering that hadn't been burnt off. Therefore, Major Norrie decided that besides patrolling well out, we had better look to our local defences in the Bowling Alley. Accordingly, we set up a program, sending out a sweep patrol twice a night. The patrol would report to Fox outpost, then turn right and follow an old overgrown trail down Fox's right ear to the valley floor. I got the job of continuing this trail east across A Company's front, blazing a new track just inside the bush line, on to Ibex outpost on our right flank. It was not a difficult patrol, but it was quite vital to A Company's security. Of course, the starting points of the patrols were varied at random. Fox and Ibex outposts duly reported their departures or arrivals to Coy HQ. We used these local patrols to train up-and-coming leaders. One never knew when we might lose a corporal or even a sergeant.

C Company had a green new boy officer, a very young and inexperienced 2nd Lieutenant from God knows where, upon whom a fair bit of effort had already been spent, trying to bring him up to 3 Battalion's standard. He had already accompanied experienced patrollers three times on fighting patrols, to teach him how patrolling was conducted in the theatre. Most of us had only been taken out twice before going solo. It was arranged with Jim Norrie that, for the young fella's solo, he would be briefed by us and sent on our local sweep patrol, where he was less likely to have a contact. He was to take a full strength fighting patrol of his own C Company platoon, to give him practice in controlling it, before being sent somewhere dangerous. Major Norrie took the unusual step of asking me to attend his briefing, which was meticulously thorough. Although still a 'one pipper', I guess that I was accepted as a senior subaltern because I had survived a patrol action and was the longest serving platoon commander in A Company at the time. After telling the new patrol commander the aim and extent of the patrol, the routine items were covered. Time out, route out, route in, radio channel to be used, call sign and so on. The major then asked me to handle the briefing on the nature of the ground to be encountered, and anything else that would assist him in the conduct of the patrol, such as the position of the standing patrols, track junctions, landmarks and any other special features to look for. Never was anyone so well briefed for such a simple task. However, leading 15 heavily armed men in no-man's land is a big responsibility, and the idea was to train him for major patrolling tasks to the same standard as the rest of the subalterns in the battalion. But his lack of maturity was of concern to us. He may have been swamped by information, but even that would not explain what happened. However, his arrogance, that I noted the moment I met him, would.

So that C Company could maintain its patrolling obligations, an arrangement had been effected. A Coy lent C Coy the services of one of our most experienced patrollers and his men. Lt Peter Goss, who had taken over No. 2 Platoon from John Hooper, was a fine man and a mature officer. He was briefed by C Company and sent with a fighting patrol of his own men to the Mound. His task was to find out what he could about it. In other words, to start sorting it out. We didn't know how the enemy used it. There was no information available as to whether or not the lonely-looking but dominating feature was incorporated in the Chinese defensive system and, if it was, to what extent. In this area, the defendable hills were further apart as no-man's land widened at the confluence of our valley and its streams with other tributaries, all running westward to the Samichon River. So it was a fairly long slog from C Company and worse if, instead of walking on the bunds, you waded directly through the expanse of neglected paddies. Peter probably travelled on the bunds. That would have doubled the distance, but Peter and his men would have arrived fresher and with dry feet. Speed was not an imperative. The later they arrived, the less alert the Chinese were likely to be. Ambushes between C Company and the Mound, that had been left alone for so long, were considered unlikely, but you never know. As for the objective itself, there was no way of getting there ahead of the enemy.

When the C Company patrol left to do our local patrol under the command of its brash young leader, I joined Jim Norrie in his CP. As OC of the battalion flying patrol that night, I could react more quickly from there. I would be able to follow the progress of C Company's patrol, which was the only fighting patrol with a dicey task and if there was a clash I could be quickly briefed. I believe that the major was glad of my company, as it was a lonely job carrying all his responsibility. Company HQ was again within my perimeter, and the whole of 3 Platoon was still on the hill, with my flying patrol standing by with stretchers, ready to go. Ray Simpson was to all intents and purposes in charge of 3 Platoon's position. The men were so on the ball that it was not necessary to breathe down their necks. They knew their job. If Peter Goss or anyone else ran into trouble, it was our task to go to his assistance. As soon as we heard a clash, I would join the flying patrol and take command. But I would not leave the position until ordered to. Therefore it made sense for me to follow the action from the company CP. In the event of trouble, Jim Norrie would give me any last minute instructions that he or Battalion considered the situation might warrant.

There were spare 31VHF sets in the CP, so I suggested to Major Jim that we tune another set into C Company's net, so that we could monitor Peter's progress as well just as a matter of interest. He agreed enthusiastically. Peter was, after all, an A Company officer. For some considerable time, the radios were silent. When patrolling in the valley, we restricted their use unless we were under orders to report progress or were in trouble. After about an hour, Major Jim and I heard one of my platoon signallers start calling the local patrol, which was the new boy's assignment. His patrol was well overdue. Eventually, 3 Platoon's signaller rang me at Company to tell me that he had not heard even a squeak from the sweep patrol. He knew that 30 minutes should have covered its time out and time in. Ibex outpost also wanted to know what had happened to them, and he couldn't enlighten them. I thanked him, saying we were also concerned and were watching the situation and to pass that on to Ibex.

Major Norrie and I were also baffled. In regard to Peter's patrol, he was breaking new ground; we did not expect to hear from him until he had gained his objective, which was a long way out. But where was the local patrol? I started to worry. I have no doubt that Jim did too. But each kept his concern to himself, probably because of the disparity in our rank. Mug after mug of tea followed each other in quickening succession. I had decided that the situation was ridiculous, but I could not figure out what to do about a disappeared patrol that was not answering its radio. Yet time had run out for such a short and straightforward domestic patrol.

Suddenly, the tension in the CP was relieved by the crackle of the set tuned to C Company's net. Over the air, Peter Goss's very calm voice reported, "We have enemy silhouetted on the slopes of the Mound. Am attacking."

Jim and I looked at each other, and breathed again. Great. A Company's local patrol was for the moment forgotten in the excitement. Seconds later, the sound of firing reached us in the CP and our spirits rose even further. Then the radio on A Company's net burst into life.

"Being attacked! Am taking casualties!"

I was already half-way up the entrance trench of the CP, when I heard Jim shout, "Get up there, Kiwi, and find out what is happening."

We both had it figured out anyway. Once out in the open, I had no trouble identifying the small arms fire involved. The 9 mm Owen guns, .303 Brens and rifles, were all going hammer and tongs. But there was a complete absence of the easily recognized higher rate of fire of burp guns, the main armament carried by Chinese patrols. The worst had happened; we had a friendly clash on our hands, I reported to the major who was almost distraught. He asked me if I could remember whether the briefing he had given the young fella had been adequate. I assured him that no one could have been more thorough.

But as commander of the flying patrol, my concern and responsibility were the wounded. I grabbed my Owen and took off. We were moving out through Fox outpost, loaded down with stretchers, when a phone message to the outpost recalled us. C Company had been so appalled at what had happened that they rushed a lot of troops straight out into the valley to pick up the casualties. Battalion decided that it did not make sense to have any more troops out there. It might add to the confusion. I could only agree and of course obey orders. But we were disappointed at not being able to help our own mates. The casualty toll was cruel.

We in the battalion were told promptly what had taken place. Peter had carried out an impeccable patrol, deep into the valley. On reaching his objective, he circled it. No mean feat, as he was right on the Chinese doorstep. On the other hand, the C Company patrol leader had apparently absorbed his briefing but chose to ignore it. After passing the track junction on Fox, he was spoken to by his sergeant, who in fact should not have been there, as it was supposed to be the lieutenant's 'solo' patrol. The sergeant suggested that they must have passed the track junction off to the right. The reply was curt and sharp.

"I am in charge and I am sick and tired of being told what to do by NCOs."

So they carried on along the Fox's nose spur, heading toward the Mound, 800 metres further on. Because they were travelling over the knolls and saddles, they reached the Mound first.

When Lt. Peter Goss spotted figures sky-lined on the slopes of the Mound, he knew that they had to be Chinese. His was the first Australian probe into the area for many months and nobody else was likely to have had a go. It was within Hill 159's boundaries and opposite the turn in the frontline. The next Commonwealth position was the Yongdong, at least 5 km to the south. It was unthinkable that the shadowy figures on the slopes of this enemy-dominated hill, which was close enough to their lines to be an outpost, were other than Chinese. He gave the order. "Enemy left. Fire!"

My recollection of the enquiry is that the initial burst killed five men of the C Company patrol and wounded another six. Taken completely by surprise, the blokes on the receiving end started to curse and swear as they struggled to react to the attack. Hearing the Australian vernacular, Goss ordered, "Stop firing!"

The range had been closing, as his men pressed forward into the attack. The cessation of the firing gave the C Company patrol a chance to steady themselves. Not unnaturally, they had opened fire probably without an order. Before they could be stopped, they had killed one of A Company's men and wounded five others. These men could fight. The total butcher's bill was therefore 6 killed and 11 wounded, including the new C Company officer. He was shot in the hand.

After the Court of Enquiry, the novice officer was sent back to the Battle School at Hara Mura, then reposted to 2 RAR in another platoon commander appointment. To avoid starting a controversy, I will content myself by commenting that I was disgusted. I believe that among the men of A Company, I was not alone. How Peter came out of the Court of Enquiry, I never heard. But instead of coming back to us, he was given command of the patrol dog training school. Of course, this unfortunate incident alerted the Chinese to our interest in the feature on their doorstep. Recce patrols confirmed that there was increased enemy movement to and from the feature. Not surprisingly. A Company was given the task of sorting the situation out.

Major Norrie started all over again. He sent Ray Simpson with a fighting patrol to recce the Mound itself. Ray did the place over thoroughly, discovering two tunnels dug into the reverse slope, at the Chinese end of the hill, obviously, providing protection from air observation and shelling. They were probably used as hides, where the Chinese could lie up all day and get out into the valley more quickly at dusk. This rear or northern face of the little feature was the only one that had not had the scrub burnt off by shellfire. Brigade decided to blow up the tunnels, but the engineers required precise details of their configuration and dimensions so the next night I took out a full fighting patrol to take measurements. The seasonal rains were just beginning. Warm, thick and very heavy, they saturated but did not chill.

We went out through Fox, down its nose and along the knolls and saddles leading to our objective. I was methodical in my use of scouts, but we encountered no opposition. At about 2200 hrs we went steadily up the southern end of the Mound and paused at the crest, not only to regain our breath, but also to assess the situation. The rain had temporarily eased off. Peering into the darkness, we could make out no silhouettes nor detect any movement or noise. Forming an extended line, with the Brens on the flanks, I moved from man to man, quietly explaining that we would have to sweep the top with bayonets fixed, as the safest means of getting to the other end. I did not want a shot fired unless the bayonet could not do the work. When all were briefed and I had taken my place in the centre, I said, "Let's go!" The whole 16 of us rose. Bayonets on rifles and Owens, we moved forward, gathering speed until in full stride. I was literally swept along with the charge. It was exhilarating and felt unstoppable. But there was no enemy to test it on.

I immediately formed a defensive perimeter on the Chinese end of the feature, then led four men down the slope to locate the tunnels. It was pitch black. The softwood scrub was chest high. About 40 metres down the slope and off to one side of the track, we found the entrance to one tunnel and, before exploring it, located another one on the other side of the track at the same level. There were no others in the vicinity. The tension was mounting. Were there Chinese in them? Both holes were about 3 metres across and went down, then inwards. The tunnels were much larger than I had been led to expect. At the first one, I crouched down, shone my torch in and craned my neck, trying to look in without getting my head blown off. A digger took over. He jumped straight in with his Owen gun in one hand and torch in the other. I followed him. The anticlimax was as unbelievable as it was unexpected. The light from our torches shone back off a heap of sodden clay. The reason that the opening was bigger than Ray Simpson had described became obvious: the continuous heavy rain had caused the roof to collapse. I jumped in first at the second tunnel, only to find that the same thing had happened there. There was now nothing sufficiently tangible or important enough left to blow up. Nature had done every bit as good a job as our engineers could have. We didn't wait to find out whether there were Chinese soldiers trapped under the mud. We weren't carrying shovels anyway. I put a team to work checking the whole rear face, at that level below the crest, but they found nothing more and we all felt a bit let down. Meanwhile, I went some distance further down the track toward the Chinese lines, on my own, to investigate some rustling in the foliage. Finding nothing in the pitch dark, I decided that there was no future in that. So I went back up the hill, collected the others at the tunnels and rejoined our firm base on the top.

Not wanting to go home empty-handed, I figured that we might pick up some useful information if we could see into the Chinese lines which, according to the map, were no more than 300 metres in front of us. All we needed was light to see by. There was a break in the rain, so I called company and gave them the co-ordinates and requested light over the enemy positions. Then we waited. As usual, the Kiwi gunners were not long in answering. But this one was a negative. "Sorry, but we do not carry illuminating shell." Major Norrie said he would try the Yanks. Time dragged on. We had by now been on our objective for some hours. Eventually, Major Norrie came on the air again. "The Americans are only too pleased to help with their medium guns. It will however, take 40 minutes to dig out the split trails to achieve the traverse required to reach across the divisional front. Come home, Kiwi."

It was 0230 hrs. We had already been out eight and a half hours, and the torrential rain had really set in. Because of the distance involved, and the time that had passed, I decided not to return by a different route through the paddies to C Company, which normally would have been prudent, but to retrace our steps back along the line of saddles and knolls. I had become convinced that the Chinese were too smart to be out in such weather, so we travelled fast, though not carelessly. I led, using the 'I' formation. If we struck trouble, we were organised and ready to fight. Had we bumped into an enemy ambush, we would have bulldozed them out of the way. We had the morale, the tactics and the drills.

After reporting to Fox outpost, I prepared to enter the company position. We were nearly home and Fox outpost had reported our approach by phone, but we did not relax. A complication was that the growth between Fox and A Company was quite thick. So visibility was poor. In fact, with the rain, it was as black as the inside of a cow. When we reached the area where we could expect to be challenged, nothing happened. We had to proceed. So as we got closer to A Company's front trenches, I made some noise by rustling the foliage, in case the picket had dozed off. By now it was 0345 hrs. There was still no challenge. I stopped the patrol and, drawing on my experience with the DLI, started to whistle "The Director", 3 Battalion's marching song, also known as "We're a Pack of Bastards." It was recognisable to any Australian in Korea, and particularly in our own battalion.

That did it. From no more than 3 metres ahead of me, possibly less, came the spine chilling rasp of a .30 calibre Browning machine-gun being cocked. I let go. At the top of my voice I yelled, "Hold your fire! You stupid bloody bastard! We're Australians. Get your officer!"

There was a grunt, and I knew that I had guessed right. One of my colleagues had broken the 'golden rule'. He had put two Korean Augmentation Troops Commonwealth or KATCOM together on picket, guarding an entrance into the company position. They at that time spoke almost no English and understood very little. They would not have much idea of what they were supposed to do, or indeed what was going on around them. They were only boys, probably no more than 16 years of age. It is unlikely that these two were the permanent gun crew of the .30 calibre Browning, otherwise it would have been already cocked. But that cut no ice with me. The platoon commander turned up and learned that I was very angry. In fact, having just faced an unnecessary and unproductive death, I had difficulty in being civil. We proceeded with no further incident.

Dick Witton carried out a few more checks on the Mound, all apparently uneventful. Battalion's interest in it faded as bigger things at the other end of the divisional sector took the attention of higher headquarters.

– *Twentytwo* –

Threat on the Left Flank

It was the end of May 1953. 2 RAR had settled in nicely on Hill 355, sweeping the valley clear with well organised and well led patrols. 3 RAR was coping well as usual on Hill 159, covering Little Gibraltar's left flank and rear. Patrols were still being sent out to the Mound, but there were no contacts with enemy patrols. With the exception of the friendly clash tragedy, there was nothing to write home about. The Chinese seemed to have lost interest in the eastern end of the COMDIV sector.

The daily sitreps reported that the Duke of Wellingtons had been fighting for their lives on The Hook. Well, that was not unusual, in that it had been a hot spot since the American marines first captured it. It was heavily attacked, lost and retaken several times. When the marines first took The Hook, they were pushed off again the same night, having dug nothing more than shallow grave-like shell scrapes instead of trenches. They 'rolled with the punch', retaking it with a counter-attack the following morning. From then on, they fought hard and often to hold it.

At the end of October 1952, divisional boundaries were altered again. The Commonwealth Division did a shift to the left and was given responsibility for the defence of The Hook. The 1st Battalion the Black Watch was put on the main Hook position, Pt. 120, with a company of the Duke of Wellington's regiment manning Pt. 146 behind it, on the continuation of the same ridgeline. The New Zealand 16th Field Regiment established an observation post on Pt. 146 which dominated The Hook, the Sami-chon Valley and the main road south to Seoul. How the Kiwi gunners got involved I do not know. But what I do know is that it was the best thing that could have happened.

The cluster of hills forming The Hook position were the south-eastern half of a low range that ran from north-west to south-east for about 6 km into the Sami-chon River valley. It was the westernmost battalion position of the Commonwealth division's sector. The Chinese held the other end of the range, that is the north-western end, to the discomfort of the United Nations' defenders. The most forward company position was on Pt. 120. The whole battalion position was called the 'The Hook' because when marked on the map the dispositions of the companies showed up in the shape of a fishhook. The Hook had such a bad reputation that it was often referred to as 'the bloody Hook'. An additional battalion would have made the deployment more relevant to the strategic and tactical importance of the position and the amount of real estate that needed to be held. Pt. 146 at the south-eastern end of the ridge, sometimes referred to as the Right Hook was, because of its dominant height, vital to The Hook's security. Had it been properly manned from the start, with another battalion, it would have given depth to the defences of the forward positions by bringing counter-attack reserves closer.

Another feature vitally relevant to its security had been left out of The Hook's defenders' deployment altogether. Three hundred metres directly north of Pt. 120 and joined to it by a wide and shallow saddle, was a 137-metre-high hill, nicknamed Warsaw. Had it been manned, it would have dominated the valley of dry paddy between the UNO positions and the Chinese positions on a range of hills 1000 metres or so to the north, across the Samichon Valley. Warsaw's northern face was a steep gradient down to the floor of the valley; its south-western side sloped gently back toward The Hook. It would have been too expensive for the Chinese to maintain as a forward position, from across the valley. But for some reason the Americans never incorporated it into The Hook position, although it was 17 metres higher than The Hook feature itself. Dominating the valley to the west and east as well as the north, it should have been our anchor. But when the COMDIV took over The Hook and its backup positions, it did not have the resources to turn Warsaw into a forward company position, so it was technically and practically in no-man's land. The Chinese were able to cross the valley at night without detection. Because of the saddle between the two features, attacking downhill from a start line on Warsaw's crest gave them the best chance of surprise. Although the Chinese did not occupy the top of the large feature, they had set up an assembly area at its base on its north side, complete with tunnels to shelter in, and directly opposite their own front line Just below the top of the hill made a most suitable

FUP, and the crest made a secure start-line. The whole set up was perfect for them, because they were out of observation until they crossed the start-line and from then on it was a downhill run into the heart of The Hook position. An unmanned Warsaw kept the guardians of Pt. 120 on their toes. Patrol clashes occurred almost every night. Each had to be quickly assessed, as to whether it was a probe or an attack. If a Brit patrol on Warsaw found the Chinese numbers were too great for them to handle, and they usually did, they fired a Very pistol flare and ran for their lives. Within 30 seconds, an artillery barrage descended onto the Warsaw feature and continued to fire until it was established whether it was a serious attack or just a probe.

On the night of 18/19 November 1952, the Black Watch commanded by Lt. Col. Rose were assaulted in strength. A Company took the brunt of it, when the forward company on Pt. 120 was attacked on three sides: from Warsaw in the north, the Ronson ridge to the west, and up the valley that ran north-east across the front of the American marines on The Hook's left flank. The Watch held, fighting doggedly as it always did.

In this battle, which started at 2100 hrs and ended around 0700 hrs the next day, the Black Watch suffered 20 killed, 54 wounded and 11 taken prisoner. But they held. No 'rolling with the punch' by them. That was when Alex Rattray was awarded his M.C.

Back on The Hook in May 1953, they were attacked a second time at 0150 hrs on the morning of the 8th, but the tough men of the Watch were in no mood to be overrun just before going home. After calling for a heavy barrage of airburst onto their own position from the whole New Zealand artillery regiment, the Scots counter-attacked before the Chinese could recover, throwing them off at the point of the bayonet. A mate of mine, another tough minded Scotsman, Captain Derek McElvogue, a gunner who had left the British army and joined the New Zealand one a year or two before, was 16th Field's 163 Battery Observation Post Officer on Pt. 146. At the height of the battle, Derek queried Colonel Rose's co-ordinates four times, when he requested an uncle target—all the field artillery guns at the Field Artillery Regiment firing together; 24 high explosire shells landing together onto one area—onto grid ref. one zero four, one zero four. 104104 were the map coordinates for the Watch's battalion headquarters. Satisfied that he had heard correctly, Derek ordered a regimental target. All the guns of the 16th Field Regiment fired five rounds gunfire onto the position at the same time. When, after three uncle targets, the surviving attackers were wandering around the position totally disoriented and shell-shocked, they were quickly dealt with by the Scots. The Black Watch did well on The Hook. Unfortunately, in this second battle Alex Rattray lost his life.

When the Australians gave The Hook any thought, we wanted to know what was so wrong there. We knew that the Allied units involved could fight, so was the position undermanned?

On the night of 12/13 May the whole battalion of The Duke of Wellington's Regiment which, as mentioned, already had one company on Pt. 146, relieved the Watch, which was played out. Brigadier Kendrew, the commander of 29 Brigade, replaced the Duke's company on Pt. 146 with two companies of the King's Regiment and kept the remainder of that battalion in close reserve to the south. The additional company not only bolstered The Hook defence, but its deployment indicated a belated appreciation of the importance of Pt. 146. It had generally been accepted that Pt. 146 supported The Hook which, because of the bloody battles, had become infamous.

What the Kiwi gunners had known all along must have now become clear to the hierarchy: that the vital ground was in fact Pt. 146. The artillery OP dominated the Sami-chon Valley to the north and to the east. To the north-west, Green Finger and Warsaw were in its sights, as was the Hook itself. It also overlooked the American marines' positions for thousands of metres to the west of the Hook. I know, I visited MacElvogue's OP on Pt.146 several times. It was the key to Seoul in this area, and The Hook position was the key to the security of Pt. 146.

The Dukes set to work with a will to repair the battered defences digging and wiring all night long, every precious night, to make the position as impregnable as possible in the limited time which, they were only too aware, was available to them. The result at the end of their two weeks grace, was a repaired and sturdy trench-line, and a barbed wire fortress on the easy going slopes of the Hook feature.

Heavy concentrated shelling started mid-morning of 28 May and plastered the new defences all day. At 1950 hrs that evening, the weight of the Chinese bombardment was turned up another notch for three minutes, before easing off as their infantry hit the wire. Though chopped up badly by the shelling, it was still an obstacle. Quickly clearing it with pole charges, the Chinese infantry poured through. The extremely heavy preliminary bombardment had collapsed many of the very deep communication trenches, making it difficult for the Dukes to get extra men to where they were needed. Small parties of brave men fought the enemy when they met him. But contemporary accounts indicate a lack of control and cohesion. The use of tunnels to shelter from heavy shell-fire proved a mistake as some of the Chinese infantry, following the barrage very closely, carried satchel charges with which they effectively collapsed the tunnel entrances, entombing those inside. Thankfully, as the battle eventually went our way, the entombed men were able to be dug out.

The arrival of a counter-attack force from the King's Regiment more or less coincided with an outflanking attack by two Chinese companies onto Pt. 121, 800 metres south of The Hook on the western flank of The Hook feature. Without a heavy bombardment or the element of surprise to help them, the Chinese were thoroughly dealt with before they even hit the wire. Another and final attempt on The Hook at 0030hrs, mounted from Betty Grable, met the same fate. Then, as the frontal attacks on the Dukes eased off, the enemy mounted a new assault, this time against Pt. 146 from Pheasant, directly north across the Samichon valley. It never got within cooee of the King's, as the Kiwi OP put 16th Field's 24 guns onto the Chinese infantry as it advanced across 1000 metres of paddy, cutting them to pieces with airburst before they got within striking distance. The Duke of Wellington's and the King's Regiment had held. Like the Watch, the Dukes had suffered casualties to the extent that, realistically, they could no longer be effective.

But they had done the job asked of them, just the same. As the man whose name the Regiment carried, remarked after the successful conclusion of the Battle of Waterloo,

"It was a near run thing."

General West moved smartly to counter the inevitable fall of the strategic position. The 29th Brigade, which was a standard three battalion brigade, was played out. It now had only two battered battalions with experience in the Korean scene, the Dukes and the Black Watch. The King's Regiment, having done its 12 month stint, was time-expired and about to head home. It had been replaced by the newly arrived 1st Bn, the Royal Scots. They were put into the quietest part of the Divisional Sector, the Yongdong position for familiarisation with the unique Korean terrain and tactics. The general reinforced the Dukes with the Royal Fusiliers, taken out of reserve from the four-battalion strong, 28 Brigade. They took over Pt. 146 and manned a blocking position to the rear. That gave General West breathing space to action his master-stroke.

Despite their setbacks, the Chinese high command had obviously decided that the acquisition of The Hook was a better bet than Little Gibraltar especially as they were well aware that the agreement on a truce was only a few weeks away. The Hook was 9 km closer to Seoul than Hill 355 was, and the hills were lower and the going easier. If they could capture The Hook complex, they would dominate the Samichon valley, thereby protecting their left flank. Which they could not have been sure of doing if they only broke through the marines' line, as a counter-attack could have been mounted from the Samichon, through The Hook.

For nearly a year, the communists had maintained pressure on the two key features at each end of the divisional sector, keeping the United Nations' forces guessing over which one they were really after. The capture of either would have opened a floodgate that would have seen a torrent of Chinese infantry and supporting units bypass the other strong point and make a thrust for Seoul, with disastrous consequences for South Korea. The Chinese would have poured in still more troops to secure their flanks and widen the gap, while their spearheading force charged on to the Imjin. The great river is an obstacle, but not a defendable line; the Chinese would have skipped over it. What happened then would have depended on the size of the counter-attack that could have been mounted by the UNO forces. The 7th Marines, now that it occupied the divisional sector to the west of The Hook, was too thinly spread to be able to help the Commonwealth Division. The United States Army's attention was diverted by their badly handled defence of positions like Old Baldy and Pork Chop Hill, next to the eastern end of the Commonwealth sector. Could the US Army have responded to a 'breakthrough' at the western end? Did they have sufficient reserves? I think not.

The Marines' problems seemed to have had a low priority with the US Army, which was running the show. But it would have added a serious dimension to the conflict if The Hook had fallen or been outflanked. I believe that, after the Chinese captured Hill 355's anti-tank position from the American 2nd Division and didn't exploit and take the whole 355 position yet kept continually attacking The Hook, the Commonwealth higher command decided that the Chinese choice for a breakthrough to Seoul was, in fact, via The Hook.

The right flank of the British division had quietened down somewhat since 28 Brigade had regained control of no-man's land, and the Canadian 25th Brigade would keep it that way. On 9 July, the Canadians started to relieve the 28th Brigade. During that night, 2 RAR was switched across the front onto The Hook, and the DLI was put in a blocking position behind. Secrecy was paramount in these important preparations to deal with the expected all-out attack on The Hook. We were deliberately not told for security reasons. The next day, we soon realised that 2 Bn had been relieved on Hill 355, but at platoon level we had no idea why nor where they had gone. That night at around 2100 hrs, a Canadian lieutenant appeared at my CP. He introduced himself and told me that he was there to relieve us. I asked him when the changeover was due to take place. He replied, "Now."

I rang Company headquarters. Jim Norrie confirmed the news, adding: "Move fast. I want you in the trucks by 0200 hrs."

My local patrols were called back in. Now it was obvious why we had not been given a major patrol task that night.

I had learnt to accept the surprising and the inevitable. We were not told what our destination was. Unlike later wars, we had no such things as transistor radios—they had not been invented—so security could be kept tight. We were actually, although we did not realise it at the time, living in a closed society. We were the battalion and the battalion was us. We had no other existence. The Canadian lieutenant was a good bloke. I saw my duty as making sure that he was properly briefed on the position that he was taking charge of. Time allowed only a passing acquaintance, but as I was leaving that CP for the last time, he took off the armoured vest that he was wearing and presented it to me.

"Thanks very much. But I can't accept that. You will need it yourself," I protested.

"Not as much as you will, fella, where you're going. Please accept it with my blessing. The Hook is the worst place on earth. If you shelter in the tunnels, they will seal you in with satchel charges. If you are outside, you will get squirted with burp for sure."

That was something that I had figured out for myself. But it was news that we were headed for The Hook.

It is a most unusual manoeuvre for a unit to be withdrawn from a front line on one flank of a division's sector to relieve a front-line unit on another flank during the same night. I learnt later that 2 RAR's switch was done the same way. They had taken over Pt. 120. Now we were going to their side, on Pt. 146. We headed west.

– *Twentythree* –
The Hook

We arrived before dawn. The last kilometre of our journey into The Hook position was along a camouflaged road. The senior officers were dropped off to attend a briefing at the HQ of the 1st Battalion the Duke of Wellington's Regiment whom we were relieving.

The platoons were transported on to a rendezvous near our predetermined company positions, where the officers were separated from the men. For the platoon commanders it was a bit confusing, as the Royal Fusiliers from our own brigade showed us to the positions, which we were taking over from the Dukes. The probable reason for that was that the Dukes had been so knocked about that they could not field enough junior officers to show us around. We were, after all, taking over front line positions that had just been badly battered along with their occupants. Why we were separated from our men was not clear, as the briefing of the platoon commanders was very cursory.

My reading of histories of the first world war had given me a healthy respect for the difficulties of operating in a salient, and I now had a feeling that we had enemy facing us from more than one direction. The Fusiliers' briefing, however, hadn't mentioned the possibility. Our men, with a few exceptions, had very likely not even heard of the term salient, let alone had it explained to them. It had mostly occurred in the trench warfare of WW1 and is hardly, if ever, referred to in the history books of WW2. But we were about to experience it ourselves. I found the platoon on a flat piece of grass-covered ground, which bore more resemblance to a lawn tennis court than a paddy. Rather cosy really. They had just had their mess tins filled with a substantial breakfast, and were happily sitting or squatting in a bunch out in the open while they started to eat. Had the war finished without my knowledge?

I reacted instinctively, not because of the briefing but because all my training and experience had made me aware that it is extremely stupid to mass troops together at meal time. During the seven months that I had been with the battalion, I never concentrated a platoon in a front-line position. I did my block. I ran toward the men, yelling out in a very strong and condemning tone to Ray Simpson, "Sergeant! Get the men under cover!"

Neither Simmo nor the diggers had ever heard me go crook. I don't think that they considered me soft. Possibly easygoing and unflappable, but not soft; so they must have been surprised at the harshness and urgency in my voice, because they moved like greased lightning. Instead of getting to their feet in the casual way that diggers have down to a fine art, they leapt up and started running for the communication trench at the far end of the flat area. With their mess tins held in front of them, it was like an egg and spoon race. As I followed, running like hell myself, I was handed my mess tin, full of breakfast. There was no time to even look at it. The whole platoon was within five or six strides of the trench, moving like the wind though to me we appeared to be in slow motion. I had caught up, and was right up there with the 'tail end Charlies' but we were still out on the flat. CRASH! There was a hell of an explosion immediately behind us. I looked around and saw the tall column of black smoke shooting up. A shell from a Chinese SP gun had exploded on the very spot that we had just vacated. The shrapnel whistled past and the blast helped propel us toward the trench. As I dived in, there was another sharp explosion and I was further assisted by the blast from the second shell. Instinctively I turned my mess tin as I rolled, thereby ending up the only man not to lose some of his breakfast. A residue of training? Or animal instinct?

I was devastated. Heartbroken that I must have lost so many good men. The dirt blown up by the second shell was still raining down when I called for a head count. I did not want to do the check myself—I feared the worst. But it had to be done. Tough old Ray Simpson responded, and he did it. I was pleased to hear his voice. I had issued the order, to be carried out by whoever was still on their feet. Ray must have been more worried than I was, if that was possible.

"No casualties, sir. We have not lost a man." Then, after a pause and some heavy breathing, in his raspy voice he enquired, "What sort of a place is this, Skipper?" Analysing the incident. The fact that they got two shells away in quick succession and we did not hear them coming is evidence that they were from a 76 mm high velocity gun. The Chinese gunners must have been so pleased to have such a passive and immobile target that they took their time to align their sights carefully. When the platoon moved unexpectedly and fast, they had no time to re-adjust their aim so fired anyway, in the hope of hitting someone. However, some good had come out of it. We all now understood exactly what we were up against in The Hook area.

With breakfast abruptly ended, we moved on into the trenches and went through the routine of the change-over. While Ray supervised the occupation of each section's fighting pits, the Fusilier 2nd lieutenant showed me over the position, which was about 80 metres above the paddy fields that stretched away to Pheasant, the easternmost hill of the enemy-held range across the valley.

To give depth to The Hook defence and also protect 2 RAR's two rear companies' right flank and rear, A Coy 3 RAR was put on Pt. 146, alongside A Coy 2 RAR to the north-west, with B Coy 3 RAR beside us to the south-east. Our other companies were deployed in close reserve, behind us to the south, ready to come to our assistance. Support Company had its specialist platoons deployed tactically. Ron Grey's 3-inch mortars were sited where they could give supporting fire to either battalion. Jack Spiers' OP was on Sausage, within the perimeter of 2 RAR's A Coy. The MMG platoon, dug in on the Yongdong battalion position, across the Samichon River to the east, was sited to fire across 3 RAR's north-eastern frontage, which would also help A Company 2 RAR. Our assault pioneers were attached to 2 RAR to help them with bunker repairs on The Hook's battered position.

One novelty for me was the tunnel system on The Hook and Pt. 146 features. The young British 2nd lieutenant was most proud to be able to show off the platoon commander's sleeping quarters. I could not believe it. A 50 metre or so long tunnel, running directly into the hill, courtesy of the New Zealand field engineers. About 30 metres in, a short branch led to a chamber, approximately 2.5 metres square, fashioned out of the limestone. The roof was wet and gleaming in the reflected light of the torch, and water streamed down the walls almost as strongly as the mighty Imjin—and he thought it a good place to sleep. I thanked him, refraining from telling him of my personal philosophy of sleeping close to the action. Admittedly the tunnel was a useful place for off-duty men to shelter in during heavy shelling, so long as adequately manned forward bunkers ensured early warning of an assault.

On leaving the tunnel, I collided with Captain Tom Channings M.B.E., who had been a close friend at college. He had apparently come looking for me.

"So there you are, Matthews," said Tom. He had just relinquished the post of adjutant of the New Zealand 16th Field Regiment, and was doing a few days in The Hook OP before going home. "I heard that you were in the theatre. Took you long enough to get here. I outrank you now. Tiger for punishment, aren't you? Joining the infantry."

Not being able to get a word in, I gave up trying. But I was mighty glad to see Tom. Our hands meeting in a hearty shake proved how much we still respected each other. He had been the senior warrant officer of our college Air Training Corp squadron, when I was RSM of the army cadet battalion. It was good to meet again, and we have managed to keep in touch for the last 50 years, something that, but for the Korean War, may not otherwise have happened.

By mid-morning, the sigs had the command post fully set up and functional, and Ray Simpson had settled the diggers into their quarters. The platoon then 'stood to' while I inspected the fighting pits and checked out the machine-gun bunkers' fields of fire, mutual support, etc, then the men's sleeping bunkers, to ensure that they were adequate. After that, their time was their own. Lunch was on its way and then they could sleep for four hours, subject, of course, to the lookouts and pickets being relieved according to roster.

A kilometre across the valley to the north the enemy held a range of hills climb in a succession of increasingly higher peaks, north-westward, across our front from the Samichon River. The Brits had given each peak a bird nickname. The previously mentioned Pheasant was the lowest one and closest to the river. Then running north-west, Goose, Crow, and Duck, etc. Any threat to 3 Battalion's two forward companies could be expected from them, so the fighting bunkers facing them were our front line. I moved the command post into a bunker in the front communication trench to give me quicker access to the whole position. About 40 metres along the communication trench to the north of the platoon CP, a steep spur ran down into no-man's land. At the bottom, an outpost was manned every night by a small standing patrol equipped with a field telephone and an 88 radio plus their personal weapons.

After 3 Platoon's drama of the first day nothing untoward happened, as far as I knew. Exploring the area late the next afternoon, absorbing the general layout of the company's deployment and its relativity to the rest of The Hook position, I was following a communication trench between my platoon position and No. 2 Platoon. Rounding a corner I came across Jack Morrison, now CSM of A Company, but again employed as a platoon commander, this time Peter Goss's platoon. He was scrambling about on the side of the hill above the communication trench, dragging a 2-inch mortar ammo box behind him.

"What the hell are you doing up there, Jack? You could get yourself shot," I called out.

"That's why I waited 'til dusk. One of the blokes thought this was a good place to sunbathe." Jack sounded very bitter. Remembering how my men had learnt their lesson about salients, I said nothing. Climbing out of the trench, I joined him in his search for remains. Remains? Little bits of very bloody meat. Jack took no notice of me and that was natural, as the big bronze ANZAC could get very upset at the loss of a digger. I couldn't carry any more pieces in my hands, so moved across to put them in the ammo box. Jack acknowledged me with a nod.

"Who was it?" I enquired.

"The new Pommy bloke," Jack replied. I didn't know the new Pommy bloke in his platoon, so grunted "Hard luck" and went back to look for the rest of him. Not much, another couple of handfuls. The steel box measuring approximately 450 x 200 x 200 mm was nearly half full of what looked like steak and kidney, fresh from the butcher.

"That's it, I reckon," said Jack, acknowledging my continuing presence. "I've got the legs down the hill. Poor bastard copped it somewhere above them. Blew him ..." He stopped. He did not intend to show any weakness in his 'big bronze ANZAC' act. "Thanks," he said grudgingly. There had never been any love lost between Jack Morrison, one of Australia's greatest soldiers, and myself. But then, he resented officers on principle with, I must qualify, the possible exception of Major Norrie.

Patrolling had to be next on the agenda. We would have felt vulnerable without it and so would battalion headquarters. I was detailed to take an ambush patrol into the flat valley to the north, between our positions and Pheasant. BHQ was in some doubt about minefields, close in on our immediate front. There were no maps or overlays showing their positions, and perimeter wire with or without the red triangles had either not been put in position or had been subsequently blown away. Obviously, previous custodians of this vital ground had laid fields indiscriminately, without recording their positions on the map. So the patrol was not sent down our own spur to get into the valley.

Instead, a ten minute hike got us back to the right flank of B Company, where we descended to the paddies. Turning left, we moved out toward the Million Dollar Fence, which ran right across the valley that spread north-west off the Samichon valley, a massive construction of wooden posts, the size of the old fashioned wooden telegraph poles, laced with enough barbed wire to ensnare the devil himself, and liberally sown with mines and 44 gallon drums of napalm. It was undervalued at a million dollars, cost-wise, but seriously overvalued as an asset; despite the fact that our medium machine-gun platoon covered it with their Vickers guns from their Yongdong position, it would not have stopped much. We flitted through the large wood and wire gateway, another intriguing feature. Like an advancing legion? No. More like new actors on a stage full of artificial props. Once through, it wasn't so bad; we were on dry paddy. The summer season was changing conditions again, but the mozzies were still out in force to the extent that their combined loud buzzing possibly affected our ability to hear slight noises. Moving position constantly was not necessary in these warmer conditions, but I had been ordered to set a series of ambushes in likely positions as much to try and establish a pattern of enemy traffic in this area as to ambush roving enemy patrols. The Chinese obviously guessed that we were out, as the broadcasts from loudspeakers on the hills were personalised for us.

"Hello, Aussies. Welcome to The Hook for your short stay."

News to us.

"You know that you should not be here, serving the warmongering interests of the Wall Street capitalists. This war will soon be over for you, when the army of the Peoples' Republic of China throw you off The Hook. It might be tonight. You are sensible men. Why not come over and join us in liberating this beautiful country from the imperialists? Is it not a beautiful country? But you cannot enjoy it if you are sitting in a paddy and your feet are wet."

On and on she went. It was always a seductive female voice peddling the nonsense. It had only one effect on me. The droning voice made me sleepy. I never discussed the issue with anyone else, but I found the lack of action the biggest bore. We were there to fight to the best of our ability, and ready and willing to do so. But short of thrashing around in the dark, how did you find the enemy? Our orders were quite rigid, as lack of co-ordinated effort would only lead to accidents. With both sides having similar aims but different techniques, there was inevitably a large element of blind man's bluff. When frustrated, small things tend to annoy. For the first time, we had been issued with anti-mosquito cream. Reasonably effective, but don't put it on the part most vulnerable to mozzie bites, your forehead. Perspiration washes it into your eyes and does it sting? We didn't wear cap comforters on patrol in the summer, because the heat was nearly as uncomfortable as the mosquitoes were annoying.

For a week or so, Simmo and I alternated in taking out fighting patrols. Then the patrolling roster changed, in that I was detailed to lead all the patrols that 3 Platoon was required to do. I got tired and so did the men. Dick Witton and Jack Morrison patrolled on the other nights. We were probing closer all the time to Pheasant and Goose and up the valley toward Green Finger and Warsaw, but encountered nothing. We were not given any news of the peace talks, so were quite unaware that a truce was imminent.

One morning, after all the housekeeping chores had been seen to, and the men not on duty were free to get some sleep and I had been expecting to do the same, Major Jim, who was also showing signs of fatigue, arrived with the CO, Lt. Col. Macdonald. After greeting me, the colonel said, "Kiwi, where can we get the best view of the valley, looking toward The Hook?" I showed him to our fighting bunker that was closest to The Hook. It overlooked the valley floor for most of the way, but the spur running down between 2 RAR's right flank and 3 Platoon's position obscured the Warsaw feature from the bunker. He was not dismayed. "I want you to find the main track through the paddies, leading from north to south, and set an ambush to intercept line crossers."

They were the people who flitted between the opposing lines to pass information to cells of sympathisers in the opposition-held territory. To get across from the Chinese lines, they operated tactically and travelled down the wide plain between Pheasant and The Hook, crossed the

Samichon River and penetrated the more thinly held Yongdong sector. Roger so far. I told the colonel that I could handle that, and asked what I should do if the line crosser did not stop when ordered to. In other words, did we have to take them alive?

"Oh, no. If they don't stop when challenged, just shoot them."

I was glad of that order, because the business of trying to cosh them in the dark was a lot of nonsense. Especially at the speed they travelled. I didn't mention it, but I figured that the smart thing to do would be to shoot the line crosser in the legs and bring him back alive.

"Also," I rubbed my eyes as he started again, "It has occurred to me that if we were to have a patrol clash between the front of A Company and say Warsaw, we could evacuate any wounded much faster by bringing them up that spur in front of us, than by having to carry them back through the Million Dollar Fence."

Fair comment in that the quicker the evacuation, the greater the chances of survival. At this stage, I was unaware myself that the spur next to this one already had a track up it and no mines or wire at the bottom. He may have been, too. He droned on, "But because it is unmanned, the spur is thoroughly covered in mines, so I have borrowed a Brit field engineer, who will accompany your patrol. I want you to take him to the bottom of the spur, and detail a digger to protect him while he clears a track up it."

I told him that I would be pleased to. Now, I thought, I might be released to get two hours sleep after lunch. I had all the info that I needed to do the job. But there would be no sleep after lunch: I would be busy organising fire support from the field artillery. That was not as simple as it had been on Hill 355, where the battalion and 16th Field had been together for at least 18 months. DFs were all organized and in place, for the main positions on The Hook, but the Australian patrolling pattern at this end of the divisional sector was still evolving. Just as my head was nodding at the thought of sleep, he began again.

"You know, Kiwi, that the Chinese have dug caves in the base of Warsaw?"

"Yes, sir. I understand that they have." I was having a hell of a time trying to keep awake. He droned on. "What if we were to continue along the valley and arrive on their doorstep? They would not expect it. Our patrol could shoot up the caves, then go straight on to Warsaw, and come in through 2 Battalion's lines." I sharpened up quickly. He was right. The way to stop the Chinese hitting The Hook from Warsaw was to gain control of it. What he had just suggested could achieve that. But why tell me? Did he want me to volunteer for what would have virtually been a suicide mission? Had the colonel said right from the start that my task was to lead a fighting patrol into the firm base that the Chinese had established at the bottom of Warsaw, I would have replied: "Yes sir. I suggest that it be a full platoon strength patrol." I would have also requested a 24 hour stand down for the platoon, so that we were fresh enough to carry it out. Had he turned down the request, I would have done the patrol anyway. But we were getting very tired and I was certainly not going to volunteer. In retrospect and after years of reconsidering it, I now think that the whole conversation was designed to bluff me and the men into believing that the war was continuing as usual. He may have been concerned that we might suspect that a cease-fire was imminent, and not press home our normal patrolling efforts. Anyway, he was quite unfazed by the fact that I did not volunteer on the spot.

I took a fighting patrol back into the valley that evening. The light was fading as we passed through B Company's position but it was not quite dark by the time I got the Brit engineer sergeant to the bottom of the spur. The track was totally choked with long grass growing through the tightest tangle of barbed wire that I have ever seen. Where the mines were could not be ascertained until the wire was removed and, as the field was a pirate one, some of the mines could have been under the wire. He had a no-win situation on his hands. I left him and his escort to it. We had our own task to fulfil.

Out in the widest part of the valley we did a few sweeps and, passing some tracks, finally locating a well-defined and wider path which had obviously been carrying more recent foot traffic than the others. It was exactly where I had expected. Well out to the north-west, about half way between Warsaw and Pheasant, it ran parallel with the original track shown on the map, which was too obvious to use. This track was ideal for again employing my new ambush formation. The diggers had been well rehearsed and took up their respective positions without a sound. We settled down. This was not one of the several 30 minute stands, at different locations. We were here for seven hours at least.

That would take us to three in the morning. As it turned out, we got back to our lines about 0400 hrs.

Some of the paddies still had stagnant water in them, so it was still open season for the mosquitoes. We sat still and let them eat us alive. The need for silence precluded slapping them. The best way to deal with them was to keep wiping your face with your free hand. I remember thinking that there must have been a pile of mozzies' bodies nearly up to my knees. Despite our counter efforts, the effect of the bites gave us all swollen hands and faces. They were more than swollen—they were puffed up and lumpy and very itchy, especially our faces.

There was no action. We had a few tense moments when there were some rustling sounds from the direction that we expected a visitor. It might have been an animal. Or it may well have been a line crosser. He would have been very alert on such a hazardous venture, and he may well have smelt us. I mean that literally, as none of us had been able to take a shower for weeks, and had little enough time or water for a decent desert bath.

The engineer had no success either. He said that he did not have time to make an impression on the minefield. He did not have to tell me why. How can you clear mines in the dark, in a tangle of barbed wire and long grass? As it turned out, nothing hinged on it.

– *Twentyfour* –

Finale

It appeared that the Chinese, on finding that we had taken up residence on The Hook features, decided that they had insufficient time to waste trying to overcome the tough and tenacious Australians. So they elected to have another go at their old foe, the 7th United States Marine Division, who had taken over their own sector again from the 25th US Division that had held it from early May until early July. Obviously, the Chinese must have figured out that if they could push the Marines back far enough, the 28th Commonwealth Brigade could be surrounded and bypassed. That would have still left them a clear corridor to Seoul. They set to with a will.

The front line took a dive south at The Hook, the COMDIV's left boundary, then swung back onto a south-west heading, across the Marines' front. The 1st Marine Regiment had dug in on a series of small hills that were the only defendable features available. They called them outposts. The closest outpost to The Hook was Detroit. Next, going west, were East Berlin and Berlin collectively known as the Berlin complex. The collection of outposts continued south-west, with such exotic names as Vegas, Elko, Reno and Carson. The whole group, including Detroit and the Berlin complex was known as the Nevada complex. The distance across the front from the Com Div to Carson was about 4 km.

Reno and Elko were conceded during June, followed by Vegas, stoutly defended by the Turks who were by then in an untenable position. Detroit and the Berlin complex then came under attack in mid July and we received information to the effect that C Coy of 2 RAR, the company next to the marines, was under assault. Its deployment as left rear company on Pt. 121 had, with the Marines having been driven back, now became the front line on the flank of the salient created. Providentially, 2 RAR had on their arrival on The Hook worked hard to restore the badly damaged defences and had built several new bunkers. Also, the British Centurion tanks were on The Hook features in considerable numbers, with more reserves further back.

Major Bill Grupen, a NZ Regular Armoured Corps NCO at that time, was seconded to the British tanks, and commanded a Centurion on Pt. 121. He was therefore in a position to witness the attacks on the Marines close up. As I understand it, our tankies joined in when necessary, although their specified task was the defence of Pt. 121. Bill told me that the WW2 vintage Sherman tanks supporting the Marines could usually take on the Chinese 76 mm high velocity self-propelled guns on even terms. As they were also flat trajectory guns, that was more or less an even contest. But the armour on the Sherman's turrets, unlike the Centurion's, was not adequate to withstand the fire from the enemy's medium artillery, so they were eventually withdrawn. Without their tanks' heavy machine-gun fire support, the Marine infantry could no longer contain the human waves and had to give ground, fighting gamely all the way. They were heavily supported by the New Zealand artillery as some of their own field artillery was on a restricted ammunition allocation at that critical time because the US Army run Supply Corps considered that the Marines had exceeded their allocation. Can you believe it? But all credit to the 1st US Marine Division. Although they were unable to hold their position against the waves of fanatical Chinese infantry, they fought, as the Marines have so often had to fight. Outnumbered to hell; lacking adequate artillery support; fought nearly to a standstill, but not quite. Although slowly forced back by weight of numbers, they kept their line intact.

Day and night attacks of increasing intensity followed. From our position, we had a grandstand view. At night time the tracer and flares made it like the 'Fourth of July', when in fact it was coming up for the 24th. As the situation became more serious for the Marines, the New Zealand 16th Field Regiment took a bigger hand. Dug in to the east, the line of flight of their shells was right over the top of our two company positions. We relished the sound of the shells roaring overhead, knowing that they were doing a vital job well. But no longer did anyone, even for a minute, venture out of a bunker without wearing his steel helmet. To bring the artillery fire to bear where required, it was necessary for the infantry to accept minimum crest clearance over their positions. We had no option. The larger proportion had VT proximity fuses but some of the shells had time-set brass nose cones. Being in trenches rather than in the open like the attacking Chinese, we did not suffer any serious casualties from shells exploding above us due to insufficient crest clearance, but a few men were clouted on the helmet. One unlucky bloke received a broken shoulder when brass nose cones fell from a faulty time-of-flight-fused shell that exploded over our position.

Then the news came in a sitrep: the Marines had been pushed back a further 1500 metres. The forward elements of the Chinese army were within 1200 metres of 3 RAR's A Echelon area. This was serious. They were behind us. We were now not only in a salient, we were almost surrounded. I could not help thinking: will we break out eastwards, across the valley to the Yongdong if things become too tough? Or attack south—taking on the enemy in a bid to not only get ourselves out, but to frustrate his success. Or will we stay as a thorn in his side, being resupplied by air?

Some military historians have suggested that if the communist forces had reached the Imjin River just north of Seoul before the truce, they would have been forced by the terms of the truce to withdraw from their late gains. I don't believe that there would have been sufficient will or moral force left in the United Nations Organization at that time to restart the war to evict them. The civilians of the member countries, unless they had a son fighting there, had forgotten that the war was still going on.

But not so in the military. Morale was high in the units where the pressure was being applied. On the central front, some South Korean divisions were again under severe attack. They held. In our sector, the US Marines and the Turks who were now attached to them, still had their tails up. The Australians, who made up the rest of the major players in The Hook area, were in fact frustrated from inaction and spoiling for a fight. The New Zealand gunners and drivers were still enjoying doing a first class job.

The strategic situation was that, if the Communist forces got past this last barrier of defendable hills north of the Imjin, South Korea would have been totally open to invasion again. Nothing could have stopped them from advancing to Seoul. The big unanswered question is whether they would have waited for a truce to be signed and the UNO troops to go home or would have pressed right on.

Patrolling by our company petered out. We did not even send out recce patrols, which could at least have given warning of an approaching force. We were still isolated from information on the progress of the peace talks, and I had long since refrained from questioning Major Jim about battalion policy. In hindsight, in view of the hierarchy's knowledge of the imminent truce, they were right to keep us in the dark.

The assaults on the US Marines continued, the NZ gunners' artillery barrages passing over our position reached a crescendo on the night of 25-26 July. The next night, the shelling eased off earlier than we had become accustomed to. Since the cessation of patrolling, I had increased the number of pickets on duty at night. During the evenings, those not on duty gathered in the fighting pits, in what had been our rear section position to watch the action, now only 1000 or so metres away behind us, and moving still further south. There was light enough from the exploding shells and the artificial moonlight provided by searchlight beams being reflected back off the clouds, for us to actually see the Marines and the waves of Chinese infantry attacking them. The attacks petered out about 0100 hrs.

We 'stood to' the morning of 27 July 1953. The platoon commanders were summoned to Company Head Quarters. We were told that a truce was to be signed at 1000 hrs that day, taking effect at 2200 hrs. Company orders later. This was good news indeed. Until the magic hour, we had to stay alert for treachery. Fair enough. The day dragged, although there was a much more relaxed atmosphere on the position. However, we kept our heads down.

The guns gradually became quieter. Even the Marines' sector was no longer being pummelled. Routine continued unabated, but in a rather studied way. By 1800 hrs we realised that the guns had indeed completely stopped firing. A Company's three man strong standing patrol that was positioned each night at the bottom of the large spur that ran down from Pt. 146 toward Pheasant across the valley, had been sent out as usual, but no recce or fighting ones. The tension grew.

Our standing patrols had always been three men strong which was considered to be quite adequate for the task of giving warning of an enemy approach up a spur.

But on the most important night of the whole war, we stuck to the roster and I sent out a comparatively junior NCO in charge of two recent reinforcements. They had, however, settled quickly into the routine in the line and appeared to be dependable. But that is no excuse. It would have been prudent for me to ensure that we sent an experienced patrol leader with sufficient men and weaponry to be able to react to any unforeseen emergency. But it never entered my tired head.

Darkness closed in, accentuating the humidity. It was not a comfortable evening, and the atmosphere was tense. Was the war really coming to a close? Or was this another lull before the storm? The evening progressed and the tension built. The standing patrol was quiet, the pickets around the platoon perimeter were maintained, and the CP was manned. I encouraged the remainder of the men to congregate in small groups in the front communication trench rather than the fighting pits and bunkers. It seemed to me important that they could talk to one another, exchange moral strength and have a chance to share the moment. 'Mateship' it is called. I spent my time circulating among the groups. The machine-guns were still in position and could be manned within seconds. Anyway it was not our style to overreact to situations. We were not paranoid about our ability to maintain our defence.

But we let ourselves down. At approximately 1930 hrs, a drama suddenly spilled over the parapet, at the top of the track where the spur met the communication trench. I saw them arrive. Our outpost at the bottom had been abandoned. The standing patrol had returned, unannounced and certainly unauthorised. They said that 12 Chinese had confronted them. The battalion record based on B Company's standing patrol's report states eight, which is more probable.

But the patrol's task was to give warning by telephone, or radio if the line had been cut. If neither worked, a few shots would have alerted us. They could have then retired with honour intact. It was not expected of them to fight a battle, although there was nothing to stop them doing so. But they sent no warning call over the field telephone, which they left behind in their panic. In addition, one man threw away his ammunition in his hysterical scramble up the hill. This had never happened to me before.

Under normal circumstances, I would have quickly got together a fighting patrol and led it out myself to re-establish the outpost, depending on other information or suspicion of the enemy's intent. Naturally, Company would have been kept informed. So long as they knew what we were doing, they would have been quite happy. But as these were not normal circumstances, I handled it the other way around.

I informed Jim Norrie straight away, then set about organizing a fighting patrol while he reported to Battalion. Within minutes I was called to the phone to talk to the CO. He too was good. There were no recriminations or time wasted in apportioning blame, just a clear instruction. I was to take out a dozen men and re-establish the outpost. The crunch of his orders was that, should the enemy patrol still be there, I was to kill every one of them provided that I was confident of getting them all. If I considered that any might escape, I was not to open fire. He was adamant about that. I would be informed when to leave our position, as Battalion was organizing supporting fire. Of course with only a couple of hours to go till the implementation of the truce, it was not just a matter of calling a DF to cut off the enemy patrol's retreat. He concluded with, "Good luck, Kiwi."

It was never mentioned, but it was a fact that the whole Chinese army could have been behind the eight men that confronted the outpost. But I thought the CO was very fair. He had given me a chance to salvage the platoon's reputation.

I hastily went about my preparations. Ray Simpson was given a list of the men that I wanted with me, and the automatic weapons that I required all of them armed with. While Ray was organising the patrol I personally sited two Brens, and briefed their teams to fire down each side of the spur in the event of a fire-fight at the bottom. My reason for this was to stop the enemy patrol from getting behind our party by climbing the sides of the spur. Despite taking that precaution I still considered it perfectly feasible to bowl the whole enemy patrol in one volley of automatic fire, and I briefed my chosen men accordingly, and they were with me. There had been no drop in their fighting spirit. I notified Company that we were ready to go, and was told that the CO was back on the phone and wanted to speak to me. His message: I as platoon commander must stay and command the position. I bet that was Brigade interfering. My sergeant was to take over the fighting patrol. I was not happy with that order. My heart was in this enterprise. But I briefed Ray Simpson on my plan. He accepted it as workable.

Then Major Norrie informed me that the New Zealand artillery had just warned Battalion that they could not fire after 2000 hrs. What did we want artillery fire for anyway?

"Well, let us go now," was my reply. I was told that we were waiting for Battalion's final authorisation. Battalion eventually came up again.

"Call it off. B Company reports movement of a small force across their front, from left to right. It is concluded that it is the same patrol, and it is moving away."

Well, we got away with it, but one cannot help thinking of the consequences had the enemy patrol been sweeping ahead of a larger force intent on attacking. On the other hand, BHQ had kept its head and 3 RAR's reputation for calm and considered reaction was intact. What of the diggers in the standing patrol? While from a military point of view they had run in the face of the enemy without firing a shot or using the field telephone to alert the position, they may have been reluctant to shoot in case they restarted the war, if they could think that profoundly. Their crimes were: panicking and not informing platoon HQ. War is stressful, but on what was to be the last night of a three-year savage war, the tension was dynamic. They were not punished.

Sharp on 2200 hrs, the air was rent by a barbaric sound from our right flank. Across the Samichon valley, the Royal Scots were cheering their heads off. The truce had become effective.

There was a temporary cessation of hostilities which has lasted for 50 years. There was no sound at all from the Australian battalions. The usually extrovert Aussies were quietly counting their blessings, and thinking of their mates who were no longer alive to share the moment. The War had stopped!

We shook hands all round.

Epilogue

The next morning it seemed that the war was indeed over. We 'stood to' as usual. With no guns rumbling the silence was unnerving. As the day dawned, we could see masses of Chinese troops assembling on the skyline almost all around us, with no hint of aggressive intent. Some waved. It was a most unusual experience. Eventually, there were thousands of them. I wondered if they were counting the comparative few of us.

With full daylight, we set to work. The first task was to dismantle the bunkers, to make it easier for working parties at a later date. Terms of the truce allowed us 40 days to send working parties back into the demilitarised zone to recover the Oregon timber and assault cable telephone wire, etc. which would be re-used in the construction of new defences on the Kansas Line. But we did have to get our reserve ammunition out before we moved off the position.

In the meantime, Battalion issued orders for the evacuation of our front-line positions. The plan was to detach the Bren groups from the platoons. Under the command of the platoon sergeants, they would cover the withdrawal of the forward companies. In the event of a breach of trust, it would be up to the Bren teams to buy time for us to return and counter-attack. I believe that, with our artillery support still available, re-occupation was feasible. Bearing in mind that each platoon position still had their seven Bren guns, and artillery fire was still available, it was tidier than leapfrogging sub-units, as would have been necessary in the case of a fighting withdrawal.

We had 72 hours from the time that the truce took effect to organise our withdrawal. That was sensible, and gave us time to clear the position of ammunition that might be needed later. The diggers worked hard for those three days. Everyone was exhausted, but in high spirits. Late afternoon of the third day, all was ready. Handshakes were exchanged with the personnel of the covering party. They took post. The rest of us departed quietly and without fuss. It was still summer and, as the photo shows, still light but fading as we moved off the position.

To my knowledge, there was no major hiccup, which was amazing considering the magnitude of the manoeuvre, involving both sides at the same time, right across the 115 mile front. It was an historic occasion.

APPENDIX 1

A platoon weapon scale in 3 RAR

Each rifle platoon had one .30 calibre air-cooled Browning medium machine-gun, seven .303 Bren light machine-guns, thirteen 9 mm Owen submachine-guns and a number of .303 SMLE No.1 Mark III bolt action rifles. These were the same model used by the British army in the first world war and by the Australians and New Zealanders in the second. Brand new from Australia's Lithgow arms factory, they were beautifully made from a tried and proven design. Although not automatic like the American Garand, they were most effective in the hands of the average infantryman as he had to make every shot count. They also had the 18-inch bayonet. Most importantly, they did not jam with battlefield grit like the Garand and the No. 4 rifle, with which the British forces in Korea were still armed, as was the New Zealand army at that time.

The generous scale of automatic weapons, often unofficially exceeded, gave us sufficient flexibility to arm our patrols with a preponderance of light automatics, thereby increasing their firepower.

In addition to the machine-guns and rifles, each platoon was equipped with a 2 inch mortar with both HE and illuminating bombs which when fired produced a useful magnesium flare supported by a silk parachute. The HE was not very effective. For local protection against vehicles or tanks we were equipped with a 3.5 inch rocket launcher.

Some platoon commanders added to the platoon's firepower by acquiring an American .30 calibre carbine. Mine was a beautiful weapon that would not let you down so long as you kept it clean. I acquired it from an American officer by swapping a pistol which I bought from a digger. As the pistol was a Smith and Wesson .38 British army issue, its history was dubious. I suspect that it was the one that was missing from the holster of the unfortunate decapitated armoured car commander. Last of our personal weapons were boxes upon boxes of hand grenades, distributed throughout the platoon position. Most people carried three or four on patrols as well. They were the British 36 Mills grenade with a four-second fuse—a most effective weapon.

Finally we were issued with a few phosphorus grenades. These, however, were not popular because of the reported Chinese statement that any enemy captured with one on his person would have it strapped to his body and the pin pulled. How valid the threat was is unknown, but nobody wanted to test the truth of it. I always had a couple in the command post, one in the steel 2-inch mortar ammo box in which I kept the maps and signals.

APPENDIX 2

Nominal roll of No. 1 Platoon, late January 1953

Beattie	Anthony	Byran	2/400531
Buchanan	Peter	Davidson	3/400790
Chandler	George	James (Square Deal George)	1/400512
Chinn	Terry		1/400544
Cocks	Bernard	Kevin (Bernie)	2/400126
Connelly	Patrick	John Michael	2/401044
Cox	Ernest	Quinn	3/400911
Cox	Colin	Digby	1/400544
Coyle	John/Jack	Patrick (Jacky)	5/400219
Francisco	Lawrence	George	6/400084
Gaebler	George	Edward	3/400634
Grose	Norman	Walter	5/400115
Gulson	Peter	Kelvedon	1/400539
Hubbard	Stanley		1/400562
Hughes	Burnett	Arthur	1/400538
Jansen	Stanley	William	3/400944
Johnson	Ian	Claude	3/400766
Kellehear	Raymond	Jack	2/401130
Kelly	Kelvin	George	2/400842
Kiesecker	Maxwell	James (Bogie)	1/400261
Kirkham	Kevin		3/400773
Lange	Brian	John	4/400096
Mackay	George	Lance	3/400697
Matthews	Samuel	Bruce (Bruce, Skipper or Kiwi)	203161
McKenzie	Edward	Thomas	3/400814
McKenzie	Kenneth	Thomas	2/401143
Miller	John		3/400681
Moss	Neville		4/400152
Newton	Ronald	Gennings	3/400812
O'Donald	Michael	(Mick)	not known
Payseno	Lester	George	2/400873

Peel	Maxwell	Keith (Jacky)	3/400903
Redenback	Frank		3/400612
Rich	Francis	John	1/400486
Robinson	Frederick	Thomas	3/400922
Simmons	Colin	Keith	5/400244
Stewart	Roy	Edmond (Honest Roy)	1/400495
Turner	Colin	Robert Charles	2/401152
Wilson	Fredrick	Thomas	5/400223
Whitney	Vic	R.	1/229

APPENDIX 3

Usual patrol formation when moving in open country.

Known as the box formation, it was very flexible. The spacings shown were not set in concrete. They were varied according to the light, weather and terrain.

+	Scout Owen		Scout Owen
30-50M			
+	Left Sec Leader Owen	Commander Owen	Right Sec Leader Owen
2M			
+	Rifleman	Radio Op Pistol	Rifleman
2M			
+	Owen gunner		Owen gunner
2M			
+	Bren gunner LMG		Bren gunner LMG
2M			
+	Bren 2ic Rifle		Bren 2ic Rifle
2M			
+	Rifleman		Rifleman

+---------- 3M ---------+----------- 3M ---------+

The **I** formation that we in 3 Platoon developed for movement along ridgelines.

+	Scout Owen
1M	
+	Scout Owen
15M	
+	Commander Owen
2M	
+	Radio Op
2M	Pistol
+	Left section leader Owen
2M	
+	Rifleman
2M	
+	Owen gunner
2M	
+	Bren gunner
2M	
+	Bren 2ic Rifle
2M	
+	Rifleman
2M	
+	Right Section leader
2M	Owen
+	
2M	Rifleman
+	
2M	Owen gunner
+	
2M	Bren gunner
+	
2M	
+	Bren 2ic Rifle
2M	
+	Rifleman

Standard ambush formation in open country, where the enemy could approach from any direction.

\+ 1.5 M +

Scout
Owen

Scout
Owen

Sec Ldr
Owen

Sec Ldr
Owen

Commander
Owen

Rifleman

Rifleman

Owen Gnr

Radio Op
Pistol

Owen Gnr

Bren Gnr

Bren Gnr

Bren 2IC
Rifle

Bren 2IC
Rifle

Rifleman

Rifleman

References

Colonel Moody's précis of the activities of the New Zealand 16th Field Regiment, during the Korean War.

The Australian Army's report on the final battles of The Hook.

The Black Watch Regiment's official report of the 1st Battalion's two battles on The Hook.

Lt. Colonel A.J. Barker's excellent account of The Duke of Wellington's stand on The Hook, in his book *Fortune Favours The Brave.*

Jack Gallaway for the informed account of the efforts of 3 RAR in the fluid early part of the Korean War in his book *The Last call of The Bugle.*

Ian McGibbon's comments quoted on page 78 of his book *New Zealand and the Korean War.*

Acknowledgements

Major Alex Weaver for writing the account of his experience with Lt. Colonel Charlie Yacopetti's fateful patrol.

Lt. Colonel Ray Burnard for his firsthand account of his brush with death and his subsequent experiences.

Corporal Clifford Gale for supplying me with a personal account of his experiences in the fateful patrol actionof 24/25 January 1953.

Mrs Bernadette Spiers, widow of the late Major Jack Spiers MiD, for supplying me with details of his remarkable career in the New Zealand Army.

Major Bill Mendrum for supplying me information on Jack Spiers' post-Korean War service in various hotspots, including Malaya, Borneo and Sarawak.

Major Bill Grupen for supplying me details of the effectiveness of the Sherman and Centurion tanks in Korea.

Geoff Churchman and Colin Bassett of transpress New Zealand for their work on this book.

My dear wife Annette, who has lived with military matters all her married life. I thank her for her patience and unflinching support, particularly with my second life in the New Zealand Territorial Force at weekends.

Our daughter, Mrs Elizabeth H. Clarke, who discovered our worthy publisher and organised me into getting on with the manuscript and knocking it into publishable shape.